WILLIAM W. GREENHALGH

THE FOURTH AMENDMENT HANDBOOK

FOURTH EDITION

AMERICAN BAR ASSOCIATION
Criminal Justice Section

Cover design by ABA Publishing

Printed in the United States of America.

23 22 21 20 19 5 4 3 2 1

Library of Congress Cataloging-in-Publication Data
Names: Benner, Laurence A., editor. | United States. Supreme Court. | American Bar Association. Section of Criminal Justice, issuing body.
Title: The Fourth Amendment handbook / Laurence A. Benner, editor.
Description: Fourth edition. | Chicago, Illinois : Criminal Justice Section, American Bar Association, [2019] | Includes bibliographical references and index.
Identifiers: LCCN 2019017832 (print) | LCCN 2019020626 (ebook) | ISBN 9781641054836 (ebook) | ISBN 9781641054829 (alk. paper)
Subjects: LCSH: Searches and seizures—United States.
Classification: LCC KF9630 (ebook) | LCC KF9630 .G68 2019 (print) | DDC 345.73/0522—dc23
LC record available at https://lccn.loc.gov/2019017832

Discounts are available for books ordered in bulk. Special consideration is given to state bars, CLE programs, and other bar-related organizations. Inquire at Book Publishing, ABA Publishing, American Bar Association, 321 North Clark Street, Chicago, Illinois 60654-7598.

www.ababooks.org

DEDICATION

Dedicated to All Students of the Fourth Amendment

I am writing this dedication on behalf of my late husband, Professor William W. Greenhalgh, who died on February 28, 1994. Bill was the director of the Criminal Justice Clinic and taught Constitutional Criminal Procedure for 31 years at Georgetown University Law Center in Washington, D.C.

The Fourth Amendment to the Constitution was Bill's passion and his life work. He fervently believed that the freedom to be free from unreasonable government intrusion, "the right to be let alone," was the most important personal freedom that we have.

Bill's heroes were those who fought to protect the rights of the citizen against unreasonable government searches and, most particularly, the framers of the Fourth Amendment. Bill would often remind all who would listen, and even some who would not, that the Fourth Amendment could only be understood in light of its history. He frequently referred to James Otis and George Mason, both of whom played key roles.

Because of the abuses wrought on the colonists by writs of assistance, which granted unlimited search authority to customs officers, James Otis recognized the need to limit discretion in government search authority. Bill agreed wholeheartedly with Otis that a "man's house is his castle." The writs of assistance, however, meant that "Custom-house officers may enter our houses when they please; we are commanded to permit their entry" based upon bare suspicion without oath. George Mason, a farmer and justice of the peace from Virginia, was one of Bill's favorites because it was George Mason who drafted the Fourth Amendment, relying upon the Virginia Declaration of Right.

Bill believed that the framers of the Fourth Amendment were profoundly influenced by the experiences of the English in the seventeenth and eighteenth centuries as they battled the abuses of the king and Parliament, who would order searches to enforce taxes, to enforce customs and printing laws, or merely to silence political dissent. Bill's favorite quote belonged to Sir William Pitt: "The poorest man may in his cottage bid defiance to all the forces of the Crown. It may be frail; its roof may shake; the wind may blow through it; the storm may enter; the rain may enter; but the King of England may not enter; all his forces dare not cross the threshold of the ruined tenement."

Bill idolized Justices Felix Frankfurter and Potter Stewart as the modern protectors of the Fourth Amendment. He believed that they, perhaps more than any other justices in the history of the Supreme Court, were committed to protecting people from the intrusions of a jealous government.

To Bill, the role of the judiciary in enforcing the Fourth Amendment could not be overestimated. Like James Otis, George Mason, and Justices Frankfurter and Stewart, he believed that judges and magistrates played a key role to check the discretion of law enforcement officers engaged in the often competitive business of criminal law enforcement. Neutral judges safeguard our rights by issuing search warrants prior to the intrusion—warrants that are based upon sworn oath, and probable cause, and issued only if the police can describe the objects of their search with particularity.

Bill zealously taught his first-year criminal justice students to understand the importance of the Fourth Amendment and their role as lawyers to protect its principles. He taught them that the Fourth Amendment had meaning only because of the gloss of history. He taught them not to consider its words in a vacuum. He taught them to exhaustively research the facts and untiringly research the case law. His terse warning was legendary: "Read, brief, and know cold."

Sara Lee Greenhalgh

CONTENTS

FOREWORD

Henry Adams wrote, "A teacher affects eternity; he never knows where his influence will end." Professor Bill Greenhalgh's life has ended, but his influence lives on in the lives and careers of scores of grateful students who remember him with affection.

More than just a teacher, Professor Greenhalgh was a force at the bar, and particularly in the American Bar Association. He was a long-time member of the Criminal Justice Section and its chairperson from 1982 to 1983. In debate, he could be counted on to cross swords with prosecutors and defense attorneys with equal fervor. He particularly enjoyed deflating the egos of the pompous, whoever they were. Some who did not know him could be angered by his sharp words and intolerance for what he saw as ill-considered opinions. But those of us who knew him well understood his intent and overlooked his occasional lack of tact, and, like his students, took his jabs no more seriously than he meant them.

After his family and his students, Professor Greenhalgh's first love was the Fourth Amendment. He named his farm in the country after it and truly enjoyed reading, analyzing, criticizing, and eventually writing about what, for many of us, can be a confounding part of the criminal law.

With this posthumous work, we can see the professor carefully trace trends and doctrines over several decades as he describes the legal justification for rules and exceptions that, for some of us, may seem to have their support more in practical politics than in sweet reason. His students, and all who knew him, will hear his voice as they read his words and will thank him with warm remembrance as they extend his influence far beyond his tenure.

Andrew L. Sonner

PREFACE TO THE FOURTH EDITION

Overview[1]

This Fourth Edition of the *Fourth Amendment Handbook* includes 45 new Supreme Court decisions, delivered from January 2010 to January 2019. This period highlighted the controversial nature of the privacy rights guaranteed by the Fourth Amendment and the mechanism for their enforcement. The justices were able to reach unanimous agreement on the outcome in less than half (44 percent) of the cases. Over one-third (36 percent) of the cases generating disagreement were resolved by a 5–4 margin.

Although the government prevailed in almost two-thirds (64 percent) of the decisions during this period, the Court nevertheless expanded Fourth Amendment protection in several cases to address threats to privacy created by the digital age. Supplementing the tools used for defining a "search," the Court used the property-based common law "trespass theory" to hold that attaching a GPS tracking device to a vehicle constituted a search. As explained below, this transforming development was initiated by Justice Scalia, who passed away on February 13, 2016. In what perhaps may be seen as his final legacy, Justice Scalia ended the domination of *Katz v. U.S.* (1967) and its reasonable expectation of privacy (REP) formula for divining when a search occurs. Using the trespass approach, the Court has extended the zone of privacy protection for "persons, houses, papers and effects" to include areas previously thought to be unprotected under the *Katz* test. The Court also recalibrated the *Katz* test itself, finding a right to privacy in electronic data stored in cell phones and in business records of a cell phone carrier that contain information revealing the user's daily movements.

While expanding the reach of the Fourth Amendment, the Court at the same time continued to weaken substantive Fourth Amendment protection in general. Employing simple "reasonableness" as the touchstone of Fourth Amendment analysis, the Court found no constitutional violation, for example, when police improperly stopped a motorist for conduct that was not an offense. The Court ruled that the Fourth Amendment was satisfied because the officer's mistake of law was "objectively reasonable." The Court also continued to sanction the use of deadly force by police in a variety of circumstances. It found, for example, that firing 15 shots into the interior of a fleeing car, killing both the driver and his passenger, was reasonably necessary in order to terminate the "threat to public safety" created by the high-speed pursuit of the minor traffic offender, whose driving after being pursued was deemed "outrageously reckless."

The Court also continued its assault upon the exclusionary rule, shrinking its application and weakening its power to deter stops made without individualized reasonable suspicion. At the same time, through the expansive use of the

1. This Preface and the new case briefs for this Fourth Edition were prepared by Laurence A. Benner, who also was a contributing editor to the Third Edition.

judicially created doctrine of qualified immunity, the Court limited the ability of juries to hold state officers accountable for violations of Fourth Amendment rights through civil law suits brought under 42 U.S.C. §1983. It also limited the civil remedy for violations by federal officers established in *Bivens v. Six Unknown Agents* (1971), ruling that "special factors" precluded extending this judicially created remedy to circumstances implicating national security.

Summary of Significant Search and Seizure Decisions

Searches

The period covered by this update began with *Ontario v. Quon* (2010), where the Court upheld an administrative search of text messages in the workplace. The Court assumed without deciding that Quon had REP in texts that were stored on a government-provided device. It found, however, that privacy expectations were diminished in the workplace. Therefore, the Court ruled that the search was reasonable because it was limited in scope to a non-criminal, work-related purpose.

Then came *U.S. v. Jones* (2012). In an opinion by Justice Scalia, which garnered five votes, the Court held that the *Katz* REP formula was not an exclusive test for determining when a government intrusion constituted a search. Resurrecting the long-discarded trespass theory from its *Katz*ian grave, *Jones* re-established physical intrusion upon a property interest as a co-equal test. It then ruled that the installation of a GPS device to the undercarriage of a Jeep constituted a search, because it was a trespass upon Jones' "effects."

Applying *Jones*, the Court held in *Grady v. North Carolina* (2015) that attachment of a GPS device to the ankle of a sex offender, following completion of his sentence, was a trespass upon the person. This, the Court held, constituted a search without regard to whether public or private movements were monitored. In *City of Los Angeles v. Patel* (2015), the City conceded that a police officer's demand to inspect a hotel's guest registry was a search under *Jones*. The Court ruled that the 1899 ordinance authorizing such suspicionless inspections was unconstitutional on its face, because there was no opportunity for pre-compliance review and thus no control on an officer's discretion to prevent harassment.

In *Florida v. Jardines* (2013) and *Collins v. Virginia* (2018) the Court also enlarged the definition of "curtilage," which is protected from trespass as part of the home. The Court ruled that curtilage also includes the area "immediately surrounding" the home, even though that area may be visible to the public. The limitations of the trespass approach to defining a search were seen in *Byrd v. U.S.* (2018). Here the Court fell back on the *Katz* test to find that a driver in lawful possession of a rental car had a reasonable expectation of privacy, even though he was not listed as an authorized driver on the rental agreement.

The Court also used the *Katz* test to limit the third-party doctrine, derived from *United States v. Miller* (1976) and *Smith v. Maryland* (1979). Under this doctrine, REP is deemed lost when information is revealed to a third party. In *Carpenter v. U.S.* (2018), a 5–4 decision, the Chief Justice ruled that cell phone users have a "legitimate expectation of privacy" in a wireless carrier's business records containing cell-site location information (CSLI), because these records capture a user's past physical movements. *Carpenter* held that the government's acquisition of CSLI records, allowed by the Stored Communications Act, was therefore a search under *Katz*, and required a warrant based upon probable cause. Interestingly, Justice Gorsuch, who replaced Justice Scalia, dissented. Although agreeing that the third-party doctrine should be discarded, Justice Gorsuch noted that no property-based interest in the carrier's records had been asserted and he disfavored the *Katz* test, finding it inappropriate.

The Court also strengthened the warrant requirement for arrestees by adopting categorical rules requiring a warrant in certain frequently encountered arrest situations. In *Riley v. California* (2014), the Court refused to expand the search incident to a custodial arrest exception to permit the warrantless search of electronic data in a cell phone found in an arrestee's pants pocket. The Court again required a warrant to obtain a phone number from a cell phone's call log in the companion case *U.S. v. Wurie* (2014). In *Missouri v. McNeely* (2013), the Court rejected the state's argument that the natural dissipation a person's blood alcohol content creates an automatic "exigent circumstance" excusing a warrant. The Court held that absent consent or proof that a judicial determination of probable cause cannot be obtained in time, a warrant is required to draw blood from a driver arrested for DUI. The Court, however, expanded the "exigent circumstances" exception to the warrant requirement in *Kentucky v. King* (2011). There, the Court ruled the police may engage in conduct that provokes the circumstances relied upon to establish the exigency, as long as their conduct does not violate or threaten to violate the Fourth Amendment.

While *Riley* and *McNeely* enhanced core privacy protection for arrestees, four other decisions afforded arrestees less protection from searches. *Florence v. Burlington* (2012) upheld suspicionless strip searches of persons arrested for minor misdemeanors if they are placed in the general jail population; *Maryland v. King* (2013) allowed warrantless DNA cheek swabs of persons arrested for "serious" offenses; and *Bernard v. Minnesota* (2016) upheld punishment of DUI arrestees for refusing to take a warrantless breath test. *Fernandez v. California* (2014) also expanded the ability of police to obtain third-party consent. There, the Court ruled that although the defendant had been present and objected to the search of his apartment at the time of his arrest, police could return to his apartment after taking him to jail and obtain valid consent from his cohabiting girlfriend.

Seizures

The Court's decisions involving unreasonable seizures also had mixed results. In *Manuel v. City of Joliet* (2017), the Court held that pretrial detention constitutes a continuing seizure until trial commences. The Court further ruled that Manuel's Fourth Amendment claim of unlawful pre-trial detention, based upon a fabricated lab report, was not extinguished by a judicial determination of probable cause following his arrest. In *Rodriguez v. U.S.* (2015), the Court held that a brief delay to walk a drug detection dog around a car after completion of a traffic stop was an unreasonable seizure. However, this decision still allows officers to walk a detector dog around the car while the "traffic safety mission" is being completed, which *Rodriguez* affirms includes the time taken to obtain a warrant check. In *Bailey v. U.S.* (2013), the Court limited the exception created in *Michigan v. Summers* (1981), which permits the police to detain occupants of a home during execution of a search warrant for contraband. Refusing to expand this exception, the Court ruled that only persons in the "immediate vicinity" of the targeted home may be seized and detained.

In two seizure cases, however, the Court relaxed the *individualized* suspicion requirement for both the probable cause and reasonable suspicion standards. In *District of Columbia v. Wesby* (2017), a civil rights action, the Court, without individualized fact finding, nevertheless found probable cause existed to arrest all 21 partygoers for unlawful entry under the "totality of the circumstances" test. In *Navarette v. California* (2014), the Court also found that reasonable suspicion existed to make a DUI stop, based upon an "anonymous" 911 call. The caller gave a detailed description of a pickup truck that she claimed had run her off the road. A short time later officers observed defendant driving a pickup matching the description and followed it for five miles without observing any irregular driving before pulling it over and discovering drugs. The Court ruled that the anonymous tip was sufficiently corroborated to give the officer reasonable suspicion the driver was intoxicated.

Perhaps the most significant seizure case, however, was *Heien v. North Carolina* (2015), which held that a traffic stop for driving with one working brake light, which was lawful under state law, did not violate the Fourth Amendment. Although the statute specifically addressing brakes clearly required only one brake light, the Court found ambiguity was created by another provision of the traffic code. Therefore, the Court ruled, the officer's mistake of law was "objectively reasonable." The ramifications of this decision remain to be seen. Justice Kagan concurred to stress that *Heien* should not apply to mistakes about constitutional law.

Remedies

The Court issued just two decisions involving the Fourth Amendment exclusionary rule, both of which further curtailed its application. Distinguishing retroactivity from remedy, *Davis v. U.S.* (2011) held that where evidence was obtained during a search conducted in good faith and in reasonable reliance upon binding appellate precedent, it would not apply the exclusionary rule to cases on direct appeal at the time the constitutional rule sought to be enforced was announced. Thus, while the new constitutional rule limiting car searches incident to arrest announced in *Arizona v. Gant* (2009) applied retroactively to *Davis*, a case then on direct appeal, the defendant had no remedy because binding precedent had previously upheld such searches.

In *Utah v. Strieff* (2016), the Court further reduced any deterrent effect the exclusionary rule may have with respect to investigatory stops made without reasonable suspicion. There an officer, who was investigating an unsubstantiated anonymous tip about drug activity at a house, stopped and detained a pedestrian seen leaving the house without any individualized suspicion of criminal activity. A warrant check revealed the pedestrian had an outstanding traffic warrant. Finding that the officer was investigating in good faith, the Court refused to apply the exclusionary rule to drugs discovered during a search incident to the arrest on the fortuitously discovered arrest warrant, ruling 5–3 that the arrest warrant "attenuated" the taint of the unlawful stop.

The Court also continued its restriction of civil remedies for Fourth Amendment violations. It ruled for the government in 80 percent of the 42 U.S.C. §1983 cases decided during the period. In 40 percent of those cases that reached the substantive merits of a claim involving officer misconduct, the Court granted the officers "qualified immunity" on the ground that the Fourth Amendment right sought to be vindicated was not "clearly established" in the "context" in which the violation occurred. Both the concept of qualified immunity and the "clearly established" right requirement, are not authorized by statute, but are judicial gloss superimposed upon a remedial Act of Congress.

As similarly noted in the Preface to the Third Edition, the Court has again remained on the sidelines regarding Fourth Amendment protection in the context of national security, where the Court gives deference to the Executive Branch. In *Clapper v. Amnesty Int'l USA* (2013), the Court, in a 5–4 decision, denied standing to non-citizen attorneys and journalists who sought to challenge surveillance of their overseas electronic communications. In *Ziglar v. Abbasi* (2017), the Court also limited the remedial cause of action created for constitutional claims against federal officers in *Bivens v. Six Unknown Agents* (1971). *Abbasi* involved a challenge to conditions of confinement by illegal aliens, federally detained in New York under a "hold until cleared" policy following the 9/11 terrorist attack. The detainees alleged they were subjected to daily strip searches and a pattern of abuse and harsh treatment. The Court held that "special factors" justified its refusal to extend the *Bivens* remedy to the "new context" of national security.

Hernandez v. Mesa (2017), another *Bivens* case, involved a cross-border shooting. There, it was alleged a Border Patrol agent, standing on the U.S. side of the border, shot and killed an unarmed 15-year-old Mexican citizen, standing in Mexico. The Court remanded the case back to the Fifth Circuit in light of *Abbasi* and that court determined that special factors similarly precluded bringing a *Bivens* action challenging the use of excessive force. On May 28, 2019, the Court granted certiorari limited to the *Bivens* issue.

By repeatedly restricting access to the judicial system in such cases, the Court avoids conflict with the Executive Branch and defers to Congress in crafting a remedy. Until Congress or the Court grapples with such controversial issues, however, the Fourth Amendment's guarantee of reasonableness will remain an illusory promise whenever a claim of national security implications can be raised, even where the alleged unconstitutional conduct occurs on U.S. soil.

Laurence A. Benner

PREFACE TO THE THIRD EDITION

The Constitution of the United States is a law for rulers and people, equally in war and in peace, and covers with the shield of its protection all classes of men, at all times, and under all circumstances.
Justice David Davis
Ex parte Milligan, 71 U.S. 2 at 76 (1866)

If the Government becomes a lawbreaker, it breeds contempt for law.
Justice Louis Brandeis
Olmstead v. United States, 277 U.S. at 485 (1928)

When the last edition of the *Fourth Amendment Handbook* went to press, the aftermath of September 11, 2001, still dominated discussions about the exercise of governmental power in the face of newly understood threats. The ink on the PATRIOT Act was barely dry; judges, lawyers, the press, and the public were still grappling with its meaning; and fundamental questions were being asked regarding just how much protection the Fourth Amendment would afford when faced with such fear-inspired challenges to its restraints.

That debate continues, but the Supreme Court has remained on the sidelines regarding the Fourth Amendment's application, not only to the numerous intrusions authorized by the PATRIOT Act (including roving wiretaps and secret searches) but also to President Bush's unauthorized electronic surveillance program. Described in a 2009 report by the Office of Inspector General as "unprecedented," the warrantless surveillance program was enjoined by a federal district court judge who found it violated both the First and Fourth amendments. The Supreme Court, however, declined review after the Sixth Circuit ruled the plaintiffs lacked standing and reversed the district court. *See ACLU v. National Security Agency,* 493 F.3d 644 (2007), *cert. denied,* 128 S. Ct. 1334 (2008).

The Supreme Court has not, however, neglected the Fourth Amendment, issuing 27 search and seizure decisions in ordinary law enforcement cases since the last edition, seven years ago. Only six of these decisions were decided by bare majorities, while almost half (12) were unanimous, indicating a fair degree of consensus. With several notable exceptions, these post-9/11 decisions have tended to restrict the amendment's application and vigor.

For example, the Court continued to cut back the scope of the Fourth Amendment's exclusionary rule and expanded the "good faith" exception to include isolated negligent errors made by police department clerical personnel. Expanding the circumstances in which police can engage in suspicionless searches and seizures, the Court upheld "informational checkpoints" and status-based searches of parolees. The Court also ruled that no suspicion is needed to justify the use of a narcotics-detector dog during a valid traffic stop, confirming earlier dicta that a dog sniff does not constitute a "search."

The Court's rulings with respect to other police practices on the street have likewise tended to favor the police. While the Court held that passengers are seized during a traffic stop and can therefore contest the validity of the stop, it also found that such seizures were reasonable for the duration of a valid traffic stop and held that, where an officer fears for her safety, passengers can be subjected to *Terry* patdown searches even though they are not suspected of any criminal activity.

The Court did, however, make Fourth Amendment jurisprudence somewhat more logical, holding that once an arrestee has been handcuffed and restrained, police may search a car as an incident to a custodial arrest only if there is reason to believe the car contains evidence relevant to the crime for which the arrest was made. When neither officer safety nor evidence-preserving rationales is present, the automatic search of the passenger compartment permitted by *Belton v. New York* is thus no longer permitted. It seems likely, however, that in most arrest situations police would be entitled to impound an arrestee's car and conduct a suspicionless inventory search in any event. Thus the Court's intellectually appealing gesture would appear to only minimally affect law enforcement's ability to search an arrestee's automobile.

The Court approved anticipatory search warrants, held that arrests made in violation of state law do not violate the Fourth Amendment, and upheld arrests for refusal to give identification when stopped on reasonable suspicion. It also decided several cases dealing with the manner in which a search is conducted or an arrest is made, upholding, for example, the use of deadly force to apprehend a fleeing traffic offender who drove recklessly. In an identity theft case where police mistakenly raided the home of an innocent family to look for computers, it condoned police conduct in ordering a woman to get out of bed and stand naked because weapons might be in the bedding; and, in a gang-related search, it validated a three-hour detention in handcuffs of an 18-year-old non-suspect female during the execution of a search warrant for weapons at her home. However, the Court did find that a strip search of a 13-year-old middle school student, based only upon reasonable suspicion that she possessed ibuprofen in violation of school rules, was beyond the pale.

The Roberts Court, which decided 16 of the new cases in this edition, appears to disfavor bright-line categorical rules for controlling police behavior. Instead, when a police practice departs from the warrant or probable cause requirements found in the literal text of the Fourth Amendment, the Court has employed a simplified version of the traditional balancing test as the touchstone for determining "reasonableness." This permits the Court, in each context, simply to determine whether the government's need to make the warrantless and/or suspicionless intrusion outweighs the liberty or privacy interest at stake. As a result of this approach, the values the framers sought to safeguard have been protected from extreme abuses, while the government has been granted a great deal of flexibility when its interests chafe against the amendment's restraints.

How much flexibility the Court can continue to grant without gutting the Fourth Amendment of its essence and vitality remains to be seen. What weigh in the balance are not just the rights of individual criminal defendants, but the liberty and privacy of all Americans.

Laurence A. Benner and
Sharon Rubinstein

ACKNOWLEDGMENTS FOR THE FOURTH EDITION

The Preface to this Fourth Edition and case briefs for 45 additional decisions, which span the period from January 2010 to January 2019, were prepared by Professor Emeritus Laurence A. Benner, with research and editorial assistance by Matthew Hobson, Jennifer Myers, Jonathan R. Benner, John Lanahan, Barbara Bergman, and Professor Emeritus Michal Belknap.

A debt of gratitude is owed to Sara Lee Greenhalgh for her continued cooperation in the release of this edition and to the many contributors to prior editions, including the Honorable Charles Moylan, the Honorable Andrew Sonner, Sarah Forbes Orwig, Sharon Rubinstein, Kimberly Rosenfield, Amie Clifford, Carol Garfield Freeman, Jack Hanna, Susan Clark and Professor Andrew Taslitz.

Special thanks also go to the Criminal Justice Section's leadership and staff, the members of the Section's Book Publishing Board, the ABA Publishing production and marketing staff, and especially Sarah Craig, Executive Editor at ABA Publishing, for their exceptional assistance, encouragement and support.

The right of the people to be secure in their persons, houses, papers, and effects, against unreasonable searches and seizures, shall not be violated, and no warrants shall issue, but upon probable cause, supported by oath or affirmation, and particularly describing the place to be searched, and the persons or things to be seized.

The Fourth Amendment to the Constitution of the United States

INTRODUCTION

A Conceptualization of the Fourth Amendment

Hon. Charles E. Moylan, Jr.

For one who first felt the magic of the Fourth Amendment many years ago at Bill Greenhalgh's feet, it was a labor of love to accept the invitation of Bill's widow and of Bill's colleagues to write a brief introduction to the masterful summary of the Fourth Amendment he had compiled just before his untimely death. His definitive collection of every Supreme Court decision touching the Fourth Amendment provided us a rich repository of individual doctrinal ornaments. What remained to be done, hopefully by way of this introduction, was to sketch with broad strokes the general shape of the tree on which the individual ornaments may then, with some sense of logical decorum, be hung.[1]

What a Fourth Amendment buff soon learns is that few of us, with the rare exception of a Bill Greenhalgh, will ever master it all.[2] What, then, do we do instead? I suggest that we develop, like an airline pilot, a set of checklists and have them readily available in the cockpit, or at the trial table, so that we can pull the appropriate one down as occasion demands and measure the circumstances of our case of the hour against the pertinent criteria. The most basic Fourth Amendment checklist of them all consists of three very simple (or, perhaps, three very profound) questions. They are 1) "Is it even there?" 2) "If so, has it been satisfied?" and 3) "If not, so what?" Those questions engage the gears of the three key Fourth Amendment issues around which we can organize all of the individual decisions: 1) the threshold of its applicability, 2) its substance or merits, and 3) the sanction for its violation.

I. The Threshold Applicability of the Fourth Amendment

The key to any true understanding is an appreciation of the vast conceptual difference between the issue of Fourth Amendment applicability and the very different issue of Fourth Amendment compliance. When dealing with the latter, our judges are the keepers of the sacred flame, the enforcers of the values written into the Bill of Rights by the framers. The Fourth Amendment demands of law enforcement good things like warrants, probable cause, exigency, and police good faith. They all, however, are but the subcriteria by which we measure something else: reasonableness. For Fourth Amendment purposes, the police have to be reasonable when they search and when they seize because the Fourth Amendment demands it of them.

The "flip-side" of the same logic, however, is that when the Fourth Amendment does not apply, the commandment to be reasonable, which exists only by virtue of the Fourth Amendment, does not apply either. In some coldly neutral world of outer space where, for a variety of reasons, the Fourth Amendment might not apply, the warranted search would be no better than a warrantless one, probable cause no better than a fishing expedition, exigency as a reason for not getting a warrant no better than police laziness, and police good faith no better than bad faith.

Before spinning our wheels, therefore, in an exercise in futility inquiring into whether the Fourth Amendment has been satisfied, we should pause at the

1. Judge Moylan's comprehensive Introduction was written before the Supreme Court's 2008 term and remains essential to understanding the proper framework for analyzing Fourth Amendment issues. Footnotes have been added where cases discussed in the Introduction have been impacted or overruled.
2. Bill Greenhalgh himself compiled a total of 288 case summaries that became the basis for the first edition of this book. As a result of two prior editions and this Fourth Edition, the total number of Supreme Court decisions reported on has now grown to 399.

threshold to inquire whether the Fourth Amendment is even applicable so as to require satisfaction. When the Fourth Amendment is applicable, we properly go on to examine the issue of its satisfaction. For that purpose, the subcriteria by which we measure reasonableness are vitally important. If the Fourth Amendment is inapplicable, on the other hand, the inquiry is at an end and those subcriteria are utterly immaterial. What, then, are the prominent respects in which the Fourth Amendment might be deemed inapplicable?

A. *Katz and the "Reasonable Expectation of Privacy"*

As we turn to examine closely the threshold of Fourth Amendment coverage, it is necessary to get a firm handle on the 1967 decision of *Katz v. United States*. *Katz* has probably had a greater impact on Fourth Amendment jurisprudence than any other single Supreme Court decision with the exception of *Mapp v. Ohio* (1961).[3] Its impact, ironically, has been exclusively at the threshold of applicability or coverage. Even there, it has not altered the substantive law with respect to coverage, but it has changed dramatically the vocabulary we use to talk about coverage. The special impact of *Katz*, moreover, has proceeded not from its majority opinion but from the concurring opinion of Justice Harlan. That concurrence has been cited and quoted with approval so regularly by subsequent decisions of the Supreme Court that it has ripened into the prevailing conventional wisdom.

The factual issue in *Katz* was a narrow one. FBI agents had warrantlessly placed an electronic eavesdropping device on the roof of a public telephone booth in Los Angeles. By the use of that "bug," they recorded the voice of Charles Katz as he illegally transmitted wagering information to contacts in Miami and Boston. There was no issue as to satisfaction of the Fourth Amendment for it was clear that the FBI agents, with ample time to have obtained a court order for the placement of the listening device, had not done so. If the Fourth Amendment applied, therefore, it had been violated. The only issue was whether the Fourth Amendment even covered the situation.

The controlling precedents of *Olmstead v. United States* (1928) and *Goldman v. United States* (1942) had held that there is no Fourth Amendment involvement unless there is a physical penetration into a constitutionally protected area. The electronic listening device in *Katz* was, like the one found to have been unoffending in *Goldman*, one that did not penetrate the structure and that did not, therefore, intrude into the constitutionally protected area. That distinction the Supreme Court repudiated, expressly overruling *Olmstead* and *Goldman* to the extent to which they had held that a physical penetration into the constitutionally protected area was the sine qua non of Fourth Amendment involvement. To do so, however, the Supreme Court had to modify significantly the way in which it described Fourth Amendment coverage.

The *Katz* decision itself, confined to its factual context, is straightforward and free of confusion. The at-times broad language of the *Katz* opinion, however, generated significant confusion and debate. Some argued that the very concept of a constitutionally protected perimeter was dead and that Fourth Amendment coverage had moved from inside that traditionally protected perimeter to the broad outside. The predicate for that notion were the seven words early in the majority opinion, "the Fourth Amendment protects people, not places." Arguing against a too-hasty conclusion that the very concept of "place" had lost its significance, however, was the follow-up reference in the majority opinion, two paragraphs after the first reference, in which it was stated, "the Fourth Amendment protects people—and not simply 'areas.'" (emphasis supplied). Justice Harlan's concurrence, moreover, carefully pointed out:

> As the Court's opinion states, "the Fourth Amendment protects people, not places." The question, however, is what protection it affords to those people. Generally, as here, the answer to that question requires reference to a "place."

The more conservative reading of *Katz*'s language about "people and places" was that it did not move Fourth Amendment coverage from inside the traditionally protected area to the broad outside, for those were not the facts of *Katz*, but that it did, rather, enhance the quality of the protection within the constitutionally protected perimeter. Justice Harlan's concurrence pointed out that for the period of its use and occupancy "an enclosed telephone booth is an area where, like a home," a person enjoys Fourth Amendment protection and is "unlike a field," where there is no such protection. That reading of *Katz* is that, within the protected telephone booth, the

3. The recent decision in *United States v Jones* (2012) has diminished the dominance of the *Katz* "reasonable expectation of privacy" formula for determining the scope of Fourth Amendment protection. While the *Katz* test continues to have vitality, *Jones* resurrected the concept of common law trespass (upon a property interest protected by the text of the Fourth Amendment) as a "co-equal test" for determining Fourth Amendment applicability.

thing protected is the privacy of the person inside the place and not the structural integrity of the "place" itself—the woodwork, the stucco, the glass. That, it was argued, was the intended meaning of protecting "people, not places." In repudiating *Olmstead* and *Goldman*, therefore, the Supreme Court had ruled that it was protecting a person inside such a protected area from such highly sophisticated and intrusive, but nonpenetrating, devices as laser beams, parabolic microphones, and detectaphones, just as traditionally it had protected against such old-fashioned and actually penetrating devices as jimmies, crowbars, and spike-mikes.

The debate between the two positions posed the classic law school issue of how to read a judicial opinion. What is the law of the case when the decision itself, on its facts, is narrow, but where the language of the opinion announcing the decision is broad? In 1984, the well-reasoned analysis of Justice Powell in *Oliver v. United States* settled the debate in favor of the narrower interpretation, pointing out that that was the only interpretation that had a base in the actual facts of the *Katz* case itself.

The far-reaching impact of *Katz* has stemmed from the concurring opinion of Justice Harlan. In groping for a way to describe Fourth Amendment coverage, he came up with the phrase "a reasonable expectation of privacy." The phrase caught on. Justice Harlan broke it down into two component parts, its subjective aspect and its objective aspect. It is initially required that an individual have an actual or subjective expectation of privacy. Thus, even in the otherwise protected venue of a man's home, "objects, activities, or statements that he exposes to the 'plain view' of others are not 'protected' because no intention to keep them to himself has been exhibited." In the years since the *Katz* opinion was promulgated, emphasis has shifted decidedly away from this subjective aspect of a reasonable expectation of privacy and to the objective aspect.

Even if an individual has an actual, subjective expectation of privacy, that does not translate into a Fourth Amendment protection unless such expectation is also one that society has objectively recognized as reasonable. "[C]onversations in the open would not be protected against being overheard for the expectation of privacy under the circumstances would be unreasonable. *Cf. Hester v. United States*." It is because of the critical significance of this objective aspect of "a reasonable expectation of privacy" that the impact of *Katz* on the threshold issue of Fourth Amendment coverage has been revealed to be more linguistic than substantive.

Where one used to ask, "Did the defendant enjoy a Fourth Amendment protection?", one now asks, "Did the defendant possess a reasonable expectation of privacy?" Those are, however, but two ways of saying precisely the same thing. Under *Katz*, a Fourth Amendment protection is defined as "a reasonable expectation of privacy." Both the Fourth Amendment protection directly or the objectively measured "reasonable expectation of privacy" are then determined by such traditional inquiries as 1) Was the place that was searched covered by the Fourth Amendment? 2) Was the searcher an agent of government? 3) Was it the defendant, and not someone else, who enjoyed the protection or the expectation and, therefore, has the standing to raise the question? and 4) Was the type of police conduct in issue a "search" or "seizure," or was it something else not covered by the Fourth Amendment?

The net effect has been simply to move such traditional inquiries one step further down in the outline. An outline that used to be:

I. Was there a Fourth Amendment protection?
   A. Coverage of place
   B. Coverage of searcher
   C. Coverage of defendant
   D. Coverage of type of police conduct

has now become:

I. Was there a "reasonable expectation of privacy"?
   A. Subjectively
   B. Objectively
      1. Coverage of place
      2. Coverage of searcher
      3. Coverage of defendant
      4. Coverage of type of police conduct

The most significant effect of the substitution of the new "reasonable expectation of privacy" language seems to be that instead of measuring coverage mechanistically—on an "all or nothing" basis—we measure it more flexibly according to the ever-shifting "totality of the circumstances."

B. Applicability to Place

There is first the problem of geographic coverage—which places are protected and which are not? Starting far back from the epicenter of the obviously protected home, we learn from *United States v. Verdugo-Urquidez* (1990) that the Fourth Amendment enjoys little, if any, extraterritoriality. Although the Supreme Court did not address whether the Fourth Amendment might apply to a search beyond our political borders of an American citizen by American law enforcement agents, it held squarely that the Fourth Amendment does not apply, even when the subsequent trial is to be held in the United States, to a search beyond our borders, even by American agents, of the home of a foreign national having no lawful connection with the United States.

Moving in closer, *United States v. Knotts* (1983) confirmed that the protection of the Fourth Amendment, even within the political boundaries of the United States, does not extend its protective umbrella over land in the public domain, such as streets, sidewalks, roads, or parks.[4]

Moving on to private property, we encounter the seminal 1924 decision of *Hester v. United States*. *Hester* promulgated the so-called "open fields doctrine." That doctrine is not, as many carelessly characterize it, an exception to the warrant requirement, for both the warrant requirement and all of its exceptions are ways of satisfying the Fourth Amendment when applicable. The "open fields doctrine," by contrast, is a way of determining that the Fourth Amendment is not applicable so as even to require satisfaction. There is a vast conceptual difference between an instance of the Fourth Amendment satisfied and an instance of the Fourth Amendment inapplicable.

Hester holds that the Fourth Amendment is a core value that protects both the home and the extended home, that we learned in burglary law to call "the curtilage," but does not protect mere private real estate beyond the family's zone of habitation. The energizing principle is that the geographic coverage of the Fourth Amendment protects the family in its habitation from the public invader even as the geographic coverage of the burglary law affords similar protection from the private invader. *United States v. Dunn* (1987), utilizing that principle of family use, helps us to draw the line between the protected home and curtilage, on the one hand, and the unprotected "open fields," on the other.

Although *Hester*'s notion of a constitutionally protected perimeter was buffeted for a time by Justice Stewart's dictum in *Katz v. United States* (1967) that "[t]he Fourth Amendment protects people, not places," Justice Powell reconfirmed *Hester*'s vitality in *United States v. Oliver* (1984). The "open fields" are not a protected place. The function of *Katz*'s "reasonable expectation of privacy" test is not to move Fourth Amendment coverage from inside the traditionally protected perimeter to the broad outside but, rather, to determine whether, within the protected perimeter, the potential protection of the Fourth Amendment translates, under *Katz*, into actual protection. That test was twice applied, in *California v. Ciraolo* (1986) and in *Florida v. Riley* (1989), to determine whether the potentially protected curtilage of a home actually enjoyed a "reasonable expectation of privacy" from aerial surveillance and, if so, from surveillance at what altitude.[5]

C. Applicability to the Person of the Searcher

The overarching principle explaining this aspect of Fourth Amendment applicability is that the entire Bill of Rights, including the Fourth Amendment, is a set of "Thou shalt not's" addressed to government as government and not to private persons. In the phrase "constitutional law," the limiting adjective "constitutional" serves a purpose. The main body of any constitution establishes the structure of a government and then spells out what that constituted government is empowered to do. A bill or declaration of rights is then frequently appended to the document to spell out precisely those things that the government may not do. Both the pluses and the minuses are directed to government as government.

From *Burdeau v. McDowell* (1921) through *United States v. Jacobsen* (1984), the Supreme Court has always been unanimous in holding that the Fourth Amendment does not apply to a search conducted by a private person in a private capacity. It is not that such a search is necessarily reasonable. Frequently, as in *Burdeau*, it is far from it. It is rather the case that a purely private search, reasonable or unreasonable, is none of the Fourth Amendment's concern. The mere fact that the evidence is offered in a criminal trial does not transform the antecedent search from private action into state action. The nonviolation of the Fourth Amendment is not limited to the satisfaction of the Fourth Amendment.

On the other hand, if the search by a private person or private corporation involves governmental cooperation or participation, then, under agency principles, "state action" is involved and the Fourth Amendment is thereby made applicable. *Smith v. Maryland* (1978); *Skinner v. Railway Labor Executives' Ass'n* (1989).

---

4. In *United States v Jones* (2012), however, five justices indicated that individuals have a reasonable expectation of privacy in the aggregate of their movements in the public domain. See also *Carpenter v United States* (2018), which held that cell phone users have a reasonable expectation of privacy in in a wireless carrier's business records containing cell-site location information, because such records capture the users past physical movements.

5. The definition of curtilage was enlarged in *Florida v Jardines* (2013) and *Collins v. Virginia* (2018) to include areas "adjacent the home" that are associated with "the activity of home life," even if the area is visible by the public.

Where state action is involved, moreover, it matters not whether the objective of the search is to gather evidence of crime or to serve "special needs" beyond the investigative norm. *New Jersey v. T.L.O.* (1985) made it clear that the Fourth Amendment applies to a search of a student by a school official even where the purpose is simply to enforce school regulations. *New York v. Burger* (1987) applied the Fourth Amendment to a search by a licensing authority, just as *O'Connor v. Ortega* (1987) applied it to a search by state hospital authorities looking merely for evidence of occupational misfeasance. What matters is not the purpose of the search but the involvement of government in the searching process.

D. Applicability to the Person of the Defendant

The entire subject of Fourth Amendment standing is simply the threshold question of the applicability of the Fourth Amendment to the person of the defendant challenging a search or a seizure. From the dawn of the Republic, American courts have been sufficiently busy that there is no time left over at the end of the day to settle questions of only academic interest. That function is left to the law schools. The mission of the courts is the resolution of the "live case or controversy." A defendant must, if timely challenged, establish that he or she enjoyed a Fourth Amendment protection in the first place before being permitted to litigate whether that protection was violated. A defendant lacks standing to vindicate vicariously the Fourth Amendment rights of someone else. A challenge of one's standing is the law's polite way of asking, "What business is it of yours?"

1. Proprietary Standing

Originally, a defendant, in order to show standing, had to establish that he enjoyed a possessory or other proprietary interest in either the place searched or the thing seized. That is still the most common way of establishing standing. That original variety of standing will be unaffected by whether one looks at the threshold of Fourth Amendment coverage in a traditional way or looks at it through the prism of *Katz*'s "reasonable expectation of privacy." The possession of a proprietary interest in the place searched—it was the defendant's house, the defendant's car, the defendant's pocket—will ipso facto represent an objectively measured "reasonable expectation of privacy." *United States v. Padilla* in 1993 reaffirmed that "a property interest," just as surely as a "reasonable expectation of privacy," is a way of establishing a Fourth Amendment protection conferring the standing to litigate a possible violation of that protection. The reasonable expectation of privacy arises from the property interest.

2. The Rise and Fall of Automatic Standing

Jones v. United States (1960)[6] dramatically liberalized the law of standing by adding two new varieties. The first was automatic standing. It dealt with an interest in the thing seized. A defendant charged with the simple possession of contraband was automatically entitled to litigate the constitutionality of the search for or seizure of that contraband. Automatic standing, however, did not long survive. It was a rule designed for the express purpose of removing a defendant "from the horns of a dilemma." The dilemma was that the very evidence offered to establish standing frequently might come back to haunt the defendant on the merits of guilt or innocence. *Simmons v. United States* (1968) eliminated the dilemma by granting a defendant the right to testify on a preliminary issue such as standing with immunity from the use of that testimony on the merits of guilt or innocence. It seemed that *Simmons* had eliminated the very reason for automatic standing to exist. After ruling on several occasions that the issue was not squarely before it, the Supreme Court, in *United States v. Salvucci* (1980) and *Rawlings v. Kentucky* (1980), recognized that the rule, indeed, should not outlive the reason for the rule.

3. Derivative Standing

The second reform of *Jones* was the creation of what is generally called derivative standing. It also deals with an interest in the place searched, but not by the owner. It is called "derivative" because it derives through the host, who enjoys proprietary standing, to all of those legitimately on the premises as the guests, licensees, or invitees of that host.

It is on the assessment of derivative standing that the flexibility emphasized by *Katz*'s "reasonable expectation of privacy" approach has had an effect and, arguably, a very salutary effect. In the wake of the *Jones* case, it was thought by many that anyone "legitimately on the premises" of the place that was searched would automatically have the full measure of Fourth Amendment standing to contest the search. Although no Supreme Court case law had held that such a mechanistic approach was necessarily called for, *Katz*'s "totality of circumstances" has guaranteed that such an assessment will not be that mechanistically inflexible. Both the three-month guest with clothes hanging in the bedroom closet and the mailman three feet inside the kitchen door collecting three cents overdue on a letter are both, to be sure, legitimately on the premises. That the first enjoys derivative standing to challenge a search of the home,

6. Not to be confused with United States v. Jones (2012).

however, by no means implies that the second should enjoy the same privilege. Measuring the totality of the circumstances guarantees that an appropriate or reasonable distinction in that regard can be drawn.

Rakas v. Illinois (1978) applied the derivative standing rule to one legitimately present in someone else's automobile and held that, under the totality of the circumstances, a "mere passenger" in an automobile does not enjoy such derivative standing. If there were something more involved than being a mere passenger, however, the strong suggestion is that derivative standing might exist. A three-week cross-country trip with one's suitcase in the trunk may confer more of an expectation of privacy than hitching a ride downtown to the office. A family member in the car may have a greater expectation of privacy in it than would a hitchhiker.

Minnesota v. Olson (1990) calibrated more finely the derivative standing of one legitimately present in someone else's home, holding that status as an overnight guest would, without more, establish such standing. By contrast, *Minnesota v. Carter* (1998) denied derivative standing to two individuals who were legitimately in an apartment for several hours, but who were there for business purposes (the packaging of drugs) rather than for residential purposes. The Supreme Court starkly contrasted the two purposes. "While the apartment was a dwelling place for [its owner], it was for these Respondents simply a place to do business." Even though the structure may be the same, the Court pointed out that "property used for commercial purposes is treated differently for Fourth Amendment purposes than residential property." This focus on the purpose for which an individual is inside the home of another underscores the Supreme Court's recent concern with the "core value" of the Fourth Amendment, which is the protection of the home, presumably when used "as a home."

4. *Target Standing and Conspirator Standing*

With the death of automatic standing, the only categories of standing that remain are proprietary standing and derivative standing. *Rakas v. Illinois* (1978) laid to rest the ghost that there had ever been such a thing as target standing, conferring standing simply on the basis of one's being the target of the criminal investigation. *United States v. Padilla* (1993) emphatically held that standing with respect to places or things owned by other members of a conspiracy could never be established merely by one's participation in that conspiracy.

5. *Who Are "The People"?*

Although raised only by dicta in *United States v. Verdugo-Urquidez* (1990), there is a fascinating question yet to be resolved in terms of which defendants may enjoy the coverage of the Fourth Amendment and which may not. Unlike the Fifth Amendment, the Fourth Amendment does not, in terms, extend to "persons." Unlike the Sixth Amendment, it does not extend to "the accused." The right to be free of unreasonable search and seizure, rather, is a right inhering in "the People." If James Madison was not merely indulging in a rhetorical flourish, pursuing a rhyme scheme or groping for iambic pentameter, what did he and his colleagues intend by that tantalizing term of art "the People"?

There is a strong suggestion of the Lockean or Jeffersonian concept of those who have entered into the "social contract" that underlies the United States of America, those whom *Verdugo-Urquidez* refers to as "a class of persons who are part of a national community or have otherwise developed sufficient connection with this country to be considered part of that community." "The people" would seem to embrace those who have theoretically entered into the social compact with each other, agreeing to assume certain obligations of membership in the political group in exchange for receiving certain benefits of such membership. What, then, of the World War II saboteur who has been put ashore on the coast of Long Island from a German U-boat or of the illegal alien who has come ashore on the coast of Florida simply to smuggle drugs? Is such a person one of "the People"? If not, is such a person nonetheless entitled to the Fourth Amendment protection that is expressly the right of "the People"?

E. *Applicability to Type of Police Conduct*

In the hands of a more liberal or more judicially activist Supreme Court, this issue of threshold applicability might never have arisen. Such a Court could plausibly have held that, whatever the words of the framers may have been, the "evolving spirit" of the Fourth Amendment embraces protection against every variety of unreasonable police harassment of a citizen. A more conservative Court, on the other hand, searching for "the original understanding" of what the framers said and of what the framers meant, could readily conclude that the Madisonian Fourth Amendment expressly covers unreasonable "searches" and unreasonable "seizures" but not other varieties of unreasonable police conduct. In such a constitutional regime, it is appropriate, therefore, to inquire whether the police conduct being challenged by a suppression motion is a "search" or a "seizure" within the contemplation of the Fourth Amendment or is something else not covered by the Fourth Amendment.

1. What Is a "Search"?[7]

United States v. Jacobsen (1984) first came to grips with the question of what is a "search" within the contemplation of the Fourth Amendment. Interestingly, it took language from *United States v. Katz* (1967) about "a reasonable expectation of privacy" and, in a subtle shift of emphasis, turned it inside out. The *Jacobsen* definition is: "A 'search' occurs whenever an expectation of privacy that society is prepared to consider reasonable is infringed." If the chemical examination of a substance, such as a field test for cocaine, is so narrowly focused that it will reveal only whether the suspect substance is or is not contraband, the examination does not constitute "a search." A suspect's expectation of privacy may be infringed, but it will not be an infringement of an expectation that society is prepared to consider "reasonable" or "legitimate." It is the binary nature of the question, "Contraband? Yea or nay?" that saves it from the clutches of the Fourth Amendment's reasonableness requirement.

If, on the other hand, a chemical or microscopic examination is broad enough to reveal noncriminal as well as criminal characteristics, such as the blood test in *Skinner v. Railway Labor Executives' Ass'n* (1989), then it is a "search" within the contemplation of the Fourth Amendment, because it may infringe expectations of privacy that society is prepared to consider "reasonable" or "legitimate." There is nothing illegitimate about an expectation that one's blood will not be tested to reveal that one is anemic or pregnant or infected with HIV.

In *Kyllo v. United States* (2001), the government argued, relying on *United States v. Place* (1983), that the use of a thermal-imaging device that only measured the heat on the outside of a building was not a search. The Supreme Court held that it was a search because of the ability of the technique to reveal possibly innocent facts about the occupants of the building, as well as possibly incriminating facts.

Most searches involve the investigative employment of the sense of sight—entering private places or opening private things in order to "take a look." On occasion, however, other senses may be implicated. In *United States v. Place* (1983), the Supreme Court held that the use of the sense of smell (typically by a drug-sniffing canine) does not constitute a search within the contemplation of the Fourth Amendment. In part, this result is explained by the fact that the suspicious odors "escape" from the protected place or container and that the literal act of smelling, therefore, occurs outside the protected area. In part, it is explained by the limited investigative focus of the canine nose; the narrow canine focus on narcotics, e.g., does not infringe expectations of privacy that are "legitimate."

Illinois v. Caballes (2005) confirmed that the use of a trained dog to sniff the exterior of an automobile to detect the presence of contraband drugs is not a search and is not, therefore, a police action requiring any justification. The only thing that implicates the merits of the Fourth Amendment is the reasonableness of the roadside detention of the vehicle and the motorist for a long enough period of time to permit the dog to arrive at the scene.

By contrast with the sense of smell, the sense of touch does constitute a search within the contemplation of the Fourth Amendment. In *Bond v. United States* (2000), the Supreme Court held that a government agent's tactile manipulation, squeezing, and probing of a soft piece of luggage, revealing a suspicious "brick" on the inside, did constitute a Fourth Amendment search. Unlike telltale odors, the "feel" of the shape of the brick never came out of the protected container; the sensory probing of the fingers, rather, went in. The *Bond* holding is consistent with all of the "frisk" cases pursuant to *Terry v. Ohio* (1968) and with the "plain feel" doctrine of *Minnesota v. Dickerson* (1993), where deploying the sense of touch through a layer or two of clothing was held to implicate the Fourth Amendment and its requirement that the touching, therefore, be reasonable.

2. What Is a "Seizure" of Property?

It was also *United States v. Jacobsen* (1984) that first came to grips with the question of what is a "seizure" of property within the contemplation of the Fourth Amendment. *Jacobsen*'s definition is: "A 'seizure' of property occurs when there is some meaningful interference with an individual's possessory interests in that property." The emphasis in that definition is on the adjective "meaningful." In *Jacobsen* itself, even the admitted seizure and destruction of trace amounts of the defendant's property was deemed not to be a "seizure" because it had "at most" only "a de minimis impact on any protected property interest." A field test for cocaine did not consume enough of the suspect's "powder" to constitute a meaningful interference with his property interest in that "powder."

3. What Is a "Seizure" of a Person?

After a decade of tacking and hauling from *United States v. Mendenhall* (1980) and *Michigan v. Chesternut* (1988)

7. See the Preface to this Fourth Edition, noting the impact of *United States v. Jones* (2012) on the determination of what constitutes a "search" under the Fourth Amendment.

through *Brower v. County of Inyo* (1989), the Supreme Court finally got a firm handle on the issue of what is a "seizure" of a person in *California v. Hodari D.* (1991). Justice Scalia achieved a successful synthesis of what had theretofore been apparently contradictory strands of case law by explaining that a seizure of the person can occur in two different contexts: 1) when the police apply actual physical force to the body of the suspect and 2) when a suspect submits to a police "show of authority."

In the first context, if the police use of actual force achieves a restraining effect on a suspect, a seizure of that suspect has occurred. The Fourth Amendment, therefore, applies and the court must inquire whether that seizure was reasonable. It matters not whether the suspect submitted to the force or continued, unsuccessfully, to resist.

When, on the other hand, no actual force is applied, a two-step process is necessary before a "seizure" of the person can be said to have occurred. The actions of the police must have been such as to constitute a "show of authority"—that is, they must have been sufficient to communicate to a reasonable fugitive that the police wanted him to stop. In addition to that "show of force," however, there must also have been an actual submission by the suspect. A "show of force" plus a submission equals a "seizure" of the person. No actual touching is required.

A "show of force" not resulting in submission, however, but in continued flight or continued resistance, on the other hand, is not a "seizure" of the person. Until the suspect is successfully restrained, voluntarily or involuntarily, there may have been an attempted seizure or an intended seizure but there has been no consummated seizure. The Fourth Amendment would not apply and the reasonableness of the police conduct, absent an actual "seizure," would be immaterial. *Brendlin v. California* (2007) makes it clear that when the police order an automobile to stop, they have effectively seized not only the person of the driver but also the person of the passenger, if the circumstances are such that a reasonable person in the passenger's position would not feel free to leave.

In *County of Sacramento v. Lewis* (1998), it was claimed that an individual who was killed in a motorcycle accident following a high-speed chase by the police had been unreasonably deprived of his Fourth Amendment right to be free of an unreasonable seizure of his person. The Supreme Court held that a high-speed chase of a suspect is not per se a seizure of the person within the contemplation of the Fourth Amendment and there is, therefore, no requirement that the Fourth Amendment reasonableness standard be satisfied with respect to the chase. When a police action, either a chase or a roadblock, results in a sudden stop of a fleeing motorist, whether that abrupt termination of the suspect's mobility constitutes a Fourth Amendment seizure of the person depends upon whether the termination of movement was "through means intentionally applied." Thus the unintended collision in *County of Sacramento v. Lewis* did not amount to a Fourth Amendment seizure of Lewis, but the intended applications of force in *Brower v. County of Inyo* (1989) and *Scott v. Harris* (2007) did constitute Fourth Amendment seizures of the crash victims and warranted examination of the Fourth Amendment merits.

F. Miscellaneous Applicability

The preceding and well-developed aspects of threshold applicability have taken on a life of their own as quasi-autonomous subdivisions of Fourth Amendment jurisprudence. The rarer and miscellaneous instances of possible coverage look to *Katz*'s "reasonable expectation of privacy," objectively measured according to the totality of the circumstances, as a general statement or formula for testing Fourth Amendment applicability. Using that approach, *Smith v. Maryland* (1979) decided that the Fourth Amendment does not apply to the use of pen registers. *United States v. Miller* (1976) used the same approach to decide that the Fourth Amendment does not protect the contents of banking records.[8] *United States v. Knotts* (1983) and *United States v. Karo* (1984), on the other hand, held that the Fourth Amendment might or might not apply to the use of an electronic tracking device, depending on the placement of the device.

One particular instance of Fourth Amendment inapplicability is where the police seize abandoned property, provided that it is truly abandoned. The situation typically involves a suspect who is being followed, perhaps even chased, by the police and who deems it discrete to throw away compromising contraband before being caught. If there has been a seizure of the person of the suspect and that is the cause of the alleged abandonment, the Fourth Amendment is applicable and the reasonableness of the seizure of the person must be assessed. If that seizure is found to have been unreasonable, then the ostensible abandonment will be deemed the fruit of the poisoned tree and the property will be suppressed.

8. *Carpenter v United States* (2018) limited both *Miller* and *Smith* and the "third party doctrine" derived from them. See Preface to this Fourth Edition.

If, on the other hand, the seizure of the person is deemed to have been reasonable or if it is determined that there has been no seizure of the person, then the abandoned property may be seized and offered in evidence without any other justification needing to be shown for the seizure. This was the clear holding of *California v. Hodari D.* in 1991. Where the property is abandoned, the Fourth Amendment does not regulate its seizure.

All of the preceding subissues—"Is the place covered?" "Is the person of the searcher covered?" "Does the defendant have standing?" "Has there been a search or a seizure?"—are simply aspects of the overarching question, "Does the Fourth Amendment even cover the situation at issue here?" If the answer to that threshold inquiry is "No," the analysis is at an end and the Fourth Amendment merits are immaterial.

II. The Substance of the Fourth Amendment

If the answer to the preceding inquiry, on the other hand, is that the Fourth Amendment does, indeed, apply, then the question of its satisfaction or violation takes its rightful place on the table.

A. The Structure of the Fourth Amendment

There is no better way to begin an examination of the content of the Fourth Amendment than by looking at the amendment's words themselves. The relationship among the various parts of the amendment may perhaps be better understood if, instead of setting out the compound sentence that is the Fourth Amendment along its customary horizontal axis, we lay it out schematically:

> The right of the people to be secure in their
> [1] persons,
> [2] houses,
> [3] papers, and
> [4] effects,
> against unreasonable searches and seizures, shall not be violated,
>
> and
>
> no Warrants shall issue, but
> [1] upon probable cause,
> [2] supported by Oath or affirmation, and
> [3] particularly describing
> [a] the place to be searched, and
> [b] the persons or things to be seized.

The amendment consists of two basic clauses. The first is called, by popular academic acceptance, the General Reasonableness Clause; the second, again by common usage, the Warrant Clause. The relationship between those clauses is critical to an understanding of the amendment. Two very different analytic approaches have, over the decades, vied for dominance. Almost as God and the devil warred over the soul of Dr. Faust, a war has been waged for the soul of the Fourth Amendment. Ironically, that war has been waged between these at times complementary but at times competing clauses of the amendment. Predictably, the fortunes of that war shift back and forth every few decades.

A consideration of that struggle over analytic approaches may be briefly deferred, however, because it is only involved when we turn to the impact of the Fourth Amendment on procedural matters involved in the investigation of crime. Indeed, the Warrant Clause itself has pertinence only to criminal investigative procedures. Probable cause 1) to believe that a crime has been committed or 2) to believe that evidence of crime will be found is only material in the context of criminal investigation. When we are looking, by contrast, at the impact of the Fourth Amendment on governmental searches and seizures for some reason other than the investigation of crime or at the permitted scope of a Fourth Amendment intrusion quite aside from its procedural propriety, we are concerned only with what is reasonable within the contemplation of the General Reasonableness Clause.

B. Objective Versus Procedural Reasonableness

The General Reasonableness Clause is the appropriate measuring rod for answering the substantive question of how far a Fourth Amendment intrusion, even a procedurally correct one, may go. *Winston v. Lee* (1985) determined that a procedurally impeccable decision to dig into the body of a suspect for a possibly incriminating bullet was, in balancing the competing interests, nonetheless substantively unreasonable. *Graham v. Connor* (1989) and *Brosseau v. Haugen* (2004), in analyzing what degree of force is reasonable in various circumstances, denominate this issue of substantive, as opposed to procedural, reasonableness as a question of "objective reasonableness." A similar analysis condemned as objectively unreasonable the common law option to shoot a fleeing burglar in *Tennessee v. Garner* (1985). Whether the intentional termination by force of a high-speed chase involving a fleeing suspect amounts to the use of excessive force is also a question to be answered by using the objective reasonableness standard. *Brower v. County of Inyo* (1989); *Scott v. Harris* (2007).

Objective reasonableness has also been determined to be the appropriate criterion for assessing the constitutionality of various vehicular checkpoints. In executing a plan involving vehicular checkpoints, it is constitutionally mandatory that the selection of targets to be stopped be absolutely random and that no aspect of the selection process be left to the discretion of the officers operating the checkpoint. When there is no particularized suspicion to justify the stopping of a vehicle, moreover, objective reasonableness demands an examination of the purpose of the checkpoint. It may well be reasonable if its primary purpose is to serve a "special need beyond the investigative norm," such as 1) the interception of illegal aliens entering the country, approved by *United States v. Martinez-Fuerte* (1976); and 2) the removal of drunken drivers from the roads, approved by *Michigan Dep't of State Police v. Sitz* (1990). Strong dicta in *Delaware v. Prouse* (1979) suggested that random checkpoints for the purpose of verifying drivers' licenses and vehicle registrations would also be deemed reasonable for the primary purpose of enhancing highway safety.

By contrast, the vehicular checkpoint in *Indianapolis v. Edmond* (2000) was held by the Supreme Court to be unreasonable because its primary purpose was the enforcement of the criminal laws against the use, possession, and transportation of narcotic drugs. In distinguishing the arguably different approach taken in *Whren v. United States* (1996), the Supreme Court contrasted the subjective purpose of an individual officer on an ad hoc basis, which is not pertinent under *Whren*, from the broad "programmatic purpose" of the entire checkpoint operation, which is pertinent. When the detection of crime is the primary purpose of a Fourth Amendment detention, however brief, nothing less than particularized suspicion is acceptable as the justification. *Illinois v. Lidster* (2004) is in illuminating counterpoint to *Indianapolis v. Edmond.* In *Lidster*, a suspicionless checkpoint stop was deemed reasonable because the purpose of the stop was not to discover a possible crime by the motorist but to seek the voluntary cooperation of the motorist in providing possible information about a crime unrelated to the motorist.

In *Atwater v. City of Lago Vista* (2001), a Section 1983 constitutional tort case involving the Fourth Amendment, the Supreme Court held that it was not objectively unreasonable for the police to make a full-blown custodial arrest, with all of its attendant consequences, for a misdemeanor as well as for a felony, even if the misdemeanor did not involve a breach of the peace and even if the misdemeanor was not a jailable offense.

Searches conducted at the national border are subject to this objective reasonable test of the scope of what may be done. In terms of the initial intrusion, the Fourth Amendment does not require any special justification at the border for a minimal seizure of the person or a minimal search of persons or property. *United States v. Montoya De Hernandez* in 1985 referred to the general absence of Fourth Amendment protection at the border, "Since the founding of our Republic, Congress has granted the Executive plenary authority to conduct routine searches and seizures at the border, without probable cause or a warrant." That same case establishes, however, that the Fourth Amendment does nonetheless impose constitutional limits on the scope or intensity of the search of a person and the controlling criterion is that of general reasonableness. While there may be some reasonable limits on a highly intrusive search of a person at the national border, *United States v. Flores-Montano* (2004) made it clear that "[c]omplex balancing tests to determine what is a 'routine' search of a vehicle, as opposed to a more 'intrusive' search of a person, have no place in border searches of vehicles." The Supreme Court approved a totally suspicionless disassembly of a vehicle's fuel tank, revealing drugs.

C. *Administrative Searches and Other Searches Serving "Special Needs Beyond the Investigative Norm"*

Whenever searches are conducted by government agents, the Fourth Amendment applies to those searches. When the detection of crime is not the purpose of the search, but some other purpose, such as an administrative search, is being pursued, probable-cause-based search warrants are not involved. The controlling criterion is that of general reasonableness. *See v. City of Seattle* (1967); *Camara v. Municipal Court* (1967); *Marshall v. Barlow's, Inc.* (1978). Although the cases sometimes refer, carelessly, to a lower standard for probable cause, they are actually describing a lower standard of reasonableness.

Where certain industries are, by the very nature of their activity, more "tightly regulated," it is reasonable for the inspectors to afford less Fourth Amendment protection. *Colonnade Catering Corp. v. United States* (1970); *United States v. Biswell* (1972); *Donovan v. Dewey* (1981). Various factors may enter into the balance, but the final analysis will always be made in terms of general reasonableness.

The warrantless entry of a home or other structure to extinguish a fire or even to discover the cause of the fire is another instance of a Fourth Amendment intrusion's being governed by the General Reasonableness Clause. *Michigan v. Tyler* (1978); *Michigan v. Clifford* (1984).

The general reasonableness standard applies whenever various types of government employees are searching for evidence for purposes other than detecting and prosecuting crime. These "special needs beyond the investigative norm" may involve the search of a student by a teacher or other school official, *New Jersey v. T.L.O.* (1985); the search of an employee's desk for evidence of misfeasance, *O'Connor v. Ortega* (1987); the search of the office of an automobile junkyard for evidence of a licensing violation, *New York v. Burger* (1987); or the search of the home of a probationer for evidence of a probation violation, *Griffin v. Wisconsin* (1987).

Although the Supreme Court seems to be pushing the "special needs" doctrine to its outer limits, *Griffin v. Wisconsin* has been a fruitful seedbed. *United States v. Knights* (2001) extended the prerogative of searching probationers from probation officers to law enforcement officials generally, although the search in that case rested on the twin bases of 1) the suspect's status as a probationer and 2) reasonable suspicion of criminal activity. One could not be sure whether the probationary status alone would have sufficed. In *Samson v. California* (2006), however, the Supreme Court approved a totally suspicionless search of a parolee by a police officer. The Court noted that, on the continuum that runs "from solitary confinement to a few hours of community service," parole is even more akin to actual imprisonment than is probation. The Court also pointed out that a parolee has a "severely diminished expectation of privacy."

D. General Reasonableness and the Special Problem of Examining Bodily Fluids for Traces of Drugs and Alcohol[9]

The wide-scale testing of large groups of persons for drugs or alcohol is another governmental activity that is controlled by the General Reasonableness Clause. For the first time in 1989, the Supreme Court addressed the Fourth Amendment implications of the mandatory testing of blood, urine, or breath to detect the presence of drugs or alcohol. *Skinner v. Railway Labor Executives' Ass'n* (1989) and *National Treasury Employees Union v. Von Raab* (1989) made it clear that the Fourth Amendment is only implicated, of course, when the testing is done by the government and is not involved when the testing is conducted by private employers.

9. See also *Missouri v. McNeely* (2013) and *Birchfield v. North Dakota* (2016) requiring a warrant, absent exigent circumstances, to draw blood, but not to test the breath, of a driver validly arrested for DUI.

As an aspect of the objective reasonableness balancing approach, the governmental need for the testing is measured against the degree of the intrusion on privacy. In *Skinner*, the problem of serious railway accidents was deemed sufficiently compelling to outweigh the limited intrusion on privacy. In *Von Raab*, the governmental interest in the drug testing of customs service employees was deemed sufficiently compelling where those employees were actively involved in drug interdiction or were required to carry firearms. Mere access to classified information, on the other hand, was not deemed to be a sufficient justification to subject employees to the testing absent particularized suspicion.

In *Vernonia School District 47J v. Acton* (1995), the Supreme Court deemed reasonable the mandatory drug testing of student athletes. In *Chandler v. Miller* (1997), by contrast, the mandatory drug testing of candidates for public office by the state of Georgia was held to be unreasonable. In *Ferguson v. City of Charleston* (2001), the testing by hospital personnel of pregnant women for the presence of cocaine in their urine was deemed to be unreasonable. It was the policy of collecting and turning over evidence thus obtained to the police and the pervasive involvement of police and prosecutors in the program that distinguished this case from most of the other cases involving "special needs beyond the investigative norm."

E. The Predicate for the Initial Intrusion Versus the Scope and the Manner of Searching

In explaining the rationale for the Plain View Doctrine, especially the fact that it only comes into play after a valid intrusion is already a fait accompli, the Supreme Court in *Coolidge v. New Hampshire* (1971) for the first time examined in detail the distinction between 1) the required predicate for initiating any intrusion into a Fourth Amendment protected area and 2) even following an intrusion that was reasonable in its inception, the reasonable scope of what then may be done and the reasonableness of the manner in which the search is conducted.

With respect to the reasonable scope of a search, the overarching rule is that the permitted scope of any search is whatever is necessary to serve the purpose of that search but, under the ever-present minimization requirement, not one bit more. The permitted scope of a search under a search warrant is to do those things the necessity for which has been spelled out in the application for the warrant. The limitations on a warranted search are mandated by the particularity clause, requiring that the warrant expressly state the place to be searched and the persons or things to be searched for and seized.

The Fourth Amendment's particularity clause is the classic example of a scope limitation. The amendment expressly provides that a search warrant shall "particularly describ[e] the things to be seized." In *Groh v. Ramirez* (2004), the Supreme Court ruled unconstitutional a search pursuant to a search warrant that failed to describe the things to be seized. In preparing an application for the search warrant, the officers had carefully prepared a list of particularly described items that were to be subject to seizure. That list, however, neither made it onto the face of the warrant itself nor was incorporated into the warrant by reference. The Supreme Court held that the subsequent restraint actually exercised by the officers, in compliance with the list they had prepared, was only self-restraint by the officers. It could not be ascertained whether the judge had ever authorized the seizure of such items, and that judicial authorization is the sine qua non of Fourth Amendment reasonableness.

United States v. Grubbs (2006) deals with an anticipatory warrant, where the application for the warrant had 1) adequately established probable cause to believe that evidence would soon be present in the place to be searched and 2) explained what the triggering event (a controlled delivery) would be. Rejecting the Ninth Circuit's decision to the contrary, the Supreme Court held that the Fourth Amendment's particularity clause does not require the triggering event to be set forth on the face of the warrant.

With respect to any of the exceptions to the warrant requirement, each exception has its own purpose to be served and, accordingly, its own scope limitations. Whatever is necessary to the service of that particular purpose is within the permitted scope of the warrantless search. Once that purpose has been served, however, the commandment of the Fourth Amendment is to terminate the search. Even while the search is still in progress, its scope should not exceed what is necessary to serve its purpose. Because one of the two purposes of a search incident to lawful arrest, for instance, is to prevent the possible destruction of evidence, it is within the permitted scope of a search incident to go into an arrestee's pocket and to secure possible evidence of crime. By contrast, the purpose of a frisk is not to secure evidence but only to detect the presence of a weapon. The scope of the frisk, therefore, is limited to a pat-down of the clothing surface and does not permit entry into the pocket to retrieve evidence of crime. The lesser intrusion is all that is required to serve the lesser purpose.

If there is probable cause to believe that stolen truck tires are being carried in an automobile, the permitted scope of the ensuing *Carroll* Doctrine (p. 13, *infra*) search would be to look anywhere in the automobile that a stolen truck tire might be but not, for instance, in the glove compartment for the simple reason that a stolen truck tire could not possibly be concealed there. If, on the other hand, the probable cause were to search the same automobile for a stolen diamond ring or for a glassine bag of heroin, the permitted scope of the *Carroll* Doctrine search would self-evidently include a search of the glove compartment. The permitted scope of a search expands or contracts with the purpose of the search. The logical limitation on the scope of any search is well encapsulated by the adage, "Don't look for an elephant in a matchbox." But look, on the other hand, anywhere that an elephant might be.

F. The Manner of Conducting a Search and the Special Problem of "Knock and Announce"

Even given a validly issued search warrant that fully complies with Fourth Amendment requirements, there still remain the possible issues of 1) whether the search conducted pursuant to that warrant is reasonable in its scope and 2) whether the manner in which the warrant is executed is otherwise reasonable. An aspect of the reasonableness of the manner in which a search warrant is executed is the requirement that the police sometimes "knock and announce" their presence. In *Wilson v. Arkansas* (1995), the Supreme Court first turned its attention to this theretofore neglected aspect of Fourth Amendment reasonableness. *Wilson v. Arkansas* held that a "knock and announce" requirement had been a part of the common law at the time the Bill of Rights was framed and was, therefore, an inherent part of the reasonableness requirement of the Fourth Amendment. The Supreme Court also recognized, however, that there could be numerous exceptions where circumstances made it unfeasible for the police to announce their presence in advance.

Richards v. Wisconsin (1997) held that the exigency-based entitlement to such an exception from the "knock and announce" requirement is something that must be established on a case-by-case basis rather than by a per se rule covering an entire category of crime. *United States v. Ramirez* (1998) applied *Richards v. Wisconsin* and held that there is no elevated or incremental level of justification required simply because a "no knock" entry results in property damage.

Even when the police are not exempted from the "knock and announce" requirement, the period of time that elapses between 1) the knocking and announcing and 2) breaking open the door is an aspect of the general reasonableness inquiry. In *United States v. Banks* (2003), the Supreme Court held that a delay of between 15 and 20 seconds was reasonable when there was reason to fear that contraband drugs might be destroyed if the police delayed their entry longer.

In *Hudson v. Michigan* (2006), the Supreme Court placed this entire subcategory of law concerning the manner of entry into a realistic perspective. In a case involving a conceded violation of the "knock and announce" law, it held that the prejudice to the suspect is not serious enough to justify the heavy cost of applying the Exclusionary Rule. What is at stake is little more than whether the police entered the place to be searched 30 seconds sooner or 30 seconds later.

Michigan v. Summers (1981) held that the police, when executing a search warrant, may detain an occupant of the house for the duration of the search, even though the occupant is not suspected of any criminal activity. Relying on *Michigan v. Summers*, the Supreme Court in *Muehler v. Mena* (2005) approved the forced detention—in handcuffs and for two to three hours—of several occupants of a house being searched, even though the detainees were not suspected of any crime. In *Los Angeles County v. Rettele* (2007), the police, while searching a house, ordered two of its occupants, who had been in bed, to get out of bed and stand naked for two or three minutes while the police made sure that no weapons were present. Again relying on *Michigan v. Summers*, the Supreme Court held that there had been no Fourth Amendment violation.

G. Probable Cause

As we turn attention to the Fourth Amendment's concern with the procedural aspects of criminal investigation, we encounter a struggle that has been going on since the early 1960s over the proper analytical framework to apply to warrantless searches under the so-called exceptions to the warrant requirement. Before getting more deeply involved in that struggle, however, it is appropriate to touch on one aspect of the Fourth Amendment that applies to warranted searches and warrantless searches alike and that is an important and unchanging factor under either analytical approach.

Whether one employs the General Reasonableness approach or the Centrality of the Warrant Requirement approach, the pivotal criterion is frequently the existence of probable cause. By the very terms of the Fourth Amendment, probable cause is indispensable to the issuance of a valid warrant. That constitutional sine qua non applies to the search warrant and the arrest warrant alike. The case law, moreover, has also established probable cause as the necessary predicate for both a reasonable warrantless search for evidence and a reasonable warrantless arrest.

The subject matter of the probable cause, of course, may differ. Probable cause for a search contemplates a probability that evidence will be found in the place to be searched. Probable cause to arrest, on the other hand, contemplates a probability that the person to be arrested perpetrated a crime. The quantitative measuring of probable cause, however, remains a constant. In the context of what was a reasonable warrantless search of an automobile, *Carroll v. United States* in 1925 attempted to get a handle on the concept:

> The Fourth Amendment does not denounce all searches or seizures, but only such as are unreasonable.
>
> . . . On reason and authority the true rule is that if the search and seizure without a warrant are made upon probable cause, that is, upon a belief, reasonably arising out of circumstances known to the seizing officer, that an automobile or other vehicle contains that which by law is subject to seizure and destruction, the search and seizure are valid.

What is generally accepted as the Supreme Court's best definition of probable cause was that articulated in *Brinegar v. United States* in 1949:

> In dealing with probable cause . . . as the very name implies, we deal with probabilities. These are not technical; they are the factual and practical considerations of everyday life on which reasonable and prudent men, not legal technicians, act. . . .
>
> "The substance of all the definitions" of probable cause "is a reasonable ground for belief of guilt." And this "means less than evidence which would justify condemnation" or conviction, as Marshall, Ch. J., said for the Court more than a century ago in *Locke v. United States.* Since Marshall's time, at any rate, it has come to mean more than bare suspicion: Probable cause exists where "the facts and circumstances within their [the officers'] knowledge,

> and of which they had reasonably trustworthy information, [are] sufficient in themselves to warrant a man of reasonable caution in the belief that" an offense has been or is being committed. (citations and footnote omitted).

In *Maryland v. Pringle* (2003), evidence of drug activity found in the passenger compartment of an automobile occupied by three persons was held to constitute probable cause for the arrest of all three.

H. The Special Problem of Temporarily "Seizing" a Residence While Obtaining a Warrant to Search It

In terms of the respective degrees of intrusiveness, the Supreme Court has drawn a distinction between 1) the temporary "seizure" of a residence in order to freeze the situation and to prevent the disappearance or destruction of evidence, while a search warrant was being obtained; and 2) the ensuing search of that residence. In *Segura v. United States* (1984), while one team of officers went to find a judge to issue a search warrant, another team of officers warrantlessly entered Segura's residential apartment and "froze" the scene. Nothing they observed in the course of their warrantless presence, however, went into the warrant application or was even communicated to the other members of the team. The warrant, under authority of which the full-blown search of the apartment was ultimately executed, was held to be, therefore, the untainted product of an "independent source." The limited presence of the officers inside the apartment was deemed to have been, for analytic purposes, the functional equivalent of having surrounded and thereby "seized" the apartment from the outside, including the prohibiting of anyone from entering the apartment. The temporary seizure of the apartment was held to have been reasonable. *Illinois v. McArthur* (2001) reached the same result under circumstances where the "seizure" of a residential trailer was from the outside and where the owner of the trailer was simply prohibited from reentering it unless he agreed to take a police monitor with him.

I. The General Reasonableness Approach Versus the Centrality of the Warrant Requirement Approach

For most of the early life of the Fourth Amendment, it was thought that the heart of its command was that the police should, in a general sense, behave reasonably whenever they search and whenever they seize, without calibrating too finely just what such reasonable behavior involved. There was a balancing between the governmental interest in investigating crime and the degree of intrusion into a citizen's privacy. A requirement that a warrant must be obtained whenever feasible was not yet the measure of reasonableness. This general balancing approach prevailed from the beginning through the time of *Harris v. United States* (1947) and *United States v. Rabinowitz* (1950).

It was with the coming of the Warren Court and its so-called "Criminal Law Revolution" that the fortunes of doctrinal war suddenly tilted in favor of the Warrant Clause. Responding to earlier urging from Justices Frankfurter and Jackson, the Warren Court determined that the most effective way to maximize Fourth Amendment protection was, whenever possible, to interpose a "neutral and detached magistrate" between "the policeman and his quarry." The Warrant Clause was, in effect, incorporated into the General Reasonableness Clause as a way of measuring reasonableness. Where it was feasible for the police to obtain a search warrant, it was deemed unreasonable per se for them not to do so. It was the various exigencies that at times made obtaining a warrant unfeasible that gave rise to the recognized exceptions to the warrant requirement. *Katz v. United States* (1967) effectively stated the proposition: "[S]earches conducted outside the judicial process, without prior approval by judge or magistrate, are per se unreasonable under the Fourth Amendment—subject only to a few specifically established and well delineated exceptions."

This new dispensation, the so-called "Centrality of the Warrant Requirement," became the dominant approach to all Fourth Amendment analysis from the early 1960s through the early 1980s. Only Justice Harlan during the decade of the '60s and Justice Rehnquist during the decade of the '70s protested against the new vision. By the 1982 term of Court, however, their protest prevailed. With the post-Warren Court, the general reasonableness approach appeared to regain its earlier ascendancy. Under the freshly invigorated old approach, the standard measure of police reasonableness frequently became the "articulable suspicion" first spelled out in *Terry v. Ohio* (1968).

For several terms of court, it appeared that the Centrality of the Warrant Requirement analysis had become a dead letter. Before an official obituary could be pronounced for the centrality approach, however, it intermittently resurfaced in such cases as *Thompson v. Louisiana* (1984) and *Welsh v. Wisconsin* (1984). The Supreme Court never supplied any articulated reconciliation or explanation of how two seemingly diametric analyses could simultaneously coexist in the same Fourth Amendment field.

From the cases, however, one can distill a plausible explanation for the tense analytic coexistence. It seems that when the Supreme Court is dealing with the "core value" of the home itself, it utilizes the Centrality of the Warrant Requirement approach, the approach that maximizes citizen protection. When, on the other hand, the Court is dealing with something other than core value, as with most street encounters, it utilizes (except where well-established precedent has already preempted the field) the general reasonableness approach, the approach that maximizes investigative efficiency. One maximizes protection, even at the cost of investigative efficiency, when dealing with core value, but not otherwise. In rejecting a "murder scene" exception to the warrant requirement, the per curiam decision in *Flippo v. West Virginia* (1999) reaffirmed the "centrality" approach: "A warrantless search by the police is invalid unless it falls within one of the narrow and well-delineated exceptions to the warrant requirement."

There is much doubt as to what the currently prevailing framework of Fourth Amendment analysis is. Even in the context of a street encounter not involving "core value," a majority opinion of the Court acknowledged adherence to the Centrality of the Warrant Requirement philosophy as late as 1993 in *Minnesota v. Dickerson*. Before too much is made of that acknowledgment, however, it must be remembered that the author of the opinion was Justice White, who, at that time, was the last active member of the Court from the Warren Court era and he retired from active service at the end of that 1992-1993 term. It appears that the current Court may well have repudiated the doctrinal approach based on the Centrality of the Warrant Requirement. If it has done so, however, it has been a deliberately cryptic repudiation by silence.

J. The Centrality of the Warrant Requirement

It was the imposition of the Exclusionary Rule on state criminal courts by *Mapp v. Ohio* in 1961 that triggered the thermonuclear growth of Fourth Amendment law over the next several decades. Because that formative period was dominated by the philosophical assumptions of the Centrality of the Warrant Requirement school of thought, that analytic framework must be the starting point for any examination of the "specifically established," "well delineated," and "tightly circumscribed" exceptions.

The virtue of entrusting to a neutral and detached judicial figure the decision of when the privacy of a citizen should yield to the investigative imperative was extolled most articulately by Justice Jackson in *Johnson v. United States* (1948). Once that view of the Fourth Amendment became the dominant view for at least the next quarter of a century, a search pursuant to a search warrant became the norm, the expected way to do business. Any departure from that norm required some exigency by way of justification.

The predicate necessary to justify the initial intrusion under a search warrant has to be spelled out in the application for the warrant. That predicate must be probable cause supported by the applicant's oath or affirmation. The best explanations of what constitutes probable cause are still to be found in such early opinions as *Carroll v. United States* (1925) and *Brinegar v. United States* (1949). *Nathanson v. United States* (1933) and *Giordenello v. United States* (1958) made it clear that the warrant-issuing magistrate may not rely on the applicant's conclusory statements but must be furnished with enough detail to determine probable cause for himself. The scope limitations on the search must then be established because the warrant must state with particularity "the place to be searched and the persons or things to be seized."

In encouraging the police to act in the preferred warranted mode rather than in the nonpreferred warrantless mode, the Supreme Court, in a very practical way, "put its money where its mouth is." It gave law enforcement an "edge" when the police take the trouble to investigate in the preferred manner. *Aguilar v. Texas* (1964) announced that in a marginal case that could tilt either way, the quantum of suspicion that will qualify as probable cause in the context of a warrant review is less than that which may be required to support warrantless activity. *United States v. Ventresca* (1965) established that reviewing courts should not deal with warrants in a "hyper-technical" way but in a "common sense" assessment of documents "normally drafted by non-lawyers in the midst and haste of a criminal investigation." It pointed out that a "grudging or negative attitude by reviewing courts toward warrants will tend to discourage police officers from submitting their evidence to a judicial officer before acting." In a variety of ways, law enforcement has been given a bonus for relying on search warrants.

In 1983, the Supreme Court decision of *Illinois v. Gates* reaffirmed and spelled out more fully than had theretofore been done the deference that reviewing courts should extend to the probable cause decisions of warrant-issuing magistrates. *Illinois v. Gates* also dismantled the highly structured framework of analysis that had developed over the course of the preceding 19 years to test hearsay information from informants, especially police "informers" from the criminal milieu, on the issue of probable cause.

Beginning with *Aguilar v. Texas* in 1964 and developing more fully in *Spinelli v. United States* in 1969, the so-called "two-pronged test" had insisted that the magistrate make two determinations before accepting hearsay from an informant. The "basis of knowledge" prong required that the magistrate be told the basis for the informant's conclusion. The "veracity" prong then required that the magistrate be shown good reason for believing the informant was credible or that his information was otherwise reliable on that particular occasion.

Illinois v. Gates abandoned that two-pronged test in favor of a less structured assessment whereby "the issuing magistrate is simply to make a practical, common-sense decision whether, given all of the circumstances set forth in the affidavit before him, including the 'veracity' and 'basis of knowledge' of persons supplying hearsay information, there is a fair probability that contraband or evidence of a crime will be found in a particular place." The duty of the reviewing court, moreover, is "simply to ensure that the magistrate had a 'substantial basis for . . . concluding' that probable cause existed."

That highly deferential standard to be used by a reviewing court, trial or appellate, when examining a magistrate's probable cause determination in the context of issuing a warrant contrasts sharply with the more rigorous standard of review employed in a warrantless setting. *Ornelas v. United States* (1996) held that when an appellate court is reviewing a trial judge's determination of either 1) reasonable articulable suspicion or 2) probable cause in a warrantless setting, the appellate court, albeit deferring to the trial judge's findings of first-level facts unless clearly erroneous, will make its own independent, de novo determination of the ultimate fact of probable cause or of articulable suspicion.

United States v. Grubbs (2006) made it clear that there is nothing unconstitutional about an anticipatory warrant. As long as the application for the warrant establishes 1) that evidence will probably be present at a future time, 2) what the triggering event will be, and 3) the probability that the triggering event will occur, the warrant may constitutionally issue.

K. Exceptions to the Warrant Requirement

The requirement that the police obtain a search warrant is not an absolute. It is "subject only to a few specifically established, well delineated, tightly circumscribed, and jealously guarded exceptions." With respect to each of the exceptions, there are the two questions of 1) what is the predicate for the initial intrusion and 2) what is the permitted scope of what may be done under the exception. The permitted scope of any search, of course, is whatever is necessary to serve the purpose of that search, but not one little bit more. To determine the scope of an exception, therefore, it is necessary to identify the purpose for which that exception was created.

1. Search Incident to Lawful Arrest

Search incident to lawful arrest is the "granddaddy" of all the exceptions, coming to us from English common law. The predicate for the initial intrusion is easy. It is the fact of a lawful arrest. There is no such creature as a search incident to an unlawful arrest or a search incident to a nonarrest. A lawful arrest is indispensable. It matters not, however, whether the arrest is for the oldest common law crime or for the newest statutory crime. It matters not whether the arrest is warrantless or with an arrest warrant. It matters not whether the arrest is for high treason, for felony, or for misdemeanor. Indeed, *Atwater v. City of Lago Vista* (2001) made it clear that, in order to justify a full-blown custodial arrest, the misdemeanor need not involve a breach of the peace and need not constitute a jailable offense. Given the fact of a lawful arrest, some warrantless search will automatically follow as an incident of that arrest.

Virginia v. Moore (2008) added a significant dimension to what the Supreme Court means and does not mean by the term "search incident to lawful arrest." Virginia officers arrested a motorist for what was unquestionably a crime in Virginia but was a misdemeanor for which the officers could only issue a summons and could not make a custodial arrest. In violation of Virginia law, the officers nonetheless arrested the motorist and then conducted a warrantless search incident to that arrest. The motorist claimed that the arrest was, therefore, not a "lawful arrest" and the Virginia Supreme Court so held. The Supreme Court disagreed, explaining that its use of the term "lawful arrest" is "with constitutional law as the reference point." "We have equated a lawful arrest with an arrest based on probable cause." For clarity's sake, the term "search incident to lawful arrest" for Fourth Amendment purposes means "search incident to constitutionally permissible arrest."

Although a lawful custodial arrest is a sufficient predicate for a warrantless search incident thereto, a stop followed by the issuance of a citation for a traffic violation is not. *Knowles v. Iowa* (1998). When the suspect is not taken into custody, there is not the same exigent need to protect the officer from possible harm. "A custodial arrest involves 'danger to an officer' because of 'the extended exposure which follows the taking of a suspect into custody and transporting him to the police station.'"

The perplexing problem with search incident law was that of determining its appropriate scope. Although the police officer may have the automatic prerogative of searching one lawfully arrested, where, between the middle of the arrestee's head and the planet Venus, does that prerogative run out? What is the principle that explains why it runs out? On this little problem, the Supreme Court "zigged and zagged" for 42 years, reversing its field between broad scope and narrow scope no less than five times between *Agnello v. United States* (1927) and *Chimel v. California* (1969).

It was for *Chimel* to bring order out of chaos. It determined that there were two historic purposes for the search incident exception: 1) to disarm the arrestee to protect the life and limb of the arresting officer and 2) to prevent the arrestee from destroying evidence that might be accessible to him. The Supreme Court then reasoned that to serve those purposes it should not tie the search incident prerogative tightly to the body or clothing of the arrestee. It was necessary to move the scope of the search incident outward so as to embrace the entire area within the reach, lunge, or grasp of the arrestee. This is now sometimes called the *Chimel* perimeter. It is sometimes called the wingspan or the wingspread of the arrestee. Whatever the labels, they describe the same area—the danger zone within which the arrestee might be able to do either of the two bad things that the exception was invented to prevent him from doing. That is the zone within which the policeman is permitted to take all necessary preventive, preemptive measures.

New York v. Belton (1981) dealt with the special problem of delineating the *Chimel* perimeter when the person lawfully arrested is still in or has just been in an automobile. Its solution was to declare, by way of a "bright-line formula," that the entire passenger compartment of the automobile would arbitrarily be deemed to be within the search incident perimeter, whether in a given case it actually was or not. In *Thornton v. United States* (2004), the Supreme Court recognized the prerogative of the police to enjoy the benefit of the expanded *Chimel-Belton* search incident perimeter in a case where the arrestee had actually left his vehicle and walked a short distance away before the officer first accosted him. He was arrested, handcuffed, and placed in the back seat of a patrol car before the officer searched the arrestee's car. The Court extended the *Belton* rule to "recent occupants" as well as actual occupants of a vehicle.[10]

2. *The* Carroll *Doctrine*

The so-called automobile exception or better-called *Carroll* Doctrine is a child of 1925. It applies not just to automobiles but to such automobile equivalents as trucks, buses, motorcycles, wagons, airplanes, and boats. On the other hand, it does not apply to every warrantless search of an automobile. A warrantless probe into the situs of an automobile or automobile-equivalent may be made theoretically under any of the exceptions to the warrant requirement. It is only when the probe is made on the basis of probable cause plus exigency that it implicates the automobile exception.

To understand the exception fully, it is necessary to master the Four Cs: 1) the eponymic case of *Carroll v. United States* (1925), 2) *Chambers v. Maroney* (1970), 3) the pertinent part of *Coolidge v. New Hampshire* (1971), and 4) *California v. Carney* (1985). The predicate for the initial intrusion is the combination of 1) probable cause to believe that there is evidence of crime in the automobile and 2) an exigency, generally based upon the mobility of the automobile.

At the very end of the 1998-1999 term, the Supreme Court appeared to be undertaking, albeit almost by stealth, a major rewriting of the *Carroll* Doctrine. The effect of the effort, if successful, would have been to write out of the doctrine any residual exigency requirement at all, at least on a case-by-case basis. The energizing rationale of *Carroll v. United States* (1925) was an exigency based on mobility. It is, of course, possible to conceptualize that exigency/mobility as something built into the automobile exception itself with no further proof of that element being required. It is also possible to conceptualize the automobile exception as something requiring the proof of the two elements of 1) probable cause and 2) exigency based on mobility in each case. The reasoning of *Carroll*, of *Chambers v. Maroney* (1970), and the holding of *Coolidge v. New Hampshire* (1971) appeared strongly to favor the latter conceptualization. An automobile up on cinder blocks and without a motor self-evidently would not trigger a warrantless *Carroll* Doctrine search.

10. *Belton* was overruled by *Arizona v Gant* (2009).

There could also quite obviously be situations where, even given the mobility of an automobile, the police still, as in *Coolidge*, had had ample opportunity to obtain a warrant beforehand.

Maryland v. Dyson (1999) was a summary disposition without benefit of oral argument. It was an unsigned opinion of less than two pages in length. In rejecting any exigency requirement at all, the basic reasoning for that rejection took up no more than a sentence. The reasoning behind the *Carroll* and *Chambers* decisions, couched in exigency, was not discussed. The square holding of *Coolidge* as to the absence of exigency and its six-page supporting analysis, 403 U.S. at 458-64, was completely ignored. The *Dyson* decision took as its point of departure the case of *Pennsylvania v. Labron* (1996). *Labron* itself was a stealth opinion, an unsigned summary disposition and an unlikely candidate to be suddenly treated as a precedential landmark.

Florida v. White (1999) also dealt with the *Carroll* Doctrine, but only obliquely. It did not involve the search of an automobile for contraband. It involved, rather, the warrantless seizure of the entire automobile itself as forfeitable contraband. The Supreme Court held that, even absent exigent circumstances, probable cause to believe that the automobile itself was forfeitable contraband (having been used for the transportation of narcotics) was just as reasonable a predicate for its warrantless seizure as probable cause to believe that it contained contraband would have been for its warrantless search.

3. *The Suitcase or Container Exception*

The doctrinally eccentric suitcase or container exception was a spin-off from the *Carroll* Doctrine, an instance of the *Carroll* Doctrine declined, but seems likely soon to be subsumed within the *Carroll* Doctrine. It was born in *United States v. Chadwick* (1977) and reconfirmed in *Arkansas v. Sanders* (1979). Prior to *Chadwick*, most of the state courts that had considered the question had concluded that warrantless searches of suitcases, boxes, and other closed containers would fit conveniently within an expanded *Carroll* Doctrine analysis. The *Carroll* Doctrine permitted warrantless searches of automobiles based on the combination of probable cause plus exigency, the exigency arising out of the automobile's mobility. If probable cause existed to believe that a container held evidence of crime and if there was an exigency based upon the ready mobility of that container, the *Carroll* Doctrine rationale would have seemed as compelling in the case of the container as in the case of the automobile. That the modality of mobility would have been ambulatory rather than vehicular would have been a distinction without a doctrinal difference.

Chadwick, however, declined the opportunity to accommodate container searches within an expanded *Carroll* Doctrine. Its basis for distinguishing between the automobile exception and the new container exception was its conclusion that the container enjoyed a greater expectation of privacy than did the automobile. As a result of that purported distinction, an anomaly developed. Probable cause plus exigency justified both the warrantless seizure and the subsequent warrantless search of an automobile. The same probable cause and the same exigency, however, justified only the warrantless seizure of a container but not a subsequent warrantless search. The container might be seized to dissipate the exigency of likely disappearance, but it then had to be held inviolate in the police property room until a proper search warrant was obtained.

The anomaly became a problem when the two doctrines overlapped. When a suspect container was located inside a suspect automobile, would *Chadwick*'s greater immunity from search "trump" *Carroll*'s greater police latitude, or vice versa? With *United States v. Ross* in 1982, the tilt started going decidedly in favor of the greater police latitude allowed by *Carroll* when the two doctrines overlapped.

In *California v. Acevedo* (1991), Justice Blackmun concluded a 14-year crusade against what he deemed to be the illogic of the container exception. The Supreme Court repudiated the notion that the expectation of privacy enjoyed by a suitcase or container that is in an automobile is any more than that enjoyed by the automobile itself. As a result of *Acevedo*, there is no vitality left to the container exception when the container is in an automobile. The handwriting is on the wall, moreover, that what remains of the exception will be repudiated when the occasion next arises.

Wyoming v. Houghton (1999) made it clear that, when there is probable cause to search an automobile for contraband or other evidence under the *Carroll* Doctrine, the police prerogative includes the right to search containers within the automobile and it makes no difference whether any particular container belongs to the driver of the automobile or to a passenger. The container's presence in the automobile as a possible repository of suspected evidence is all that is required. The prerogative to search a container belonging to a passenger, however, does not imply the prerogative to search the person of the passenger.

4. *Exigent or Emergency Circumstances*

Warden v. Hayden (1967) gave birth to what was at first called the "hot pursuit" exception. It has since been realized that it is better perceived as an exigent circumstances or emergency circumstances exception generally, with hot pursuit simply as one instance of a much larger phenomenon. *Michigan v. Tyler* (1978) broadened the exception to include the emergency entrance of a fire scene both by firemen and by arson investigators. *Mincey v. Arizona* (1978) employed the exception to explain the emergency warrantless entry by the police to neutralize a murder scene. The police prerogative warrantlessly to enter a fire scene or a murder scene while the original exigency is still operative dissipates, however, as soon as the emergency itself dissipates.

In *Brigham City, Utah v. Stuart* (2006), a 3 a.m. complaint about a loud and raucous party brought the police to the backyard of a private residence. They could hear shouting inside the house. Through a screen door and windows they could see four adults and a juvenile fighting with one person being hit and bleeding from the mouth. Overruling the Supreme Court of Utah, the U.S. Supreme Court held that the emergency circumstances exception permitted the warrantless entry. Utilizing the *Whren v. United States* rationale, the Court ruled that a subjective intent by the officers to make arrests would be immaterial as long as the objective facts supported an emergency circumstances entry.

The emergency dealt with by this exception involves injury or threat of injury to persons. Whereas the lesser threshold of an automobile will yield to the lesser exigency that evidence may disappear, the greater threshold of the home will not. Even that greater threshold, however, will yield to the greater exigency of a threat to life or limb.

The scope limitation is generic. It is permitted to do whatever is necessary to deal with the exigency or emergency, but nothing more.

5. *Stop and Frisk*

The stop and frisk exceptions are vintage 1968 products of *Terry v. Ohio* (1968) and *Sibron v. New York* (1968). A stop is a junior varsity seizure of the person. A frisk is a junior varsity search of the person. Because both of these lesser intrusions infringe sufficiently on a citizen's right not to be stopped and not to be frisked, they fall within the coverage of the Fourth Amendment and must be reasonable to be permitted. Because, however, they are less intrusive than full-blown seizures and searches of the person, they may be deemed reasonable upon predicates less substantial than probable cause. The newly articulated, less substantial predicate is now generally called "articulable suspicion," sometimes "good cause to believe," sometimes "reasonable suspicion," and sometimes "particularized suspicion."

Although the stop and the frisk require the same quantitative justification as articulable suspicion, different qualitative justifications are required. Because the governmental purpose of the stop is crime-related, the predicate for a stop must be articulable suspicion that a crime has occurred, is then occurring, or is about to occur. Because the governmental purpose of the frisk, by contrast, is to protect the life and limb of the stopping officer, the predicate for the frisk is articulable suspicion that the person stopped may be armed.

The scope limitation on the stop is that it remain right at the spot or very close to where the stop first occurred. The temporal scope limitation is that the stop only last a short while. What is a reasonable length of time for a stop must be determined on an ad hoc basis. In *United States v. Sharpe* (1985), a 20-minute detention was deemed reasonable, whereas in *United States v. Place* (1983), a 90-minute detention was deemed unreasonable.

The scope limitation on the frisk is that it be confined to the pat-down of the clothing surface of the person being frisked. That is all that is required to detect the presence of offensive weapons. That is all that is necessary, therefore, to serve the purpose of the frisk.

In terms of not how intensive but of how extensive the scope of a frisk may be, frisk law looks to search-incident law as a controlling analogy. Because the single purpose of a frisk—disarming the stoppee—is identical to one of the two purposes of a search incident—disarming the arrestee—it follows that the permitted frisk perimeter logically must be co-terminus with *Chimel v. California*'s permitted search incident perimeter. As with search-incident law, frisk law, to serve its purpose of disarming a possibly dangerous suspect, must look to the wingspan; the wingspread; the reach, lunge, or grasp of the stoppee. Where the stoppee is in or immediately outside of an automobile, moreover, *Michigan v. Long* (1983) does for the permitted frisk area what *New York v. Belton* (1981) did for the permitted search incident area. By way of a bright-line formula, the geographic area in which the frisk may be conducted includes the passenger compartment of the automobile.

In the immediate wake of *Terry v. Ohio* and *Sibron v. New York*, other cases soon made it clear that the stop-and-frisk prerogative of the police may be applied to motorists as surely as it may be applied to pedestrians. *Adams v. Williams* (1972); *United States v. Cortez* (1971). An entire genre of cases has developed involving stops and frisks at airports. *United States v. Mendenhall* (1980); *Florida v. Royer* (1983); *Florida v. Rodriguez* (1984); *United States v. Sokolow* (1989).

In 1983, *United States v. Place* made it clear that articulable suspicion under *Terry* is enough not only to stop a person but to detain suspicious luggage as well.

Illinois v. Wardlow (2000) established that sudden and unprovoked flight at the approach of the police, particularly in a "high-crime area," may alone constitute reasonable articulable suspicion for a *Terry* stop. "Nervous, evasive behavior is a pertinent factor in determining reasonable suspicion. Headlong flight is the consummate act of evasion; it is not necessarily indicative of wrongdoing, but it is certainly suggestive of such."

Florida v. J.L. (2000), on the one side, and the cases of *Adams v. Williams* (1972) and *Alabama v. White* (1990), on the other side, effectively "bracket the target" with respect to the reasonableness of a stop based on an unsolicited "tip" from an informant with no "track record" of proven reliability. In both *Florida v. J.L.* and *Adams v. Williams*, there was no significant police corroboration of the "tip." In *Florida v. J.L.*, which held the stop to be unreasonable, the tipster was anonymous, whereas in *Adams v. Williams*, which affirmed the validity of the stop and frisk, the tipster was at least known to the police. *Alabama v. White* shared with *Florida v. J.L.* the common denominator of an anonymous tipster. In *Alabama v. White*, which held the stop to be reasonable, there was independent police corroboration of "predictive behavior." In *Florida v. J.L.* the police corroboration, which was held to have been inadequate to establish articulable suspicion, was only with respect to the description and location of the suspect and not with possibly criminal behavior.

It is clear under *Terry* that the police may question a suspect after a reasonable stop. As *Hiibel v. Sixth Judicial District Court* (2004) pointed out, however, "Although it is well established that an officer may ask a suspect to identify himself in the course of a *Terry* stop, it has been an open question whether the suspect can be arrested and prosecuted for refusal to answer." In this case, Hiibel was reasonably stopped pursuant to *Terry*. He was ultimately convicted under a Nevada state law for refusing to identify himself after being asked to do so. The Supreme Court held that, even if the Fourth Amendment does not affirmatively compel self-identification in the course of a *Terry* stop, neither does it confer an affirmative privilege on the suspect to refuse to identify himself. The compulsion was pursuant to state law and was held to be not unreasonable.

6. The Plain View Doctrine (Plus Plain Feel)

The Plain View Doctrine, emerging from the plurality opinion of Justice Stewart in *Coolidge v. New Hampshire* (1971), is sui generis. Unlike the other exceptions to the warrant requirement, it does not authorize the most minimal of searches. It is exclusively a seizure doctrine. It is nonetheless a legitimate exception to the warrant requirement for the reason that the Fourth Amendment proscribes unreasonable seizures as surely as it proscribes unreasonable searches.

Under the Plain View Doctrine, the police may warrantlessly seize an item when three conditions are satisfied: 1) there has been a prior valid intrusion into the constitutionally protected area, 2) an item is spotted in plain view, and 3) there is probable cause to believe that the item is evidence. It was once thought by many observers that the probable evidence spotted in plain view had to have been spotted inadvertently, but *Horton v. California* (1990) dispelled that false impression. It was *Arizona v. Hicks* (1987) that explicated most fully the requirement that the probable cause must exist before any even partial seizure or further examination of the item be undertaken.

Although some commentators characterize an inventory as an exception to the warrant requirement, it is hardly that at all. Under pure inventory theory, inventorying is not part of the criminal investigation process but, more innocuously, simply an aspect of the general police caretaking function. When an inventory turns up evidence of crime, the inventory itself, if legitimate, serves as the prior valid intrusion for a Plain View Doctrine seizure when probable evidence is then spotted in the course of making the inventory.

Minnesota v. Dickerson (1993) recognized, by way of analogy to the Plain View Doctrine, the concept of a plain-feel doctrine. The police, while conducting a properly limited frisk of a suspect, were able to detect through a layer of clothing the presence of contraband inside a pocket. Having thus acquired probable cause through the tactile sense, the entry into the pocket to effectuate the seizure of known contraband was deemed reasonable.

The *Minnesota v. Dickerson* rationale arguably might expand *Coolidge*'s second requirement so as to embrace all of the senses and not merely those of sight and touch. On the other hand, a possible problem with "plain smell" or "plain hearing" analogues to "plain view" or "plain feel" is that suspicious smells or suspicious sounds might emanate outward from inside a protected threshold. That would present problems of crossing a threshold not involved when applying the Plain View Doctrine (where the threshold has already validly been crossed) or its plain feel analogue.

7. Consent

The consent "exception" is doctrinally slippery. Some Fourth Amendment commentators once preferred to think of consent as an instance of Fourth Amendment inapplicability rather than as an instance of Fourth Amendment satisfaction. Their theory was that any constitutional right, including a Fourth Amendment protection, may be waived. The appropriate waiver standard was that of voluntariness as explained by *Schneckloth v. Bustamonte* (1973). The key questions for a consent analysis were: 1) "Who?" and 2) "How?" Who gave consent and did that person have legal authority to do so? If so, how was the consent obtained? As an instance of threshold applicability, consent or waiver would be measured objectively. Did the consenting party actually have authority to do so and was the consent actually voluntary?

We learned from *Illinois v. Rodriguez* (1990), however, that a consent search implicates the Fourth Amendment merits and, therefore, constitutes an exception to the warrant requirement rather than an instance of the Fourth Amendment having been rendered inapplicable. Because the reasonableness of police conduct is the core concern of the Fourth Amendment, consent issues must be measured subjectively through the eyes of the policeman as of the time of the search or seizure. The critical issues, therefore, are: 1) not whether the consenting party actually had lawful authority to consent but whether the policeman reasonably assumed that to be the case and 2) not whether the consent was actually voluntary but whether the policeman reasonably assumed it was. In *Illinois v. Rodriguez*, it was determined that the person who ostensibly consented to the police entry of the appellant's apartment actually had no lawful authority to do so. The policeman, who relied upon that apparent consent, was mistaken but his mistake was held to be "reasonable under the circumstances." The Supreme Court observed, "[I]n order to satisfy the 'reasonableness' requirement of the Fourth Amendment, what is generally demanded of the many factual determinations that must regularly be made by agents of the government—whether the magistrate issuing a warrant, the police officer executing a warrant, or the police officer conducting a search or seizure under one of the exceptions to the warrant requirement—is not that they always be correct, but that they always be reasonable." In *Rodriguez,* quoted with approval from *Hill v. California* in 1971, where police officers had mistakenly arrested the wrong person but where "the officers' mistake was understandable and the arrest a reasonable response to the situation facing them at the time."

A year later in *Florida v. Jimeno*, the Supreme Court reiterated that the pivotal criterion is the reasonableness of the officer's behavior on the basis of the circumstances as they appear to the officer. The *Jimeno* Court observed, "The touchstone of the Fourth Amendment is reasonableness. The standard for measuring the scope of a suspect's consent under the Fourth Amendment is that of 'objective' reasonableness—what would the typical reasonable person have understood by the exchange between the officer and the suspect?"

Cases involving third-party consent present a doctrinally difficult area. When two or more persons are co-tenants of a residence or co-owners of an automobile, a duffel bag, or a safe deposit box, each one bears the risk that the other will consent to police entry or police examination. In cases such as *United States v. Matlock* (1974), *Illinois v. Rodriguez* (1990), and *Frazier v. Cupp* (1969) (a duffel bag shared by two cousins), consent to enter or inspect by one party defeated the Fourth Amendment expectation of privacy of the other party. In those cases, however, the party who was the ultimate defendant was not available to protest to the consensual entry. In *Georgia v. Randolph* (2006), by contrast, a wife invited the police into the house as her husband stood at the door and protested against their entry. The Supreme Court held that "a physically present inhabitant's express refusal of consent to a police search is dispositive as to him, regardless of the consent of a fellow occupant."[11]

8. What the Police May Do in the Context of a Traffic Stop

As if carried on the tide of the resurging general reasonableness analysis, a number of cases, beginning with the 1995-1996 term, have, in practical effect, created a new category of permitted warrantless intrusions. The category, moreover, is defined by the nature of the police activity—a traffic stop—rather than by the doctrinal justification for the intrusion. Although an automobile or, at least, some vehicle is a sine qua non for a traffic stop, the automobile exception is seldom doctrinally involved (*but see Wyoming v. Houghton* (1999)). The traffic stop case may just as readily involve search-incident law (*Knowles v. Iowa* (1998)), *Terry*-stop law (*Whren v. United States* (1996)), consent law (*Ohio v. Robinette* (1996)), or no traditional doctrinal category at all (*Maryland v. Wilson* (1997)).

11. *Fernandez v California* (2014) held, however, that after arresting an objector at his home and transporting him to jail, police could return and obtain, from a cohabitating girlfriend, valid consent to search the objector's home.

The most significant of the traffic stop cases is unquestionably *Whren v. United States* (1996). As long as the police have articulable suspicion under *Terry v. Ohio* to believe a traffic infraction has occurred, their subsequent stop of the vehicle is objectively justified even if the enforcement of the traffic laws was not their true subjective purpose. In *Whren*, the stopping officers were members of the narcotics squad and were not traffic officers. The police thus may opportunistically seize upon a traffic violation in order to serve other investigative purposes, provided that there is an actual objective basis for the traffic stop.

The *Whren* rationale was closely followed in *Devenpeck v. Alford* (2004). A warrantless arrest is not unconstitutional if the facts known to the arresting officer objectively establish probable cause to arrest for some crime, even if such crime is not closely related to the crime the officer had subjectively in mind when making the arrest.

As early as 1977, *Pennsylvania v. Mimms* established that, when an officer lawfully stops a vehicle for a traffic infraction or otherwise, he may, for his own protection, order the driver to alight from the vehicle. *Maryland v. Wilson* (1997) extended that police prerogative to ordering passengers to alight from a vehicle as well. Neither the driver nor the passengers may be frisked, however, unless there is articulable suspicion to believe that they may be armed. The driver, of course, may be detained at the scene for the course of the traffic stop. *Brendlin v. California* (2007) seems unquestionably to confirm that when the police stop a vehicle, even if only for a traffic violation, they have the authority to detain passengers at the scene as well.

Ohio v. Robinette (1996) began as a routine traffic stop. After the purpose of the traffic stop had been served, the officer engaged Robinette in further conversation and ultimately obtained permission to search Robinette's vehicle. The voluntariness of the consent turned upon whether Robinette had been detained in violation of the Fourth Amendment once the purpose of the traffic stop had been served or whether he remained in conversation with the officer voluntarily. The Supreme Court rejected the bright-line requirement of the state of Ohio that a motorist in such a situation must be affirmatively advised of his right to leave. The case was remanded to determine whether the ultimate consent was actually voluntary or not.

Knowles v. Iowa (1998) began as a traffic stop case but ultimately turned on the principle that the issuance of a traffic citation is not the equivalent of a lawful custodial arrest and that there may not, therefore, be a warrantless search incident to the issuance of a citation. The reasons that generate the search incident exception are not present in a noncustodial setting.

Wyoming v. Houghton (1999) also began as a traffic stop. When the stopping officer developed probable cause to believe that there was evidence of narcotics in the car, however, analysis was triggered under the *Carroll* Doctrine. The holding was that a *Carroll* Doctrine search of an automobile implies the right to search any pertinent container in the automobile, regardless of the ownership of the container.

L. *The Sui Generis Nature of the Law of Arrest*

An illustration of the different ways in which the Supreme Court handles 1) an intrusion involving the Fourth Amendment's core value and 2) an intrusion involving less than core value is in its treatment of the law of arrest. Although an arrest is, to be sure, a seizure of the person, the Supreme Court has at times treated the arrest situation very differently from the way it treats the search for or seizure of physical evidence.

With respect to the search for evidence, the Court has held that it is unreasonable to search without a warrant unless some exigency makes it impossible, or at least very difficult, to obtain a warrant. In 1976, however, in *United States v. Watson*, it held that a warrantless arrest on the street, provided that it is based on probable cause, is reasonable even though there was ample time and opportunity to obtain an arrest warrant and even though the police could give no reason for having failed to obtain one. Basically, a warrantless street arrest is reasonable because that is the way it has always been done.

Four years later, in *Payton v. New York*, by way of contrast, the Supreme Court held that a warrantless arrest, even though based on probable cause, would not be reasonable if made within a home, absent some extreme exigency. From the vantage point of the person arrested, a warrantless arrest outside the home would appear to be just as grievous an intrusion as a warrantless arrest inside the home. The Supreme Court justified its insistence upon the warrant in the one situation but not in the other on the special protection afforded by the Fourth Amendment to the home itself. It explained that "the 'physical entry of the home is the chief evil against which the wording of the Fourth Amendment is directed.'"

An individual who has suffered a warrantless arrest on the street, however, is nonetheless entitled to some after-the-fact judicial intervention. *Gerstein v. Pugh* (1975) held that, following a warrantless street arrest, the individual arrested is entitled to a probable cause hearing before a judge "promptly." *County of Riverside v. McLaughlin* (1991) fine-tuned that notion of promptness by holding that the individual arrested should receive the probable cause hearing presumptively within 48 hours of the arrest. The *County of Riverside* decision was applied again by the Supreme Court in *Powell v. Nevada* (1994).[12]

III. The Sanction for a Fourth Amendment Violation

Given a violation of the Fourth Amendment, it becomes a policy question for society to decide what, if anything, it chooses to do about it. Its choices are theoretically infinite: nothing at all; a criminal prosecution of the policeman; a tort action, state or federal, against the policeman, the police department, the municipality, or the state; the evidentiary exclusion of the fruits of the violation; the total dismissal of all charges; the shooting of the policeman, etc. Haltingly over the decades, the Supreme Court settled on the exclusionary rule of evidence.

A. The Exclusionary Rule

The exclusionary rule operates to exclude from admission in a trial all evidence that is determined to be the product of an unconstitutional search or seizure. When a defendant makes a timely motion to exclude, a hearing will be conducted outside the presence of the jury, frequently pretrial, on the Fourth Amendment issue. If it is determined that the search and the seizure satisfy Fourth Amendment standards, the evidence is received. If, on the other hand, it is determined that the search or the seizure violated the Fourth Amendment, then the fruits of that unconstitutionality are suppressed and cannot be used, at least in the state's case-in-chief on the merits of guilt or innocence.

In *Weeks v. United States* (1914), the Court first employed the exclusionary rule in a federal prosecution. It seemed to do so, however, under its supervisory power over the federal court system. In *Wolf v. Colorado* (1949), it first held that the Fourth Amendment was part of the due process of law guaranteed by the Fourteenth Amendment even against state action. Justice Frankfurter, however, declined to apply the exclusionary rule to the states, reasoning that it was not part of the constitutional right per se and leaving it to the states to implement the amendment as they deemed appropriate.

There followed a troubled 12-year interim between *Wolf* in 1949 and *Mapp* in 1961. During the early part of that period, both state investigators and federal investigators availed themselves of the so-called "Silver Platter Doctrine." Even if state investigators had violated the Fourth Amendment, they were still free to offer the evidence to federal prosecutors on a silver platter and to have the evidence introduced in federal court. Conversely, federal investigators could violate the Fourth Amendment and offer the fruits of such violation to state prosecutors on a reciprocal silver platter. The Supreme Court shut off the "Silver Platter Doctrine" first in one direction in *Rea v. State* (1956), forbidding federal law enforcement officials from offering Fourth Amendment-violative evidence to their state counterparts, and then in the other direction in *Elkins v. United States* (1960), excluding from federal trials all evidence obtained when state investigators violated the Fourth Amendment. With that, the handwriting was on the wall for *Mapp*.

It was with *Mapp v. Ohio* (1961) that the Supreme Court finally applied the exclusionary rule of evidence to the states. Though *Mapp* seemed to treat the exclusionary rule as part of the constitutional protection, *Stone v. Powell* (1976) made it clear that the "exclusionary rule was a judicially created means of effectuating the rights secured by the Fourth Amendment." Subsequent cases have treated the exclusionary rule as an expedient implementing device. Periodically, opinions such as that of Justice White in *Malley v. Briggs* (1986) raise the specter that if a viable alternative to the exclusionary rule—such as an effective federal tort remedy—could be designed, then *Mapp*'s rationale for adopting the exclusionary rule would be seriously undermined.

A glaring deficiency in the *Mapp* opinion was its failure to identify the governmental purpose of the exclusionary rule. At least three possibilities existed. An exclusionary rule could be designed to be remedial in nature, treating the exclusion of unlawfully seized evidence as part of the defendant's con-

12. In *Manuel v City of Joliet* (2017), the Court held that pretrial detention constitutes a continuing seizure until trial and ruled that Fourth Amendment protection is not extinguished by a judicial determination of probable cause at the *ex parte* hearing under *Gerstein v. Pugh* (1975).

stitutional entitlement. The rule could, on the other hand, be designed to serve the imperative of judicial integrity, concerned that the image of the court system itself not be tarnished by tainted evidence. Yet a third purpose could be the prophylactic one of general deterrence, discouraging future violations by denying violators the fruits of their unconstitutionality. That deterrence, in turn, could be aimed at judges and police broadly or it could be narrowly focused on the more limited mission of "policing the police."

The opinion of Justice Clark in *Mapp* did, to be sure, at one point or another mention in passing each of the three possible rationales for an exclusionary rule. At no point, however, did it identify any of the rationales, mentioned only in the course of general discussion, as an energizing or sufficient condition for the rule. In the wake of the *Mapp* opinion, it was unclear whether all three rationales collectively were necessary to justify exclusion, whether any two of them in combination would have been sufficient, whether any one alone would be an adequate basis for an exclusionary rule, and, if so, which one. Until the purpose of the rule could be identified, there was no way to determine which applications in which situations would efficaciously serve that purpose and which applications might incur the loss of probative evidence without achieving any desired end in return.

The necessity for identifying the purpose of the rule was soon to arise because that purpose would be a major factor in determining whether the new constitutional principle should be only prospective in application or fully retroactive. In *Linkletter v. Walker* (1965), the Supreme Court premised its decision not to make *Mapp* fully retroactive on its holding that the exclusive purpose of the rule was the deterrent purpose of "policing the police." With *Linkletter v. Walker*, the Supreme Court committed itself, perhaps unwittingly, to the major premise of a significant syllogism that was yet to be constructed.

Seizing on *Linkletter*'s statement of the exclusionary rule's exclusive purpose, a series of Supreme Court decisions in the mid-1970s austerely cabined the application of the rule. Liberals characterized those decisions as "a retreat from *Mapp*;" conservatives characterized them as the disinclination to apply *Mapp* more broadly than required by *Mapp* itself. Whatever the characterization, the results were the same. *United States v. Calandra* (1974) declined to extend the exclusionary rule to grand jury proceedings. *United States v. Janis* (1976) declined to extend the rule to civil cases. *United States v. Ceccolini* (1978) declined to extend the rule to bar the use of a live witness whose identity had only been discovered by virtue of a Fourth Amendment violation. *United States v. Havens* (1980) declined to extend the exclusionary rule to the use of evidence in rebuttal for impeachment purposes. *Pennsylvania Bd. of Probation and Parole v. Scott* (1998) declined to extend the exclusionary rule to the use of evidence at a parole violation hearing.

The inevitable syllogism, which had been remorselessly building since the articulation of its major premise in 1965, appeared fully constructed in 1984 in *Massachusetts v. Sheppard* (1984) and *United States v. Leon* (1984). The "good-faith" exception to the exclusionary rule announced that, if the officer in good faith obtained a search warrant, no deterrent effect would be achieved by excluding the evidence even if a judge had made a mistake in issuing the warrant. Its cold logic was difficult to refute. If the only purpose of the exclusionary rule is to deter unreasonable police conduct, then one hits the police with the sanction of exclusion when they are unreasonable but not otherwise. If the Supreme Court has been urging, as it has, the police for 30 years to eschew making unilateral decisions and to defer to the judgment of the neutral and detached magistrate, then the police officer who does just that has been eminently reasonable. If the behavior of the officer is truly the only thing being monitored by the rule, it would be irrational to punish the officer for the judge's mistake in issuing a bad warrant.

Indeed, the vigorous dissent of Justice Brennan in *Sheppard* and *Leon* recognized the internal force of the majority's logic. If the major premise as to the exclusive purpose of the rule is true, the majority's conclusion follows validly. That is why Justice Brennan quarreled not so much with the logical validity of the result as he did with the truth of the major premise. Justice Brennan would have treated exclusion as part of the constitutional entitlement of a defendant and not simply as a prophylactic device to police the police. If the exclusion of unconstitutionally seized evidence is part of the entitlement of the defendant, then the good-faith exception to the exclusionary rule makes no sense at all. If, on the other hand, the only purpose of the exclusionary rule is to police the police, then the good-faith exception makes eminently good sense. The good-faith battle, if it is to be intelligently fought, must be fought not over the conclusion reached in 1984 but over the major premise announced in 1965.

In both *Sheppard* and *Leon*, the mistake had been made by a judge. In *Illinois v. Krull* (1987), the Supreme Court applied the good-faith exception to the exclusionary rule to a situation where an officer had reasonably followed an Illinois statute that was later held to be an unconstitutional violation of the Fourth Amendment. The mistake in that case was that of the state legislature, not that of the officer, and no deterrent purpose would have been served by punishing the officer for the legislature's mistake. Using similar reasoning, the Supreme Court gave an officer the benefit of the good-faith exception in *Arizona v. Evans* (1995), when he arrested a suspect on the basis of an arrest warrant that was no longer outstanding. It was held in that case that the mistake in not keeping accurate computerized records had been that of a courthouse clerk in the judicial branch of government and not that of the officer. Again, the focus of the Supreme Court was not on whether a Fourth Amendment violation had occurred but on whether the officer, whose conduct is the exclusive concern of the exclusionary rule, had acted unreasonably.

Only time will tell whether the 5-4 opinion of the Supreme Court in *Hudson v. Michigan* (2006) was simply one of those random "things that go bump in the night" or was as truly portentous as its words suggest. In *Hudson,* the prosecution conceded that there had been a violation of the Fourth Amendment's "knock and announce" requirement. The only issue was that of what the sanction should be for such a violation. The majority opinion held that the exclusion of evidence would not serve any meaningful deterrent purpose and that a "knock and announce" violation is not serious enough to justify the admittedly heavy cost of the exclusionary rule. The majority opinion of Justice Scalia, however, to which five justices subscribed, can only be read as a broad attack on the wisdom and efficacy of the exclusionary rule and of *Mapp v. Ohio* generally. One of the five justices, Justice Kennedy, wrote a concurring opinion in which he stated that "the continued operation of the exclusionary rule . . . is not in doubt" but he disavowed nothing in the majority opinion's scathing dissection of the rule in aspect after aspect. Something seems to be "blowin' in the wind."

B. The "Fruit of the Poisoned Tree" Doctrine

A related exclusionary principle, although not literally the Exclusionary Rule of the Fourth Amendment, is the "Fruit of the Poisoned Tree" Doctrine. That doctrine is not a part of the Fourth Amendment specifically but involves the sanction for violations of constitutional protections generally. It is a doctrine that was first recognized in *Silverthorne Lumber Co. v. United States* in 1920, which received its colorful name in *Nardone v. United States* in 1939, and reached fruition in *Wong Sun v. United States* in 1963. Its concern is not with the exclusion of the direct product of the constitutional violation, something handled by other constitutional provisions, but with the second-generation exclusion of the indirect or derivative fruits of the earlier violation. In the words of Justice Holmes in *Silverthorne*, "The essence of a provision forbidding the acquisition of evidence in a certain way is that not merely evidence so acquired shall not be used before the Court but that it shall not be used at all."

The primary constitutional violation may be of the Fourth Amendment, as in *Brown v. Illinois* in 1975, or in *Wong Sun* in 1963. In *Kaupp v. Texas* (2003), a confession was excluded not because it violated the Fifth Amendment but because it was the unattenuated fruit of an unconstitutional seizure of the person in violation of the Fourth Amendment. The primary taint may, on the other hand, just as readily be a tainted confession, as in *Brewer v. Williams* in 1977, or a tainted lineup as in *United States v. Wade* in 1967. A Fifth Amendment or Sixth Amendment violation could have suppressible physical evidence as its fruit just as surely as a Fourth Amendment violation could lead to the suppression of a confession or an identification.

There are three classic exemptions from the exclusionary effect of the Fruit of the Poisoned Tree Doctrine. They are frequently referred to colorfully as "ways of unpoisoning the fruit." They are not that. They are, rather, ways of determining that the fruit was not actually poisoned in the first place. One of them, first articulated in *Wong Sun* in 1963, is referred to as "attenuation of taint." That is where there is so much intervening time or so many intervening events between the alleged cause and the alleged effect that proximate causation cannot be said to exist with any certainty. The issue, according to *Wong Sun*, is "whether, granting establishment of the primary illegality, the evidence to which instant objection is made has been come at by exploitation of that illegality or instead by means sufficiently distinguishable to be purged of the primary taint."[13]

---

13. The "attenuation doctrine" was expanded in *Utah v Strieff* (2016), which held that where officer was investigating an anonymous tip in good faith, the taint of an unlawful stop was "attenuated" by discovery of an outstanding arrest warrant for a traffic violation. Drugs discovered during a search incident to the custodial arrest made on the basis of the outstanding traffic warrant were therefore admissible as untainted fruit.

The second exemption is referred to as "independent source." Where the alleged fruit follows the alleged poisoned tree in point of time but is nonetheless shown to have proceeded from an independent source, the fruit is not tainted and should not, therefore, be suppressed. Both *Segura v. United States* in 1984 and *Murray v. United States* in 1988 are cases in which the evidence was found to have come from an independent source. The third and final exemption is known as "inevitable discovery" and was well illustrated by the case of *Nix v. Williams* in 1984. The derivative evidence was discovered as a result of the constitutional violation but would inevitably have been discovered in any event.

Where the proximate causation is established, however, and where the primary constitutional violation has been of the Fourth Amendment, the Supreme Court has been somewhat inconsistent in applying the full exclusionary rigors of the Fruit of the Poisoned Tree Doctrine. Where the unattenuated product of an illegal Fourth Amendment detention has been a confession, as in *Wong Sun*, in *Dunaway v. New York* (1979), and in *Taylor v. Alabama* (1982), or fingerprints, as in *Davis v. Mississippi* (1969), the Supreme Court has insisted on the exclusion of the derivative evidence. Where, on the other hand, the derivative evidence from a Fourth Amendment violation is used to impeach testimonial credibility, as in *United States v. Havens* (1980), or leads to the development of live witnesses, as in *United States v. Ceccolini* (1978), the Supreme Court has not insisted upon the suppression of those fruits.

IV. Independent State Grounds

It may be noted that this introduction has not mentioned the subject of independent state grounds. This is not because it is not a potentially important aspect of search and seizure law. It is only because this is an introduction to Bill Greenhalgh's book, which is not about search and seizure law generally but about the Fourth Amendment specifically. There are, by definition, no independent state grounds when it comes to an exclusively federal constitutional phenomenon.

The topic, however, is a very important one. There are strong reasons a state might wish to turn to its own constitution in order to provide greater protection from questionable searches and seizures than is provided by the federal Constitution. There are also strong reasons a state might wish to refrain from multiplying the constitutional challenges to evidence or, at least, might wish to approach such multiplication with caution. The possibility, pro and con, is fraught with profound implications. It is, however, beyond the scope of the Fourth Amendment and, therefore, the topic for another introduction to another book.

A CHRONOLOGY OF SUPREME COURT JUSTICES

The Supreme Court of the United States
1914-2019

Chief Justices, 1914-2019

Name	*Appointed By*	*Oath Taken*	*Years Served*
White, Edward Douglass	Taft	12/19/1910	1910-1921*
Taft, William Howard	Harding	07/11/1921	1921-1930
Hughes, Charles Evans	Hoover	02/24/1930	1930-1941
Stone, Harlan Fiske	Roosevelt, F.	07/03/1941	1941-1946*
Vinson, Fred Moore	Truman	06/24/1946	1946-1953
Warren, Earl	Eisenhower	10/05/1953	1953-1969
Burger, Warren Earl	Nixon	06/23/1969	1969-1986
Rehnquist, William H.	Reagan	09/26/1986	1986-2005*
Roberts, John G., Jr.	Bush, G.W.	09/25/2005	2005-

*Earlier service as associate justice

Associate Justices, 1914-2019

Name	*Appointed By*	*Oath Taken*	*Years Served*
McKenna, Joseph	McKinley	01/26/1898	1898-1925
Holmes, Oliver Wendell	Roosevelt, T.	12/08/1902	1902-1932
Day, William R.	Roosevelt, T.	03/02/1903	1903-1922
Lurton, Horace H.	Taft	01/03/1910	1910-1914
Hughes, Charles E.	Taft	10/10/1910	1910-1916
Van Devanter, Willis	Taft	01/03/1911	1911-1937
Lamar, Joseph R.	Taft	01/03/1911	1911-1916
Pitney, Mahlon	Taft	03/18/1912	1912-1922
McReynolds, James C.	Wilson	10/12/1914	1914-1941
Brandeis, Louis D.	Wilson	06/05/1916	1916-1939
Clarke, John H.	Wilson	10/09/1916	1916-1922
Sutherland, George	Harding	10/02/1922	1922-1938
Butler, Pierce	Harding	01/02/1923	1923-1939
Sanford, Edward T.	Harding	02/19/1923	1923-1930
Stone, Harlan Fiske	Coolidge	03/02/1925	1925-1941†
Roberts, Owen Josephus	Hoover	06/02/1930	1930-1945
Cardozo, Benjamin Nathan	Hoover	03/14/1932	1932-1938

†Promoted to Chief Justice

Name	*Appointed By*	*Oath Taken*	*Years Served*
Black, Hugo Lafayette	Roosevelt, F.	08/19/1937	1937-1971
Reed, Stanley Forman	Roosevelt, F.	01/31/1938	1938-1957
Frankfurter, Felix	Roosevelt, F.	01/30/1939	1939-1962
Douglas, William Orville	Roosevelt, F.	04/17/1939	1939-1975
Murphy, Frank	Roosevelt, F.	02/05/1940	1940-1949
Byrnes, James Francis	Roosevelt, F.	07/08/1941	1941-1942
Jackson, Robert H.	Roosevelt, F.	07/11/1941	1941-1954
Rutledge, Wiley Blount	Roosevelt, F.	02/15/1943	1943-1949
Burton, Harold Hitz	Truman	10/01/1945	1945-1958
Clark, Thomas Campbell	Truman	08/24/1949	1949-1967
Minton, Sherman	Truman	10/12/1949	1949-1956
Harlan, John Marshall	Eisenhower	02/28/1955	1955-1971
Brennan, William J.	Eisenhower	10/16/1956	1956-1990
Whittaker, Charles Evans	Eisenhower	03/25/1957	1957-1962
Stewart, Potter	Eisenhower	10/14/1958	1958-1981
White, Byron Raymond	Kennedy	04/16/1962	1962-1993
Goldberg, Arthur Joseph	Kennedy	10/01/1962	1962-1965
Fortas, Abe	Johnson, L.	10/04/1965	1965-1969
Marshall, Thurgood	Johnson, L.	10/02/1967	1967-1991
Blackmun, Harry A.	Nixon	06/09/1970	1970-1994
Powell, Jr., Lewis F.	Nixon	01/06/1972	1972-1987
Rehnquist, William H.	Nixon	01/07/1972	1972-1986†
Stevens, John Paul	Ford	12/19/1975	1975-
O'Connor, Sandra Day	Reagan	09/25/1981	1981-2006
Scalia, Antonin	Reagan	09/26/1986	1986-
Kennedy, Anthony M.	Reagan	02/18/1988	1988-
Souter, David H.	Bush	10/09/1990	1990-2009
Thomas, Clarence	Bush	10/23/1991	1991-
Ginsburg, Ruth Bader	Clinton	08/10/1993	1993-
Breyer, Stephen G.	Clinton	08/03/1994	1994-
Alito, Samuel A. Jr.	Bush, G.W.	01/31/2006	2006-
Sotomayor, Sonia	Obama	08/08/2009	2009-
Kagan, Elena	Obama	08/07/2010	2010-
Gorsuch, Neil M.	Trump	04/10/2017	2017-
Kavanaugh, Brett M.	Trump	10/06/2018	2018-

†Promoted to Chief Justice

FEATURES OF THIS BOOK

Professor Greenhalgh's chronology of the Fourth Amendment is meant for student, researcher, and practicing lawyer alike. Although the format is self-explanatory, the following points deserve mention:

Reading the Introduction

Judge Moylan's introduction is intended to provide a conceptual framework for the case analyses that follow. Judge Moylan begins his discussion by delineating a three-part approach to Fourth Amendment cases:

1. Is the Fourth Amendment applicable here?
2. If so, what does it require in these circumstances?
3. When its requirements have not been met, what should the sanction be?

In the course of his essay, Judge Moylan reviews some of the twists and turns in Fourth Amendment jurisprudence and makes predictions about the future.

Supreme Court Roster, 1914–2019

A roster of the Supreme Court is also included so that members of the Court and cases can be placed in their historical contexts.

Table of Abbreviations

Because of the space limitations inherent in presenting information in a chart format, Professor Greenhalgh used a "shorthand" for many frequently recurring terms. An extensive table of abbreviations precedes the survey.

Survey

The survey is set up in a chart format that provides the case name, charge on arrest, authority for arrest, articles seized, warrant clause applicability, exceptions to the warrant clause, and the decision. Supreme Court cases involving a substantive analysis of the Fourth Amendment have been briefed for inclusion. These case briefs provide a quick overview of the facts involved, the decision of the Court, and, using the Court's own terminology, the rationale for the decision.

Overruled Cases Noted

The history of the Fourth Amendment is ever-evolving. Over the span of the last 88 years, there have been many reversals in Fourth Amendment doctrine. Those cases included in the chart that have been overruled are flagged below their names.

Table of Cases

An alphabetized table of cases appears at the end of the survey to help locate cases within the survey.

This book is intended as a handy reference for all who use it. Either as a starting point for research, a quick means of review, or a checklist in court, the format is designed for greatest usefulness.

TABLE OF ABBREVIATIONS

(A)AG	(Assistant) Attorney General
AFDC	Aid to Families with Dependent Children
AJC	Announced the judgment of the court
Amd.	Amendment
Bivens	Bivens v. Six Unknown Agents (1971)
CCA	Circuit Court of Appeals
c/j	Concurring in the judgment
CJ	Chief Justice
c/p	Concurring in part
D	Defendant
DA	District Attorney
DEA	Drug Enforcement Agency
DIG	Dismissed as Improvidently Granted
DOC	Delivered Opinion of the Court
d/p	Dissenting in part
DUI	Driving under the influence
EPA	Environmental Protection Agency
FBI	Federal Bureau of Investigation
FOPT	Fruit of the Poisoned Tree
FRCP	Federal Rules of Criminal Procedure
IASG	Independent and Adequate State Grounds
INS	Immigration and Naturalization Service
IRS	Internal Revenue Service
J(J)	Justice(s)
j/p	Joining in part
LEP	Legitimate expectation of privacy
MPD	Metropolitan Police Department
NA	Not applicable
NPA	National Prohibition Act
OR	Overruled on these or other grounds
PC	Probable cause
PL	Plurality opinion

PWID	Possession with intent to distribute
RAS	Reasonable articulable suspicion
REP	Reasonable expectation of privacy
RSP	Receiving stolen property
RTC	Right to counsel
SIVA	Search incident to valid arrest
TOC	Totality of the circumstances
USDC	United States District Court

Case Name	Charge on Arrest	Authority for Arrest	Articles Seized	Warrant Clause	Exceptions to Warrant Clause	Decision
Weeks v. United States, 232 U.S. 383 (1914) (OR: *Mapp v Ohio*, 367 U.S. 643 (1961))	Use of the mails to distribute lottery tickets	No arrest warrant; no crime in progress; indictment issued ex post facto	Personal papers taken from defendant's home	No warrant	None	Papers returned to defendant; conviction reversed; case remanded because papers improperly seized had been entered into evidence; federal exclusionary rule is born. USDC reversed. (9-0; Day, J., DOC.)
Ocampo v. United States, 234 U.S. 91 (1914)	Claim that arrest and trial of plaintiffs without preliminary finding of PC violated the Philippine Bill of Rights	Information	NA	No warrant	None	Under Philippine statute, determining PC need not be confined to judicial officer; delegating investigative duty to prosecuting attorney does not invalidate otherwise valid statute, and where prosecuting attorney presents an information following due investigation, the accused is not entitled by right to preliminary examination. Supreme Court of Philippine Islands affirmed. (9-0; Pitney, J., DOC.)
Schenck v. United States, 249 U.S. 47 (1919)	Conspiracy to violate Espionage Act	Indictment	Leaflets urging draft resistance	Search warrant	None	Leaflets properly introduced into evidence. USDC affirmed. (9-0; Holmes, J., DOC.)
Silverthorne Lumber Co. v. United States, 251 U.S. 385 (1920)	Contempt of court for failing to produce company records and books pursuant to a grand jury subpoena	Defendants arrested under indictment and detained at home while company searched for evidence to present to grand jury	Books, papers, documents, and employees under color of invalid subpoena	No warrant	None	Knowledge gained from illegally seized evidence cannot, standing alone, serve as a basis for issuing a valid subpoena. Judgment of USDC reversed. (7-2; Holmes, J., DOC; White, C.J., Pitney, J., dissent.)
Gouled v. United States, 255 U.S. 298 (1921) (abrogation recog'd by *Warden v. Hayden*, 387 U.S. 294 (1967))	Conspiracy and use of the mails to defraud the United States	Indictment	Four documents taken from defendant's office	Three documents seized under search warrant; fourth document seized without warrant by stealth	None	On certification, held papers inadmissible. Search warrant may issue only when interest of public or complainant in the article is primary, or when the article is contraband; it may not issue merely to secure evidence. Mere evidence rule is born. (9-0; Clarke, J., DOC.)

Case Name	Charge on Arrest	Authority for Arrest	Articles Seized	Warrant Clause	Exceptions to Warrant Clause	Decision
Amos v. United States, 255 U.S. 313 (1921)	Removing whiskey without paying revenue tax and selling whiskey on which no tax had been paid	Indictment	Whiskey	No warrant	Invalid consent when officers, under color of law, demanding entrance are admitted into home by defendant's wife	Evidence improperly admitted. USDC reversed; remanded. (9-0; Clarke, J., DOC.)
Burdeau v. McDowell, 256 U.S. 465 (1921)	Civil suit for return of property in the hands of assistant attorney general (AAG)	No arrest	Private books, papers, memoranda stolen by private parties allegedly under control of AAG; AAG disavows	No warrant	Private party	Reverses order of USDC to return articles to defendant. No bar on the government using illegally obtained evidence so long as it is obtained by a private party. (7-2; Day, J., DOC; Holmes & Brandeis, JJ., dissent.)
Essgee Co. of China v. United States, 262 U.S. 151 (1923)	Violation of import law; corporate and individual defendants	Warrant	Corporate papers and books	Subpoena duces tecum	No Amd. V exception for personally inculpatory corporate records held by a corporate officer	Corporate officer holding individually inculpatory corporate papers must produce them under subpoena. USDC admitted papers into evidence properly; affirmed. (9-0; Taft, C.J., DOC.)
Carroll v. United States, 267 U.S. 132 (1925)	Transportation of alcoholic beverages in violation of National Prohibition Act (NPA)	Arrested during commission of crime based on sufficient PC; whiskey, which was being transported at time of arrest, uncovered during search of car	Alcoholic beverages	No warrant	Automobile exception	Evidence properly admitted. USDC affirmed. Automobile exception born. (Taft, C.J., DOC; McReynolds & Sutherland, JJ., dissent.)
Steele v. United States (Steele I), 267 U.S. 498 (1925)	Action for return of seized liquor	No arrest	Liquor	Search warrant for 611 W. 46th Street used for 609 W. 46th Street as well, since the two addresses were shared space	None	Evidence properly secured and need not be returned. USDC affirmed. (9-0; Taft, C.J., DOC.)

Case Name	Charge on Arrest	Authority for Arrest	Articles Seized	Warrant Clause	Exceptions to Warrant Clause	Decision
Steele v. United States (*Steele II*), 267 U.S. 505 (1925)	Possession of liquor in violation of NPA	Information	Liquor	Search warrant; PC is question for the court to decide, not the jury	None	Evidence properly secured and admitted. USDC affirmed. (9-0; Taft, C.J., DOC.)
Dumbra v. United States, 268 U.S. 435 (1925)	Motion to quash search warrant	No arrest	Alcoholic wines	Search warrant	None	Warrant properly issued because of sufficient PC; USDC refusal to quash search warrant affirmed. (9-0; Stone, J., DOC.)
Agnello v. United States, 269 U.S. 20 (1925)	Possession and sale of cocaine without registration or payment of tax	Arrest during commission of crime	Cocaine seized at home of one of defendants while he was being arrested several blocks away	No warrant	Invalid SIVA	Evidence improperly admitted. CCA affirmance of conviction reversed. (9-0; Butler, J., DOC.)
Byars v. United States, 273 U.S. 28 (1927) (OR by implication: *Elkins v. United States*, 364 U.S. 206 (1960))	Possession of counterfeit alcoholic beverage stamps	Indictment	Counterfeit alcoholic beverage stamps	State search warrant issued to state law enforcement officers; federal officer participated in search	None	Federal participation in illegal search by state officer based on insufficient PC, evidence improperly admitted. Silver platter doctrine is applicable. CCA reversed. (9-0; Sutherland, J., DOC.)
McGuire v. United States, 273 U.S. 95 (1927)	Possession of intoxicating liquor	Information	Intoxicating liquor	Search warrant	None	On certification from CCA, after conviction, held evidence was properly admitted. Even though federal officers destroyed most of the liquor—keeping samples for evidence—Court does not extend trespass ab initio principle from civil to criminal context. (9-0; Stone, J., DOC; Butler, J., c/j.)
Maul v. United States, 274 U.S. 501 (1927)	Vessel at sea employed in trade other than licensed; vessel not duly registered	Arrest during commission of crime	American vessel at sea	No warrant	Vessel on high seas beyond 12-mile limit	Brandeis's concurring opinion finds authority for seizure implied as incident to police duties of ocean patrol imposed on Coast Guard rather than "laws respecting the revenue." CCA affirmed. (9-0; Van Devanter, J., DOC; Brandeis & Holmes, JJ., concur.)

Case Name	Charge on Arrest	Authority for Arrest	Articles Seized	Warrant Clause	Exceptions to Warrant Clause	Decision
United States v. Lee, 274 U.S. 559 (1927)	Conspiracy to violate NPA	Arrest during commission of crime	71 cases of grain alcohol; cases were seized on American vessel more than 12 miles from shore	No warrant	SIVA. Coast Guard may inspect American vessel beyond the 12-mile limit if PC exists	CCA reversed USDC conviction holding search illegal because beyond 12-mile limit. CCA reversed. (9-0; Brandeis, J., DOC.)
Segurola v. United States, 275 U.S. 106 (1927)	Transportation of intoxicating liquor	Arrest during commission of crime	Intoxicating liquor	No warrant	SIVA	Objection too late. CCA affirmed. (9-0; Taft, C.J., DOC.)
United States v. Berkeness, 275 U.S. 149 (1927)	Civil suit to abate nuisance—violation of Alaska Dry Law	NA	Liquor	Search warrant invalidly issued because insufficient PC	None	Mere possession of liquor at home not violative of NPA. USDC judgment excluding evidence, upheld by CCA, affirmed. (9-0; McReynolds, J., DOC.)
Marron v. United States, 275 U.S. 192 (1927)	Violation of NPA	Indictment	Intoxicating liquor, ledger, and papers	Search warrant for liquor invalid due to lack of particularity	SIVA as to ledger and bills in care of bartender	Evidence properly admitted. Conviction, upheld by CCA, affirmed. (9-0; Butler, J., DOC.)
Gambino v. United States, 275 U.S. 310 (1927)	Transportation of intoxicating liquor	Crime committed in presence of arresting officers (state police)	Intoxicating liquor	No warrant	Invalid automobile exception	Admission of liquor wrongfully seized by state officers and then turned over to federal officers for prosecution violates defendant's rights under Amd. IV and V; cooperation between state and federal officials was contemplated under NPA but prosecution, in effect, ratified arrest, search, and seizure. CCA reversed. (9-0; Brandeis, J., DOC.)
Olmstead v. United States, 277 U.S. 438 (1927) (OR by implication: *Berger v. New York*, 388 U.S. 41 (1967) and *Katz v. United States*, 389 U.S. 347 (1967))	Conspiracy to violate NPA	Indictment	Information from defendant's conversations on the telephone	No warrant	Wire taps are not a search or seizure within the meaning of Amd. IV	Evidence properly admitted. Conviction, upheld by CCA, affirmed. (5-4; Taft, C.J., DOC; Brandeis, Holmes, Butler, & Stone, JJ., dissent. Quotable dissent by Brandeis.)

Case Name	Charge on Arrest	Authority for Arrest	Articles Seized	Warrant Clause	Exceptions to Warrant Clause	Decision
Go-Bart Importing Co. v. United States, 282 U.S. 344 (1931)	Possession, transportation, and sale of intoxicating liquor	Arrest warrant	Office papers and records secured from defendants at time of their arrest by false statement that a warrant had issued	Arrest warrant invalidly issued based on insufficient PC	Invalid SIVA distinguishing *Marron v. United States*, 275 U.S. 192 (1927)	Evidence must be returned to defendants; conviction, upheld by CCA, reversed. (9-0; Butler, J., DOC.)
Husty v. United States, 282 U.S. 694 (1931)	Possession and transportation of intoxicating liquor	Arrest during commission of crime	Intoxicating liquor	No warrant	SIVA of automobile reasonably believed to contain contraband	Evidence properly admitted. Mobility of vehicle justifies search if PC exists. CCA reversed and remanded for resentencing in view of sentences authorized under Jones Act. (9-0; Stone, J., DOC.)
United States v. Lefkowitz, 285 U.S. 452 (1932)	Conspiracy to violate NPA, including use of premises for sale and solicitation of orders	Arrest warrant issued by United States commissioner	Lists of names and addresses, bills directed to customers, letters of solicitation, and other papers	Arrest warrant	Invalid SIVA due to exploratory search distinguishing *Marron, supra*	USDC denied defendant's motion for return of the papers, CCA reversed; CCA affirmed. (8-0; Butler, J., DOC; Cardozo, J. took no part.)
Taylor v. United States, 286 U.S. 1 (1932)	Illegal possession of intoxicating liquor	Evidence uncovered during search; investigating agents smelled alcohol coming from garage, broke in, uncovered cache, and made arrest	122 cases of liquor	No warrant	None	Evidence improperly admitted. Conviction, upheld by CCA, reversed. (9-0; McReynolds, J., DOC.)
Grau v. United States, 287 U.S. 124 (1932)	Unlawful manufacture and possession of liquor	Indictment	Still, its appurtenances, and 350 gallons of whiskey	Search warrant invalid because insufficient PC (no allegation of sale on premises)	None	Evidence of seized goods improperly admitted. Conviction, upheld by CCA, reversed. (7-2; Roberts, J., DOC; Stone & Cardozo, JJ., dissent.)
Sgro v. United States, 287 U.S. 206 (1932)	Possession and sale of intoxicating liquor	Information	Intoxicating liquor	Search warrant expired under NPA after 10 days; cannot be revived absent new proof PC exists	None	Evidence of seized liquor improperly admitted. Conviction, upheld by CCA, reversed. (7-2; Hughes, C.J., DOC; McReynolds, J., c/p; Stone & Cardozo, JJ., dissent.)

Case Name	Charge on Arrest	Authority for Arrest	Articles Seized	Warrant Clause	Exceptions to Warrant Clause	Decision
Nathanson v. United States, 290 U.S. 41 (1933)	Importation of liquor without payment of import duties	Information filed after seizure	Intoxicating liquor	Search warrant issued was invalid because of insufficient PC (mere allegation of belief)	None	Evidence of seized liquor improperly admitted. Conviction, upheld by CCA, reversed. (9-0; McReynolds, J., DOC.)
Scher v. United States, 305 U.S. 251 (1938)	Possession and transportation of distilled alcohol on which tax had not been paid	Arrest during commission of crime	Distilled alcohol on which tax had not been paid	No warrant	Automobile exception	Evidence properly admitted. CCA, conviction, affirmed. (9-0; McReynolds, J., DOC.)
Goldman v. United States, 316 U.S. 129 (1942) (OR: *Katz v. United States*, 389 U.S. 347 (1967))	Conspiracy to violate Bankruptcy Act	Indictment	Information from defendant's conversations obtained by use of detectaphone	No warrant	Detectaphone use not a violation of Amd. IV	Evidence properly admitted. Conviction, upheld by CCA, affirmed. (5-3; Roberts, J., DOC; Stone, C.J., Frankfurter & Murphy, JJ., dissent; Jackson, J., took no part.)
United States v. White, 322 U.S. 694 (1944)	Contempt of court for refusing to produce allegedly inculpatory union records under subpoena	No arrest	Defendant sentenced to 30 days imprisonment	Subpoena duces tecum	No expectation of privacy in records of artificial entity or corporation	No LEP exists in records of artificial entity or corporation. CCA reversed. (9-0; Murphy, J., DOC; Roberts, Jackson, & Frankfurter, JJ., concur.)
Oklahoma Press Pub. Co. v. Walling, 327 U.S. 186 (1946)	NA	NA	NA	Subpoena duces tecum issued by administrator	Investigation authorized by Congress, for a purpose Congress can order, and articles sought were specified and relevant to the inquiry	Subpoena to produce corporate records, allowing administrator to determine compliance with Fair Labor Standards Act, not violative of Amd. IV. CCA affirmed. (7-1; Rutledge, J., DOC; Murphy, J., dissents; Jackson, J., took no part.)
Davis v. United States, 328 U.S. 582 (1946)	Unlawful possession of gasoline rationing coupons	Arrest pursuant to defendant's employee selling gasoline without coupons at 20 cents above ceiling price	168 gasoline rationing coupons	No warrant	Valid consent (1st party) search during normal business hours	Evidence properly admitted. Conviction, upheld by CCA, affirmed. (6-2; Rutledge, J., DOC; Frankfurter & Murphy, JJ., dissent; quotable Frankfurter dissent; Jackson, J., took no part.)

Case Name	Charge on Arrest	Authority for Arrest	Articles Seized	Warrant Clause	Exceptions to Warrant Clause	Decision
Zap v. United States, 328 U.S. 624 (1946)	Presenting false claims against the United States government	Claim for payment of $4,000 submitted by defendant as cost for test flight (which actually cost $2,500); the "payment" check was received, absent warrant, by the FBI from defendant's employee pursuant to Navy Department audit	$4,000 check	No warrant	Consent (1st party)	Defendant consented to waive Amd. IV and V rights when he signed government contract. Evidence properly admitted. Conviction, upheld by CCA, affirmed. (5-3; Douglas, J., DOC; Frankfurter, Murphy, & Rutledge, JJ., dissent; Jackson, J., took no part.)
Harris v. United States, 331 U.S. 145 (1947) (OR: *Chimel v. California*, 395 U.S. 752 (1969))	Unlawful possession, concealment, and alteration of Selective Service notice of classification and registration certificates	Arrest warrant for forged checks	Selective Service notice of classification and registration cards	Arrest warrant	SIVA for defendant's 4-room apartment	If validly on the premises, officers may search the place under the arrestee's control as long as it is not an exploratory search. Conviction, upheld by CCA, affirmed. (5-4; Vinson, C.J., DOC; Frankfurter, Murphy, Rutledge, & Jackson, JJ., dissent. Quotable dissent by Frankfurter, whose appendix therein inspired this project.)
United States v. Di Re, 332 U.S. 581 (1948)	Knowingly possessing counterfeit gasoline rationing coupons	Arrest by state officers in the company of federal investigator	Counterfeit gasoline rationing coupons	No warrant	Mere presence at the scene is insufficient PC for either automobile or SIVA exceptions	"A search is not to be made legal by what it turns up... it is good or bad when it starts and does not change character from its success." CCA reversal of conviction, affirmed. (7-2; Jackson, J., DOC; Vinson, C.J., Black, J., dissent.)
Johnson v. United States, 333 U.S. 10 (1948)	Violation of federal narcotics law	Arrest by state officers in the company of federal officer during commission of crime	Opium, opium pipe	No warrant	Invalid SIVA	Sanctuary seizure (seizure in a dwelling) requires, absent consent or exigent circumstances, approval by a neutral and detached magistrate. Conviction, upheld by CCA, reversed. (5-4; Jackson, J., DOC; Vinson, C.J., Black, Reed, & Burton, JJ., dissent.)

Case Name	Charge on Arrest	Authority for Arrest	Articles Seized	Warrant Clause	Exceptions to Warrant Clause	Decision
Trupiano v. United States, 334 U.S. 699 (1948) (OR: *United States v. Rabinowitz*, 339 U.S. 56 (1950))	Violating Internal Revenue Code via ownership of a still	Crime committed in presence of officers	Still, alcohol, mash, and other distilling equipment	No warrant	Invalid SIVA	Valid arrest does not legalize warrantless search or seizure. In seizing articles, officers must secure and use search warrant wherever reasonably practicable. Conviction, upheld by CCA, reversed. (5-4; Murphy, J., DOC; Vinson, C.J., Black, Reed, & Burton, JJ., dissent.)
McDonald v. United States, 335 U.S. 451 (1948)	Conducting a lottery in violation of DC Criminal Code	Crime committed in presence of officers	Adding machine (instrumentality), numbers slips (contraband), and money (fruits of the crime)	Sufficient PC for issuance of search warrant, bur warrant not obtained	Invalid SIVA	Sanctuary seizure requires, absent exigent circumstances, approval by a neutral and detached magistrate; burden is on government to show exception to the warrant clause. Conviction, upheld by CCA, reversed. (6-3; Douglas, J., DOC; Jackson, J., concurs (quotable); Vinson, C.J., Burton & Reed, JJ., dissent.)
Wolf v. Colorado, 338 U.S. 25 (1949) (OR: *Mapp v. Ohio*, 367 U.S. 643 (1961))	Conspiracy to commit abortion	Police arrested Dr. Wolf on basis of statements concerning one of his patients	Books containing patient records for 1943 and 1944 up to arrest	No warrant	State court has authority, in prosecution of state crime, to admit evidence obtained by unreasonable search and seizure	Amd. IV, but not its exclusionary rule, is incorporated to the states through Amd. XIV. Conviction, upheld by state Supreme Court, affirmed. (6-3; Frankfurter, J., DOC; Rutledge, Murphy, & Douglas, JJ., dissent.)
Lustig v. United States, 338 U.S. 74 (1949) (OR by implication: *Elkins v. United States*, 364 U.S. 206 (1960))	Violation of counterfeiting statutes	State arrest warrant for violation of Camden ordinance requiring "known criminals" to register with the police	"Similitude" of $100 bill and other items indicating counterfeit production of currency	Invalid state arrest warrant based on insufficient PC	Silver platter doctrine does not apply because of federal involvement in the search	As long as a federal agent participates in a search before the object of that search is accomplished, it is a federal search and the exclusionary rule applies. Conviction, upheld by CCA, reversed. (PL; Frankfurter, J., AJC; Reed, Jackson, & Burton, JJ., Vinson, C.J., dissent.)

Case Name	Charge on Arrest	Authority for Arrest	Articles Seized	Warrant Clause	Exceptions to Warrant Clause	Decision
Brinegar v. United States, 338 U.S. 160 (1949)	Importation of intoxicating liquor contrary to the laws of the state (federal misdemeanor)	Officers staked out at MO-OK border spotted defendant's heavily loaded car coming from Missouri; officers also knew defendant had reputation as bootlegger and prior arrests for bootlegging	12 cases of liquor	No warrant	Automobile exception	Officers must have personal knowledge for misdemeanor PC. PC requires "more than bare suspicion and exists when facts and circumstances within officer's knowledge and of which they had reasonably trustworthy information are sufficient to warrant a man of reasonable caution in the belief that an offense has been or is being committed." CCA affirmed. (6-3; Rutledge, J., DOC; Burton, J., concurs; Jackson, Frankfurter, & Murphy, JJ., dissent.)
United States v. Rabinowitz, 339 U.S. 56 (1950) (OR: *Chimel v. California* 395 U.S. 752 (1969))	Possession and sale of postage stamps bearing forged overprints	Arrest warrant for forged postal stamps	573 postage stamps bearing forged overprints	Arrest warrant	SIVA for single-room business establishment	Relevant test is not whether it is practicable to obtain search warrant but whether search was reasonable. Conviction, reversed by CCA, upheld. *Trupiano v. United States*, 334 U.S. 699 (1948), overruled. (5-3; Minton, J., DOC; Frankfurter & Jackson, JJ., dissent; Black, J., dissents; Douglas, J., took no part.)
United States v. Jeffers, 342 U.S. 48 (1951)	Purchasing, selling, and distributing narcotics	Contraband seized from hotel room of defendant's aunts	19 bottles of cocaine (only 2 of which had U.S. tax stamps) and 1 bottle of codeine (with U.S. tax stamp)	No warrant	Invalid 3d party consent search; hotel detective cannot consent to search of hotel room	Defendant has standing to move to suppress evidence seized in his aunts' hotel room because he held a key. Property rights in contraband attach for exclusionary rule purposes. CCA affirmed. (6-2; Clark, J., DOC; Vinson, C.J., Reed, J., dissent; Minton, J., took no part.)

Case Name	Charge on Arrest	Authority for Arrest	Articles Seized	Warrant Clause	Exceptions to Warrant Clause	Decision
Stefanelli v. Minard, 342 U.S. 117 (1951)	Bookmaking; suit in equity, under Civil Rights Act, to enjoin county prosecutor from using evidence seized by state police that, if seized by federal officers, would violate Amd. IV	NA	Bookmaking implements	NA	In state court for state crime, Amd. XIV does not forbid admission of evidence obtained by state officers' unreasonable search	Federal courts should refuse to intervene in state criminal proceedings to suppress evidence even when it is procured by illegal search and seizure. Dismissal of suit, upheld by CCA, affirmed. (7-1; Frankfurter, J., DOC; Black & Clark, JJ., concur; Douglas, J., dissents; Minton, J., took no part.)
Rochin v. California, 342 U.S. 165 (1952)	Possessing a preparation of morphine	Arrest during commission of crime	Remains of 2 capsules of morphine in the stomach contents of the defendant	No warrant	Invalid plain view exception	Manner in which LA County Deputy Sheriff effectuated defendant's arrest—breaking into defendant's home, forcibly trying to remove capsules from his mouth, then having his stomach pumped—"shocks the conscience" and violates the due process clause. (8-0; Frankfurter, J., DOC; Black & Douglas, JJ., concur; Minton, J., took no part.)
Frisbie v. Collins, 342 U.S. 519 (1952)	Habeas corpus proceeding to obtain release from imprisonment for state murder conviction	Michigan police kidnapped defendant from Chicago to stand trial for murder in Michigan	Defendant	No warrant	*Ker/Frisbie* doctrine: the Court will ignore how a person comes before the court as long as no evidence is seized	Court's authority to try person for crime not impaired by fact that he has been brought within court's jurisdiction by reason of forcible abduction; reiteration of holding in *Ker v. Illinois,* 119 U.S. 436 (1886). USDC denial of writ, reversed by CCA, reinstated. (9-0; Black, J., DOC.)

Case Name	Charge on Arrest	Authority for Arrest	Articles Seized	Warrant Clause	Exceptions to Warrant Clause	Decision
On Lee v. United States, 343 U.S. 747 (1952)	Selling and conspiracy to sell opium	Indictment	One pound of opium, incriminating admissions	No warrant	Eavesdropping by police via informant wearing a wire; Court extends *Goldman v. United States*, 316 U.S. 129 (1942)	Admissions gained by police eavesdropping via informant wearing wire do not violate Amd. IV where no trespass was involved; informant entered defendant's place of business with defendant's consent. CCA affirmed. (5-4; Jackson, J., DOC; Frankfurter, Burton, Douglas, & Black, JJ., dissent.)
Walder v. United States, 347 U.S. 62 (1954)	Four illicit narcotics transactions	Indictment	NA	NA	None	Exclusionary rule cannot be used as a shield for perjury; government may attack defendant's credibility on direct examination with contradictory affidavit filed in successful rule 41(e) motion in prior indictment. Conviction, upheld by CCA, affirmed. (7-2; Frankfurter, J., DOC; Douglas & Black, JJ., dissent.)
Irvine v. California, 347 U.S. 128 (1954)	Horserace bookmaking and related state offenses	Following use by police of eavesdropping device in defendant's home, defendant was arrested and found to have on his person a federal wagering tax stamp bearing personal information	Incriminating statements obtained via microphone planted by police in defendant's bedroom	No warrant	Silver platter doctrine, eavesdropping; reaffirming *Wolf v. Colorado*, 338 U.S. 25 (1949), the Court extends *On Lee, supra.*	Police misconduct insufficient to "shock the conscience" of the Court. Conviction, upheld by state appellate court, affirmed. (PL; Jackson, J., AJC, joined by Warren, C.J., Reed & Minton, JJ.; Clark, J., concurs; Black, Douglas, Frankfurter, & Burton, JJ., dissent.)
Rea v. United States, 350 U.S. 214 (1956)	Unlawful acquisition and possession of marijuana	Indictment in federal prosecution dismissed; federal officer then gave information to state law enforcement sufficient for a state arrest warrant to issue	Marijuana	Invalid federal search warrant due to insufficient PC and lack of oath or affirmation	Silver platter doctrine does not bar federal court from enjoining federal agent from testifying in state court	Proceeding to enjoin federal agent from testifying in state court and proffering illegally seized contraband evidence as basis for state prosecution of dismissed federal offense upheld under Supreme Court's supervisory power over federal law enforcement. CCA reversed. (5-4; Douglas, J., DOC; Harlan, Reed, Burton, & Minton, JJ., dissent.)

Case Name	Charge on Arrest	Authority for Arrest	Articles Seized	Warrant Clause	Exceptions to Warrant Clause	Decision
Kremen v. United States, 353 U.S. 346 (1957)	Relieving, comforting, and assisting a fugitive from justice	Arrest warrant for one of three defendants	Contents of cabin, removed to FBI office over 200 miles away, and documents on the persons of defendants	No warrant	SIVA with respect to the documents on the persons of the defendants only	Seizure and removal of the contents of the cabin excessive SIVA. Reversed; remanded. (Per curiam; Burton & Clark, JJ., dissent; Whittaker, J., took no part.)
Miller v. United States, 357 U.S. 301 (1958)	Conspiracy to commit violations of federal narcotics law; violations of federal narcotics laws	Arrested by federal officers in the company of MPD during the commission of crime	$100 marked currency	No warrant	Invalid SIVA due to failure of officers to give notice of their authority and purpose before breaking down defendant's door; no exigent circumstance exception	Federal officers must announce authority and purpose before breaking in. Brennan, J., in his first Amd. IV opinion, applies 18 USC § 3109 to search warrant, arrest warrant, and warrantless arrests. CCA reversed. (7-2; Brennan, J., DOC; Harlan, J., c/j; Clark & Burton, JJ., dissent.)
Giordenello v. United States, 357 U.S. 480 (1958)	Receiving and concealing heroin with knowledge of unlawful importation	Arrest warrant	Heroin	Arrest warrant	Invalid SIVA due to defective arrest warrant	Affidavit for warrant must contain facts enabling neutral and detached magistrate to draw inferences from which PC determination may be made. PC as alternative to warrant must be raised below. CCA reversed. (6-3; Harlan, J., DOC; Clark, Burton, & Whittaker, JJ., dissent.)
Jones v. United States, 357 U.S. 493 (1958)	Violation of federal liquor laws stemming from possession of illegal still	Arrest during commission of crime	Boiler, fuel burner, and 15 barrels	Daytime search warrant executed, which had expired prior to agents' 9:00 p.m. raid	Invalid SIVA; distinguishes *Rabinowitz v. United States,* 339 U.S. 56 (1950).	Nighttime sanctuary seizure must comply with rule 41(c) warrant requirement; question whether warrantless nighttime sanctuary seizure can be justified by PC is left open because government failed to raise the issue below. CCA reversed. (7-2; Harlan, J., DOC; Black, J., concurs; Clark & Burton, JJ., dissent.)

Case Name	Charge on Arrest	Authority for Arrest	Articles Seized	Warrant Clause	Exceptions to Warrant Clause	Decision
Draper v. United States, 358 U.S. 307 (1959)	Knowingly concealing and transporting narcotics	Arrest during commission of crime	Two envelopes containg 865 grains of heroin and a hypodermic syringe	No warrant	SIVA	Confidential informant of known reliability gave federal officer sufficiently detailed description of defendant and his movements to establish PC. (6-1; Whittaker, J., DOC; Douglas, J., dissents; Warren, C.J., Frankfurter, J., took no part.)
Frank v. Maryland, 359 U.S. 360 (1959) (OR: *Camara v. Municipal Court*, 387 U.S. 523 (1967))	Refusing to allow city health inspector access to a dwelling to investigate health hazard in violation of Baltimore city ordinance; ordinance challenged on Amd. IV, XIV grounds	Arrest warrant	NA	Arrest warrant	Health inspection or other regulatory scheme to ensure public welfare where there are procedural safeguards and PC	History of Maryland health inspections and other regulatory schemes, with carefully circumscribed procedural safeguards, does not violate Amd. IV or due process. Baltimore crim. ct. affirmed. (5-4; Frankfurter, J., DOC; Douglas, Black, & Brennan, JJ., Warren, C.J., dissent.)
Henry v. United States, 361 U.S. 98 (1959)	Unlawful possession of three cartons of radios stolen from interstate shipment	Arrest during commission of crime	Three cartons of radios	No warrant	Invalid SIVA due to insufficient PC for arrest	Suspicion is not enough to establish PC for arrest, and an arrest is not justified by what the subsequent search turns up. Conviction, upheld by CCA, reversed. (7-2; Douglas, J., DOC; Black, J., concurs; Clark, J., Warren, C.J., dissent.)
Abel v. United States, 362 U.S. 217 (1960)	Conspiracy to commit espionage	Administrative arrest by U.S. Immigration and Naturalization (INS) officers, accompanied by FBI agents, preliminary to deportation	Graph paper containing coded message, 2 forged birth certificates, bank book, hollow pencil containing microfilm, and a cipher pad	Administrative deportation warrant (INS); no warrant (FBI)	Russian spy (exchanged for Francis Gary Powers); relying on *Rabinowitz v. United States*, 339 U.S. 56 (1950), deportation proceedings subject to lesser constitutional safeguards than criminal prosecutions	INS's arrest of defendant pursuant to deportation warrant does not bar FBI from continuing its investigation, including search of defendant's vacated hotel room, for weapons and documents connected with defendant's illegal alien status. CCA affirmed. (5-4; Frankfurter, J., DOC; Douglas, Black, & Brennan, JJ., Warren, C.J., dissent.)
Jones v. United States, 362 U.S. 257 (1960) (OR: *United States v. Salvucci*, 448 U.S. 83 (1980))	Violation of federal narcotics laws	Arrest during execution of search warrant	Heroin and drug paraphernalia	Search warrant, affidavit based on hearsay is valid as long as there is a substantial basis for crediting the hearsay	None	Birth of automatic standing rule for possessory offenses. Conviction, upheld by CCA, vacated and remanded to hear suppression motion. (9-0; Frankfurter, J., DOC; Douglas, J., c/p, d/p.)

Case Name	Charge on Arrest	Authority for Arrest	Articles Seized	Warrant Clause	Exceptions to Warrant Clause	Decision
Elkins v. United States, 364 U.S. 206 (1960)	Intercepting and divulging telephone conversations; conspiracy to do so	Indictment; based on evidence seized by state officers—without involvement of federal officers—engaged in unreasonable search and seizure	Tape and wire recordings, recording machine	Search warrant (federal) obtained during state proceedings (subsequently dismissed) to search safe deposit box where state officials secured illegally obtained evidence	Silver platter doctrine overruled	Relying on "underlying constitutional doctrine" of *Wolf v. Colorado*, 338 U.S. 28 (1949), federal exclusionary rule extended to evidence illegally obtained by state officials when proffered in federal prosecutions. Conviction, upheld by CCA, vacated and remanded. Appendix traces state exclusionary rules pre- and post-*Wolf*. (5-4; Stewart, J., DOC; Frankfurter, Harlan, Clark, & Whittaker, JJ., dissent.)
Rios v. United States, 364 U.S. 253 (1960)	Unlawful receipt and concealment of narcotics	Arrest during commission of crime	Heroin	No warrant	Valid SIVA if government claim of point of arrest is found factual	Silver platter doctrine may turn on point of arrest. State prosecution dismissed due to insufficient PC to justify arrest; federal prosecution based on silver platter doctrine. CCA judgment vacated, remanded, in light of *Elkins*. (5-4; Stewart, J., DOC; Frankfurter, Harlan, Clark, & Whittaker, JJ., dissent.)
Wilson v. Schnettler, 365 U.S. 381 (1961)	Injunction proceeding to restrain admission into evidence of narcotics seized by federal officers incident to a warrantless arrest in a state prosecution as well as officers' testimony	Arrest during commission of crime	Narcotics	No warrant	SIVA; PC to make arrest absent; warrant not challenged	Federal courts below dismissed civil injunction for failing to state a claim for which relief could be granted under FRCP 12(b)(3). Absent allegation in complaint of lack of PC, CCA affirmed. (6-3; Whittaker, J., DOC; Stewart, J., concurs; Douglas & Brennan, JJ., Warren, C.J., dissent.)
Silverman v. United States, 365 U.S. 505 (1961)	Gambling violations under DC code	Indictment	Inculpatory statements of defendants obtained by eavesdropping MPD using a spike mike	No warrant	None; *Olmstead v. United States*, 277 U.S. 438 (1927), *Goldman v. United States*, 316 U.S. 129 (1942), and *On Lee v. United States*, 343 U.S. 747 (1952), distinguished	With owner's consent, police in vacant row house adjacent to defendant's home insert spike mike through the party wall making contact with heating duct of defendant's home and turning heating system into conductor of sound. Intrusion into constitutionally protected area violates Amd. IV. (9-0; Stewart, J., DOC; Douglas, J., concurs.)

Case Name	Charge on Arrest	Authority for Arrest	Articles Seized	Warrant Clause	Exceptions to Warrant Clause	Decision
Chapman v. United States, 365 U.S. 610 (1961)	Illegal operation of a distillery	Arrest during commission of crime	Still, 1,300 gallons of mash	No warrant	Invalid (3d party) consent; landlord cannot waive tenant's Amd. IV rights	Referring to *Taylor v. United States*, 286 U.S. 1 (1932) and *Johnson v. United States*, 333 U.S. 10 (1948), when there is no probability of material change in premises during time necessary to secure warrant, mere presence of suspicious odors does not strip petitioner of constitutional guarantees against unreasonable search. CCA reversed. (8-1; Whittaker, J., DOC; Black & Frankfurter, JJ., c/j; Clark, J., dissents.)
Mapp v. Ohio, 367 U.S. 643 (1961)	Possession and control of obscene material	Arrest during warrantless sanctuary search and seizure based on insufficient PC	"Lewd and lascivious" books and pictures	No warrant	*Wolf v. Colorado,* 338 U.S. 25 (1949) state court option to reject exclusionary rule overturned	All evidence obtained by illegal search and seizure is inadmissible in state courts. Amd. IV exclusionary rule applies to the states through Amd. XIV. State conviction, upheld by Ohio Supreme Court, reversed; remanded. (6-3; Clark, J., DOC; Black & Douglas JJ., concur; Harlan, Frankfurter, & Whittaker, JJ., dissent.)
Marcus v. Search Warrants of Property at 104 East Tenth Street, Kansas City, Missouri, 367 U.S. 717 (1961)	Due process challenge to Missouri statutory procedure for issuing search warrants to seize allegedly obscene material	NA	11,000 copies of 280 allegedly obscene publications	Search warrant, defective due to failure to particularize the things to be seized	None	Lack of procedural safeguards renders Missouri statutory procedure violative of due process as applied. Missouri Supreme Court reversed; remanded. (9-0; Brennan, J., DOC; Black & Douglas, JJ., concur.)
Lanza v. New York, 370 U.S. 139 (1962)	Refusing to testify before a state legislative committee	Indictment	Defendant's statements made during conversation with his brother in prison anteroom, intercepted through electronic listening device; transcript of conversation, passed on to committee	No search warrant	None	At least 2 questions asked by the committee—and which petitioner refused to answer—were unrelated to intercepted conversation; constitutional claim asserted by petitioner is simply not tendered by the record. Court of Appeals of NY affirmed. (7-0; Stewart, J., DOC; Harlan, J., concurs; Brennan & Douglas, JJ., Warren, C.J., memorandum opinions; Frankfurter & White, JJ., took no part.)

Case Name	Charge on Arrest	Authority for Arrest	Articles Seized	Warrant Clause	Exceptions to Warrant Clause	Decision
Wong Sun v. United States, 371 U.S. 471 (1963)	Transportation and concealment of narcotics in violation of 21 USC § 174	Statement by informant, Hom Way, that a laundry proprietor, "Blackie" Toy, somewhere on Leavenworth Street (covering 30 blocks of San Francisco) was source for heroin	Heroin, incriminating statements	No warrant	None	Pt. I, insufficient PC for Toy's arrest; Pt. II, Toy's statements excluded as FOPT (*Nardone v. United States,* 308 U.S. 338 (1939)); Pt. III, narcotics taken from Yee excluded as FOPT; Pt. IV, Toy's conviction set aside for lack of competent supporting evidence; Pt. V connection between Wong Sun's arrest and statement was so attenuated as to dissipate taint—statement properly admitted. CCA reversed; remanded. (5-4; Brennan, J., DOC; Douglas, J., concurs; Clark, Harlan, Stewart, & White, JJ., dissent.)
Lopez v. United States, 373 U.S. 427 (1963)	Attempted bribery of IRS agent	Indictment	Bribe offers and cash, obtained by IRS decoy wearing a wire	No search warrant	Consent (1st party)	Admitting recording of defendant's bribe attempts to corroborate IRS agent's testimony not violative of Amd. IV. (6-3; Harlan, J., DOC; Warren, C.J., c/j; Brennan, Douglas, & Goldberg, JJ., dissent.)
Ker v. California, 374 U.S. 23 (1963)	Possession of marijuana in violation of California Health and Safety Code	Known drug dealer under surveillance made sale to undercover officer; used same modus operandi the next night with defendant who was suspected of dealing drugs	Marijuana	No warrant; officers entered defendants' apartment with passkey without knocking or announcing their purpose	1. SIVA for drugs 2. Exigent circumstances for entry a. Drugs might be distributed by time warrant secured b. Officers had experienced destruction of evidence by prior suspects after knocking and announcing under Cal. Crim. Pro. § 844	For warrantless sanctuary seizures based on exigent circumstances, "reasonableness" is governed by state law. Pt. I, criteria; Pt. II, PC; Pt. III, entry; Pt. IV, SIVA; Pt. V, co-defendant's car. Cal. Court of Appeal affirmed. (PL; Clark, J., AJC; Harlan, J., c/j Brennan, Douglas, & Goldberg, JJ., Warren, C.J., dissent.)
Fahy v. Connecticut, 375 U.S. 85 (1963)	Willfully injuring a public building by painting a swastika on a synagogue	During traffic stop, officer saw paint and brush in defendant's car; after learning of crime, officer conducted warrantless search and seizure in defendant's garage and arrest warrant issued	Can of black paint, paint brush, incriminating statements	No search warrant, no arrest warrant at time of search and seizure in defendant's garage	None	Admission of illegally seized evidence, along with its collateral use through resulting incriminating statements, cannot be harmless error. *Wong Sun v. United States*, 371 U.S. 471 (1963), is extended to the states. Connecticut Supreme Court of Errors reversed. (5-4; Warren, C.J., DOC; Harlan, Clark, Stewart, & White, JJ., dissent.)

Case Name	Charge on Arrest	Authority for Arrest	Articles Seized	Warrant Clause	Exceptions to Warrant Clause	Decision
Stoner v. California, 376 U.S. 483 (1964)	Armed robbery	Defendant's check-book found in parking lot adjacent to crime scene; two stubs drawn to hotel in Pomona; Pomona police mug shots of defendant positively identified by eyewit-nesses	Gun, cartridges, clip, gray jacket, horn-rimmed glasses	No warrant	Invalid SIVA since search was too attenuated in time and space to be incident to arrest; invalid consent	Relying on *Lustig v. United States*, 338 U.S. 74 (1949), and *United States v. Jeffers*, 342 U.S. 48 (1951), LEP of hotel guest in room cannot be waived by 3d party consent; search must be contemporaneous with arrest to be SIVA. Conviction, upheld by California Court of Appeal, reversed. (9-0; Stewart, J., DOC; Harlan, J., c/p, d/p.)
Preston v. United States, 376 U.S. 364 (1964)	Vagrancy initially; conspiracy to rob a federally insured bank ultimately	Telephone complaint of men loitering in car parked in business district from 10 p.m. to 3 a.m.; officer, finding men unemployed and with 25 cents among them, made arrest for vagrancy	Caps, women's stockings, rope, pillow slips, snap-on license plate from trunk of impounded car; 2 loaded revolvers from glove compartment	No warrant	Invalid SIVA; invalid automobile exception	Warrantless search of impounded car too remote in time and place to be incident to arrest. Rationale for the automobile exception—mobility—inapplicable to impounded vehicle. Failure to obtain search warrant was unreasonable. CCA, reversed; remanded. (9-0; Black, J., DOC.)
Rugendorf v. United States, 376 U.S. 528 (1964)	Knowingly receiving, concealing, and storing stolen furs transported in interstate commerce	Fruits of crime detected pursuant to execution of search warrant, which particularly described articles based on confidential informant statements to affiant	81 furs	Search warrant	None	Search warrant based on hearsay is sufficient as long as there is substan-tial basis for crediting hearsay; confidential informant need not be identified. Confrontation clause attack on withholding informant's identity not raised below. (5-4; Clark, J., DOC; Douglas, Brennan, & Goldberg, JJ., Warren, C.J., dissent.)
Clinton v. Virginia, 377 U.S. 158 (1964)	Feloniously receiving money from a prostitute and knowingly placing a woman in a house of prostitution	Surveillance of apartment used for prostitution via spike mike inserted into medicine cabinet from apartment house next door	Incriminating statements	No warrant	None	Relying on *Silverman v. United States*, 365 U.S. 505 (1961), penetration of spike mike into the defendant's apartment violated constitutionally protected space. Conviction, upheld by Virginia Supreme Court, reversed. (8-1; per curiam; Clark, J., concurs; White, J., dissents.)

Case Name	Charge on Arrest	Authority for Arrest	Articles Seized	Warrant Clause	Exceptions to Warrant Clause	Decision
Aguilar v. Texas, 378 U.S. 108 (1964) (OR: *Illinois v. Gates*, 462 U.S. 213 (1983))	Illegal possession of heroin	Executing a search warrant, police were refused admittance; hearing a commotion within, they broke in and seized defendant in the act of destroying evidence	Heroin	Search warrant invalid due to insufficient PC	None	Relying on *Nathanson v. United States*, 290 U.S. 41 (1933), Supreme Court extends *Giordenello v. United States*, 357 U.S. 480 (1958) to search warrants. Expanded 2-prong test for basis of knowledge and reliability of informant. Texas Court of Criminal Appeals reversed; remanded. (6-3; Goldberg, J., DOC; Harlan, J., concurs; Clark, Black, & Stewart, JJ., dissent.)
Beck v. Ohio, 379 U.S. 89 (1964)	Possession of clearing house slips	Defendant's prior criminal record and mug shot along with unsubtantiated "reports" from unknown informant that defendant engaged in clearing house operation	Clearing house slips	No warrant	Invalid SIVA; distinguishes *Draper v. United States*, 358 U.S. 307 (1959)	Police knowledge of defendant's appearance and prior record, standing alone, is insufficient basis for PC; officers' good faith is not enough. Conviction, upheld by Ohio Court of Appeals and Ohio Supreme Court, reversed. (6-3; Stewart, J., DOC; Clark, Black, & Harlan, JJ., dissent.)
Stanford v. Texas, 379 U.S. 476 (1965)	Possession and use of documents concerning the Communist Party of Texas, in violation of Texas statute	Texas Suppression Act, which outlaws the Communist Party, allows search warrants to issue for potentially violative written instruments	2,000 books, pamphlets, and papers	Search warrant invalid due to failure to particularize	None	Relying on *Marron v. United States*, 275 U.S. 192 (1927), and *Marcus v. Search Warrants*, 367 U.S. 717 (1961), particularity requirement of Amd. IV "is to be accorded the most scrupulous exactitude when the 'things' are books, and the basis for their seizure is the ideas they contain." Texas court order vacated; remanded. (9-0; Stewart, J., DOC.)
United States v. Ventresca, 380 U.S. 102 (1965)	Possessing and operating an illegal distillery	Crime committed in officers' presence when they executed search warrant	Still, distillery paraphernalia, non-tax-paid liquor	Search warrant	None	Affidavit of Alcohol and Tobacco Tax Division investigator based on personal observation and other officers' observation is sufficient for PC finding. Amd. IV PC requirement should be interpreted in a common-sense rather than a hypertechnical manner. Conviction, overturned by CCA, reinstated. (7-2; Goldberg, J., DOC; Douglas, J., Warren, C.J., dissent.)

Case Name	Charge on Arrest	Authority for Arrest	Articles Seized	Warrant Clause	Exceptions to Warrant Clause	Decision
One 1958 Plymouth Sedan v. Pennsylvania, 380 U.S. 693 (1965)	Forfeiture procedure under Pennsylvania Liquor Control Act	Plymouth sedan spotted by Pennsylvania liquor control agents on highway stakeout going from Camden, New Jersey, into Philadelphia "low in the rear"	1958 Plymouth sedan (31 cases of liquor not bearing Pennsylvania tax stamps)	No warrant	None	Relying on *Boyd v. United States*, 116 U.S. 616 (1886), exclusionary rule applies to forfeiture hearings. *United States v. Jeffers*, 342 U.S. 48 (1951), and *Trupiano v. United States*, 334 U.S. 699 (1948), distinguished as criminal cases involving per se rather than derivative contraband. Judgment of Pennsylvania Supreme Court reversed; remanded. (9-0; Goldberg, J., DOC; Black, J., concurs.)
Jaben v. United States, 381 U.S. 214 (1965)	Income tax evasion	Indictment	NA	Complaint filed with U.S. commissioner under § 6531 of Internal Revenue Code of 1954 giving government a 9-month extension to 6-year statute of limitations for filing criminal charges	None	Complaint to U.S. commissioner under IRC § 6531 must show PC; sufficient detail based on personal knowledge of IRS agent can justify PC finding. Conviction, upheld by CCA, affirmed. (6-3; Harlan, J., DOC; White & Black, JJ., concur; Goldberg & Douglas, JJ., Warren, C.J., c/p, d/p.)
Linkletter v. Walker, 381 U.S. 618 (1965) (Disapproved of: *Griffith v. Kentucky,* 479 U.S. 314) (1987)	Simple burglary	Surveillance of defendant, suspected of involvement in burglary, resulted in sighting defendant carrying oxygen tank into building and climbing onto roof; burglar tools and guns found on roof	Burglar tools, guns, other evidence seized from defendant's home and business	No warrant	Louisiana court found SIVA proper	In federal habeas corpus action, *Mapp v. Ohio*, 367 U.S. 643 (1961), is not to be applied retroactively since the exclusionary rule's purpose is prophylactic rather than remedial. Denial of habeas, upheld by CCA, affirmed. (7-2; Clark, J., DOC; Black & Douglas, JJ., dissent.)
James v. Louisiana, 382 U.S. 36 (1965)	Possession of narcotics	Defendant's prior record basis for surveillance; police approached car in which defendant was passenger and saw him stuff a white tablet wrapped in cellophone in his mouth and run	Morphine, narcotics paraphernalia seized at defendant's home	No warrant	Invalid SIVA since search of defendant's house occurred two blocks from site of arrest	Relying on *Stoner v. California*, 376 U.S. 483 (1964), a search is only incident to arrest if it is contemporaneous and confined to the immediate vicinity. No extension of *United States v. Rabinowitz,* 339 U.S 56 (1950) and *Harris v. United States*, 331 U.S. 145 (1947). Conviction, upheld by Louisiana Supreme Court, reversed; remanded. (9-0; per curiam.)

Case Name	Charge on Arrest	Authority for Arrest	Articles Seized	Warrant Clause	Exceptions to Warrant Clause	Decision
Riggan v. Virginia, 384 U.S. 152 (1966)	Conducting a lottery	Crime committed in the presence of officers when they entered to execute a search warrant	Numbers slips and paraphernalia	Search warrant invalid due to insufficient information in affidavit to sustain PC finding	None	Relying on *Aguilar v. Texas*, 378 U.S. 108 (1964), conviction reversed. Virginia Supreme Court of Appeals reversed. (5-4; per curiam; Clark, Black, Harlan, & Stewart, JJ., dissent.)
Schmerber v. California, 384 U.S. 757 (1966)	Driving an automobile under the influence of intoxicating liquor	Officer smelled alcohol on breath and saw defendant's bloodshot eyes; because passenger suffered injury in accident caused by traffic violation, officer had state felony grounds for warrantless arrest	Defendant's blood for blood alcohol count (BAC) analysis	No warrant	SIVA under exigent circumstances	Narrow decision. Warrantless seizure not violative of Amd. IV due to exigent circumstances. Blood drawn not violative of Amd. V proscription against self-incrimination or Amd. VI RTC because it is nontestimonial. No violation of due process where hospital physician draws blood for BAC from defendant who refuses breathalyzer. Appellate Department of CA Superior Court affirmed. (5-4; Brennan, J., DOC; Harlan & Stewart, JJ., concur; Black, Douglas, & Fortas, JJ., Warren, C.J., dissent.)
Lewis v. United States, 385 U.S. 206 (1966)	Possession and sale of marijuana	Indictment	Marijuana, incriminating statements	No warrant	Consent (1st party)	Distinguishing *Gouled v. United States*, 255 U.S. 298 (1921), undercover agent posing as customer for marijuana transactions did not violate Amd. IV because he was invited into defendant's home. (8-1; Warren, C.J., DOC; Brennan & Fortas, JJ., concur; Douglas, J., dissents.)
Osborn v. United States, 385 U.S. 323 (1966)	Endeavoring to bribe a member of a jury panel in a prospective federal criminal trial	Indictment	Incriminating statements recorded by undercover agent	No warrant; court order; FBI authorized by two federal judges to give undercover agent a wire	Consent of one party	Relying on *Lopez v. United States*, 373 U.S. 427 (1963), particularity requirement of Amd. IV was met. Conviction, upheld by CCA, affirmed. (8-1; Stewart, J., DOC; Douglas, J., dissents.)

Case Name	Charge on Arrest	Authority for Arrest	Articles Seized	Warrant Clause	Exceptions to Warrant Clause	Decision
Hoffa v. United States, 385 U.S. 293 (1966)	Attempting to bribe jurors in prosecution for violation of Taft-Hartley Act	Indictment	Incriminating statements made by defendant in hotel suite heard by government informant	No warrant	Consent of one party	Government informant's testimony concerning conversations between defendant and informant or in his presence in which defendant voluntarily confides his wrongdoing does not violate Amd. IV, V, or VI rights. Conviction, upheld by CCA, affirmed. (8-1; Stewart, J., DOC; Douglas, J., concurs; Warren, C.J., dissents.)
Cooper v. California, 386 U.S. 58 (1967)	Selling heroin in violation of California Health and Safety Code § 11611	Crime committed in the presence of officer when defendant sold heroin to undercover officer	Two bundles of heroin, defendant's car (impounded for forfeiture), brown paper in which heroin was wrapped (seized from impounded car)	No warrant	Statutory forfeiture provision (precursor of inventory search exception)	Distinguishing *Preston v. United States*, 376 U.S. 364 (1964), and applying *United States v. Rabinowitz*, 339 U.S. 56 (1950), analysis, search was not unreasonable. Conviction, upheld by California District Court of Appeal under harmless error analysis, affirmed. (5-4; Black, J., DOC; Douglas, Brennan, & Fortas, JJ., Warren, C.J., dissent.)
McCray v. Illinois, 386 U.S. 300 (1967)	Possession of narcotics	Police received information from reliable source that defendant was selling heroin and informant identified him; when police approached defendant, he walked away rapidly	Heroin	No warrant	SIVA	Confidential informant of known reliability gave police enough specific detail to provide PC for arrest. Identity of informant need not be disclosed as long as magistrate is informed of circumstances supporting informant's credibility. Conviction, upheld by Illinois Supreme Court, affirmed. (5-4; Stewart, J., DOC; Douglas, Brennan, & Fortas, JJ., Warren, C.J., dissent.)
Warden v. Hayden, 387 U.S. 294 (1967)	Armed robbery	Officers notified of crime in progress—armed robbery suspect in flight	Shotgun, pistol, ammunition; jacket, cap, trousers ("mere evidence" taken from washing machine in defendant's basement)	No warrant	Exigent circumstances (hot pursuit)	Warrantless sanctuary seizure not violative of Amd. IV due to exigent circumstances. *Gouled v. United States*, 255 U.S. 298 (1921) and the "mere evidence" rule overruled. CCA reversed. (8-1; Brennan, J., DOC; Black, J., c/j; Fortas, J., Warren, C.J., concur; Douglas, J., dissents.)

Case Name	Charge on Arrest	Authority for Arrest	Articles Seized	Warrant Clause	Exceptions to Warrant Clause	Decision
Camara v. Municipal Court, 387 U.S. 523 (1967)	Defendant's writ of prohibition against the criminal court pursuant to his arrest for refusing to allow city housing inspector access to his apartment to conduct routine housing code inspection	San Francisco Housing Code allowing city inspectors right of entry to inspect any "building, structure, or premises" pursuant to their official duties	NA	No warrant	None	Overruling *Frank v. Maryland*, 359 U.S. 360 (1959), barring emergencies, a search warrant must issue for administrative searches if occupant refuses to allow entry. District court of appeal judgment vacated; remanded. (6-3; White, J., DOC; Clark, Harlan, & Stewart, JJ., dissent.)
See v. City of Seattle, 387 U.S. 541 (1967)	Refusing to allow fire department inspector to enter and inspect defendant's locked commercial warehouse	Seattle Fire Code imposes criminal liability on those refusing to grant fire inspectors access	NA	No warrant	None	Applying *Camara, supra*, analysis, warrant clause protection is extended with respect to administrative searches of businesses. Conviction, upheld by Washington Supreme Court, reversed. (6-3; White, J., DOC; Clark, Harlan, & Stewart, JJ., dissent.)
Berger v. New York, 388 U.S. 41 (1967)	Conspiracy to bribe the chairman of the New York State Liquor Authority	Indictment	Conversations, under New York eavesdrop statute	No warrant	None	Distinguishing *Osborn v. United States*, 385 U.S. 323 (1966), New York eavesdrop statute facially violates Amd. IV since it fails to ensure particularity or PC. Conviction, upheld by NY Court of Appeals, reversed. (6-3; Clark, J., DOC; Douglas, J., c/p; Stewart, J., c/j; Black, Harlan, & White, JJ., dissent.)
Katz v. United States, 389 U.S. 347 (1967)	Interstate wire transmission of wagering information	Indictment	Defendant's conversations on a public telephone obtained via FBI bugging device placed outside the phone booth	No warrant	Telephone booth exception rejected	Amd. IV protects people and not places; warrantless searches are unreasonable per se. *Osborn v. United States*, 385 U.S. 323 (1966), is distinguished, *Olmstead v. United States*, 277 U.S. 438 (1927), and *Goldman v. United States*, 316 U.S. 129 (1942), are not to be followed. Conviction, upheld by CCA, reversed. (7-1; Stewart, J., DOC; Harlan (famous concurrence), White, Douglas, & Brennan, JJ., concur; Black, J., dissents; Marshall, J., took no part.)

Case Name	Charge on Arrest	Authority for Arrest	Articles Seized	Warrant Clause	Exceptions to Warrant Clause	Decision
Harris v. United States, 390 U.S. 234 (1968)	Robbery	Defendant's car was seen leaving the scene of a robbery, and police traced the car to defendant	Automobile registration card belonging to victim of the robbery seized from defendant's impounded vehicle	No warrant	Inventory	Officer following MPD regulations for protection of impounded vehicles—search, remove, and secure valuables, place property tag on steering wheel, roll up windows and lock doors—is not conducting a search for Amd. IV purposes. Conviction, upheld by CCA en banc, affirmed. (8-0; per curiam; Douglas, J., concurs; Marshall, J., took no part.)
Simmons v. United States, 390 U.S. 377 (1968)	Armed robbery of federally insured savings and loan	Indictment	Co-defendant Garrett's suitcase, containing gun holster, sack, coin cards, and bill wrappers, seized from co-defendant Andrews's mother's basement	No warrant	None	Testimony given to establish standing for suppression motion cannot be admitted into evidence (witness immunity) on issue of guilt over an objection. Conviction of co-defendant Garrett reversed, remanded; conviction of Simmons affirmed. (6-2; Harlan, J., DOC; Black & White, JJ., c/p, d/p; Marshall, J., took no part.)
Dyke v. Taylor Implement Mfg. Co., 391 U.S. 216 (1968)	Criminal contempt under Tennessee law for violating terms of injunction issued in connection with labor dispute	Police received complaint that shots were fired at home of nonstriking Taylor Implement Co. employee, then followed a suspicious car that sped away from the officers	Air rifle, pursuant to inventory search of vehicle parked outside county jail	No warrant	Invalid SIVA	Distinguishing *Cooper v. California*, 386 U.S. 58 (1967), warrantless inventory search may be unreasonable due to insufficient PC. Conviction, upheld by Supreme Court of Tennessee, reversed; remanded. (7-2; White, J., DOC; Harlan & Stewart, JJ., concur; Black & Douglas, JJ., dissent.)
Bumper v. North Carolina, 391 U.S. 543 (1968)	Rape and felonious assault	At the hospital, victims identified defendant's picture from photo array; later, victims chose defendant from police lineup	Defendant's rifle in defendant's grandmother's house, where he lived, was seized by police who claimed they had a search warrant	No warrant	Invalid consent (3d party)	When an officer claims to have a warrant, the occupant has no right to resist, and where there is coercion there cannot be consent. Conviction, upheld by North Carolina Supreme Court, reversed; remanded. (7-2; Stewart, J., DOC; Harlan, J., concurs; Black & White, JJ., disssent.)

Case Name	Charge on Arrest	Authority for Arrest	Articles Seized	Warrant Clause	Exceptions to Warrant Clause	Decision
Sabbath v. United States, 391 U.S. 585 (1968)	Knowing importation and concealment of cocaine	Drug courier with cocaine interdicted at Mexican border by customs agents; agents accompanied him (now wearing wire) to defendant's apartment; hearing drug transaction, agents entered through unlocked front door without announcing authority and purpose	Ounce of cocaine and tin foil used for drug packaging	No warrant	None	Relying on *Miller v. United States,* 357 U.S. 301 (1958), unannounced sanctuary intrusions, proscribed by 18 U.S.C. § 3109, are no less unannounced and violative of § 3109 because officers open an unlocked door rather than forcing entry. Conviction, upheld by CCA, reversed; remanded. (8-1; Marshall, J., DOC; Black, J., dissents.)
Terry v. Ohio, 392 U.S. 1 (1968)	Carrying a concealed weapon	Officer observed defendant and two other males behaving suspiciously; he approached and questioned them and, suspecting they were armed, frisked defendant and felt a revolver	Two revolvers and bullets	No warrant	Investigative stop, premised on RAS, may, in the interest of safety, lead to a limited patdown of outer clothing for weapons	Narrow holding; a patdown search of outer clothing for weapons during an investigative stop premised on RAS is limited in scope and not unreasonable under the circumstances. District Court of Appeals affirmed. (8-1; Warren, C.J., DOC; Harlan & White, JJ., concur; Black, J., c/j; Douglas, J., dissents.)
Sibron/Peters v. New York, 392 U.S. 40 (1968)	Possession of heroin (Sibron); possession of burglar's tools (Peters)(consolidated cases)	Officer observed Sibron talking with known addicts over eight-hour period; officer confronted Sibron, who reached in his pocket; officer did the same and discovered heroin (Sibron); after officer saw two men outside apartment, confronted them and they fled, he apprehended Peters, frisked him, discovered burglar tools (Peters)	Heroin (Sibron); burglar's tools (Peters)	No warrants	None (*Sibron*); SIVA (*Peters*)	Search of Sibron was invalid due to lack of PC and insufficient RAS that Sibron was armed—it was warrantless general search for narcotics. New York Court of Appeals reversed (Sibron); frisk of Peters, limited in scope to weapons, justifiable under SIVA due to sufficient PC. New York Court of Appeals affirmed (Peters). (8-1; Warren, C.J., DOC; White, Fortas, & Douglas, JJ., concur; Harlan, J., c/j; Black, J., c/p, d/p.)

Case Name	Charge on Arrest	Authority for Arrest	Articles Seized	Warrant Clause	Exceptions to Warrant Clause	Decision
Mancusi v. DeForte, 392 U.S. 364 (1968)	Conspiracy, coercion, and extortion by abusing union office to compel jukebox owners to make payoffs	Indictment	Union papers	No warrant; subpoena duces tecum issued by district attorney	None	Defendant has standing to object to Amd. IV violation in shared union office, an area in which there was reasonable expectation of freedom from governmental intrusion. Subpoena is not search warrant because signed by DA rather than neutral and detached magistrate. CCA affirmed. (7-2; Harlan, J., DOC; Black & Stewart, JJ., dissent.)
Recznik v. City of Lorain, 393 U.S. 166 (1968)	Keeping a gambling place and exhibiting a gambling device	Police received tip that gambling was taking place, saw a number of parked cars, entered through the back door, and saw craps game in progress	Table, chips, dice, money	No warrant	None	Warrantless sanctuary search invalid due to insufficient PC. Conviction, upheld by Ohio Court of Appeals, reversed; remanded. (5-4; per curiam; Stewart & White, JJ., would deny cert; Black & Harlan, JJ., dissent.)
Spinelli v. United States, 393 U.S. 410 (1969) (OR: *Illinois v. Gates*, 462 U.S. 213 (1983)	Traveling to St. Louis, Missouri, from suburban Illinois with intent to commit gambling activities proscribed by Missouri law	Five days of FBI surveillance based on informant's tip; when defendant left apartment, agents made arrest, demanded keys, searched apartment	Bookmaking paraphernalia, scratch sheets, bet tabs, pay and collection sheets, bookmaking records, ledgers, accounts, three boxes of uninstalled telephones	Search warrant held invalid due to insufficient PC in affidavit	None	Implementing *Aguilar v. Texas*, 378 U.S. 108 (1964), 2-prong test, where underlying circumstances set forth are only bald assertions of suspicion, affidavit lacks PC. Using *Draper v. United States*, 358 U.S. 307 (1959), as benchmark, informant's tip may be unreliable if insufficient in detail. CCA reversed. (6-3; Harlan, J., DOC; White, J., concurs; Black, Stewart, & Fortas, JJ., dissent.)
Alderman v. United States, 394 U.S. 165 (1969)	Conspiracy to transmit murderous threats in interstate commerce (Alderman); conspiracy to transmit to Soviet Union information relating to national security of United States (Ivanov and Butenko) (consolidated cases)	Indictment (Alderman); FBI surveillance observed crime committed in the presence of officers (Ivanov and Butenko)	Conversations obtained via electronic eavesdropping (both); national security documents and espionage paraphernalia (Ivanov and Butenko)	No warrant	None	Amd. IV rights are personal rights that may not be vicariously asserted. Homeowner has automatic standing to move to suppress evidence obtained by illegal police entry into his dwelling. Judgment of CCA vacated; remanded. (7-1; White, J., DOC; Harlan & Fortas, JJ., c/p, d/p; Black, J., dissents; Marshall, J., took no part.)

Case Name	Charge on Arrest	Authority for Arrest	Articles Seized	Warrant Clause	Exceptions to Warrant Clause	Decision
Kaufman v. United States, 394 U.S. 217 (1969) (OR by implication *Stone v. Powell*, 428 U.S. 465 (1976))	Armed robbery of a federally insured savings and loan	Officers apprehended defendant, who possessed stolen cash and checks, in Alton, IL	Revolver, stolen travelers' checks, money order receipt, traffic summons, gasoline receipt	No warrant	None	Claim of illegal search and seizure is cognizable in § 2255 proceedings. CCA reversed. (5-3; Brennan, J., DOC; Black, Harlan, & Stewart, JJ., dissent; Marshall, J., took no part.)
Desist v. United States, 394 U.S. 244 (1969)	Conspiring to import and conceal heroin	Electronic surveillance of defendants in New York, Florida, and Georgia served as basis for information in affidavit for warrant; officers executing warrant found heroin	Conversations in hotel room obtained via electronic eavesdropping; heroin from defendant's trailer home	Search warrant for trailer home, automobile, and sheds; no search warrant for electronic eavesdropping	None	Under *Katz v. United States*, 389 U.S. 347 (1967), warrantless electronic eavesdropping violates Amd. IV. But *Katz* departed from precedent and this case took place before *Katz*; *Katz* is to be applied only prospectively. Convictions, upheld by CCA, affirmed. (5-3; Stewart, J., DOC; Black, J., c/j; Douglas, Harlan, & Fortas, JJ., dissent; Marshall, J., took no part.)
Stanley v. Georgia, 394 U.S. 557 (1969)	Possession of obscene material	Investigation of defendant's alleged bookmaking activities led to issuance of search warrant for his home; when warrant was executed, officers found obscene material	Three reels of 8 mm film	Search warrant	None	Georgia statute imposing criminal liability for mere possession of obscene material in the privacy of one's home violates Amd. I. Georgia Supreme Court reversed. (9-0; Marshall, J., DOC; Black, J., concurs; Stewart (lack of particularity), Brennan, & White, JJ., c/j.)
Davis v. Mississippi, 394 U.S. 721 (1969)	Rape	Defendant one of 24 black males fingerprinted in police dragnet; 60 other black men questioned; defendant had worked for victim, was presented to victim, but was never identified as rapist	Second set of defendant's fingerprints taken after he had been unlawfully detained	No warrant	None	Adopting rule in *Bynum v. United States*, 262 F.2d 465 (D.C. Cir. 1958), where fingerprints obtained from defendant were the product of unlawful detention under Amd. IV and XIV, prints must be excluded from evidence. Conviction, upheld by Mississippi Supreme Court, reversed. (6-2; Brennan, J., DOC; Harlan, J., concurs; Black & Stewart, JJ., dissent; Fortas, J., took no part.)

Case Name	Charge on Arrest	Authority for Arrest	Articles Seized	Warrant Clause	Exceptions to Warrant Clause	Decision
Frazier v. Cupp, 394 U.S. 731 (1969)	Second-degree murder	RAS for custodial interrogation ripened into PC when defendant confessed	Defendant's blood-stained clothing from duffel bag he shared with co-defendant	No warrant	Consent ("joint party")	Joint user of duffel bag may consent to its search. Denial of habeas corpus by CCA, affirmed. (8-0; Marshall, J., DOC; Warren, C.J., Douglas, J., c/j; Fortas, J., took no part.)
Chimel v. California, 395 U.S. 752 (1969)	Burglary of a coin shop	Arrest warrant, held invalid below	Coins, medals, tokens from drawers in defendant's upstairs bedroom seized during hour-long search of defendant's entire house	Arrest warrant, no search warrant	Invalid SIVA (excessive scope)	Overruling *United States v. Rabinowitz*, 339 U.S. 56 (1950), and *Harris v. United States*, 331 U.S. 145 (1947), scope of sanctuary SIVA is limited to arrestee's person and area within his immediate control, from which he might obtain weapons or destroy evidence. California Supreme Court reversed. (7-2; Stewart, J., DOC; Harlan, J., concurs; Black & White, JJ., dissent.)
Von Cleef v. New Jersey, 395 U.S. 814 (1969)	Conspiring to maintain a building for the purposes of committing acts of lewdness; possessing obscene material	Police undercover sting operation of sexual sadomasochism "consultation service"	Books, magazines, catalogues, mailing lists, private correspondence, photographs, drawings, and film seized during 3-hour search of 16-room house	No warrant	Invalid SIVA	Citing *Kremen v. United States*, 353 U.S. 346 (1957), mass warrantless seizure is too pervasive to be reasonable. Conviction, upheld by New Jersey Superior Court Appellate Division, reversed. (7-2; per curiam; Black & White, JJ., concur in grant of cert. but dissent from reversal without hearing; Harlan, J., c/j.)
Shipley v. California, 395 U.S. 818 (1969)	Robbery	Based on informant's tip, police entered defendant's home with his wife's consent and found rings taken in robberies; defendant arrested as he got out of his car	Rings, jewelery case seized from defendant's house after his arrest outside	No warrant	Invalid SIVA	SIVA too remote in space to be reasonable. Conviction, upheld by California Court of Appeal, reversed. (7-2; per curiam; Black, J., concurs in grant of cert. but dissents from reversal without hearing; White, J., dissents.)

Case Name	Charge on Arrest	Authority for Arrest	Articles Seized	Warrant Clause	Exceptions to Warrant Clause	Decision
Colonnade Catering Corp. v. United States, 397 U.S. 72 (1970)	Refusal to permit inspection of liquor storeroom by Alcohol and Tobacco Tax Division IRS agents	Suspicion of agents (who were patrons) that liquor served at catering hall was in refilled bottles	Liquor from locked storeroom seized when agent broke the lock and entered over the owner's protests	No warrant	None	Addressing administrative searches of "licensing programs" question left open in *See v. City of Seattle*, 387 U.S. 541 (1967), when Congress authorizes inspection but sets no rules governing procedure that inspectors must follow, Amd. IV's Warrant Clause applies. CCA reversed. (6-3; Douglas, J., DOC; Burger, C.J., Black, & Stewart, JJ., dissent.)
United States v. Van Leeuwen, 397 U.S. 249 (1970)	Illegally importing gold coins into the United States	RAS to delay mailing 1st-class package ripens through investigation into PC	Two packages were opened, inspected, resealed, and mailed	Search warrant	None	Amd. IV privacy interest in the mails was not disturbed until neutral and detached magistrate approved a warrant, and based on facts of case, a 29-hour delay between mailing of package and issuance of warrant was not unreasonable. CCA reversed. (9-0; Douglas, J., DOC.)
Vale v. Louisiana, 399 U.S. 30 (1970)	Possession of heroin	Officers with arrest warrant, staking out defendant's house, witnessed drug transaction; arrested defendant on sidewalk near front steps of his house	Quantity of heroin seized from rear bedroom of defendant's house	Arrest warrant, no search warrant	Invalid SIVA	Not addressing *Chimel v. California*, 395 U.S. 752 (1969), retroactivity question and relying on *Shipley v. California*, 395 U.S. 818 (1969), retroactivity question and relying on *Shipley*, search of the house was too remote from site of arrest to be SIVA. Louisiana Supreme Court reversed. (6-2; Stewart, J., DOC; Black, J., Burger, C.J., dissent; Blackmun, J., took no part.)
Chambers v. Maroney, 399 U.S. 42 (1970)	Armed robbery	Eyewitness accounts of blue compact station wagon with 4 men (one wearing green sweater, one wearing trench coat) broadcast over police radio; car and suspects fitting description sighted and stopped	Two .38 revolvers (1 loaded with dumdum bullets), glove containing coins, cards bearing name of victim of similar robbery (from car); ammunition for .38, including dumdum bullets (from defendant's home)	No search warrant for search of car at police station; search warrant for defendant's home	Automobile	Reaffirming *Carroll v. United States*, 267 U.S. 132 (1925), PC to search car at point of arrest still existed at station house; since car was not impounded, mobility rationale of *Carroll* makes search reasonable. CCA denial of writ of habeas corpus, affirmed. (8-0; White, J., DOC; Stewart, J., concurs; Harlan, J., c/p, d/p; Blackmun, J. took no part.)

Case Name	Charge on Arrest	Authority for Arrest	Articles Seized	Warrant Clause	Exceptions to Warrant Clause	Decision
Wyman v. James, 400 U.S. 309 (1971)	42 U.S.C.§ 1983 suit by mother and child whose AFDC benefits were terminated due to her refusal to allow home visits by case worker	New York State Social Services Law mandates home visits by caseworkers as a condition of receiving AFDC benefits	AFDC benefits denied by a New York City Department of Social Services hearing officer	No warrant	Home visits by caseworkers for dispensation of AFDC benefits	Distinguishing *Camara v. Municipal Court*, 387 U.S. 523 (1967), and *See v. City of Seattle*, 387 U.S. 541 (1967), unreasonableness is Amd. IV standard and home visits at issue are not unreasonable and not searches for Amd. IV purposes. Declaratory and injunctive relief granted by USDC, reversed, remanded. (6-3; Blackmun, J., DOC; White, J., concurs; Douglas, Marshall, & Brennan, JJ., dissent.)
Whiteley v. Warden, 401 U.S. 560 (1971)	Breaking and entering, being a habitual criminal	Laramie patrolman relied on police radio bulletin describing defendant	Tools and old coins	No search warrant or arrest warrant in Laramie; arrest warrant (obtained in Saratoga and basis for radio message) invalid due to conclusory affidavit providing insufficient PC	None	Relying on *Aguilar v. Texas*, 378 U.S. 108 (1964), *Spinelli v. United States*, 393 U.S. 410 (1969), and *Draper v. United States*, 358 U.S. 307 (1959), complaint lacking any factual data to support informant's tip cannot be cleansed by good faith reliance of arresting officer in another jurisdiction. CCA denial of writ of habeas corpus, reversed and remanded. (7-2; Harlan, J., DOC; Black, J., Burger, C.J., dissent.)
United States v. White, 401 U.S. 745 (1971)	Narcotics violations	After one month of controlled buys recorded via kel set on informant, defendant arrested after police observed him receive brown briefcase containing heroin	Incriminating statements, heroin	No warrant	None	Reaffirming *Desist v. United States*, 394 U.S. 244 (1969), relying on *Hoffa v. United States*, 385 U.S. 293 (1966), *Lewis v. United States*, 385 U.S. 206 (1966), and *Lopez v. United States*, 373 U.S. 427 (1963), and declaring eavesdropping dictum in *On Lee v. United States*, 343 U.S. 747 (1952) a secondary holding, a reasonable warrantless investigative effort without electronic eavesdropping does not become unreasonable by mere presence of a wire. CCA reversed. (PL; White, J., AJC; Black & Brennan, JJ., c/j; Douglas, Harlan, & Marshall, JJ., dissent.)

Case Name	Charge on Arrest	Authority for Arrest	Articles Seized	Warrant Clause	Exceptions to Warrant Clause	Decision
Williams v. United States, 401 U.S. 646 (1971)	Concealing illegally imported heroin (Williams); selling narcotics (Elkanich) (consolidated cases)	Arrest warrant (Williams); PC (Elkanich)	Heroin (Williams); marked bills (Elkanich)	No search warrant (both); no arrest warrant (Elkanich)	SIVA	*Chimel v. California*, 395 U.S. 752 (1969), is to be applied prospectively. Pre-*Chimel* SIVA must be reasonable under *United States v. Rabinowitz*, 339 U.S. 56 (1950) and *Harris v. United States*, 331 U.S. 145 (1947) standards. (PL; White, J., AJC; Stewart filed separate statement; Brennan & Black, JJ., c/j; Harlan & Marshall, JJ., c/p, d/p; Douglas, J., took no part.)
Hill v. California, 401 U.S. 797 (1971)	Robbery and kidnapping	Defendant implicated in robbery by arrested roommate; SIVA of defendant's car, driven by his roommate, produced fruits of robbery; at defendant's apartment, police arrested Miller, who they mistakenly believed was defendant	Starter pistol, 2 switch blades, .22 revolver, camera, two hood masks, automatic pistol and ammo clip, 2 pages from defendant's diary containing admission of participation in robbery	No warrant	SIVA due to good faith mistake by officers with sufficient PC to arrest Hill	Officers arresting Miller under good faith mistake that he was Hill had sufficient PC for warrantless sanctuary SIVA of Hill's apartment under pre-*Chimel v. California*, 395 U.S. 752 (1969), standard. California Supreme Court affirmed. (6-2; White, J., DOC; Black, J., concurs; Harlan & Marshall, JJ., c/p, d/p; Douglas, J., took no part.)
Coolidge v. New Hampshire, 403 U.S. 443 (1971) (OR in part: *Horton v. California*, 496 U.S. 128 (1990))	First-degree murder by assault with a deadly weapon, murder by the same means in the course of committing kidnapping	Police, after investigating crime, obtained an arrest warrant as well as search warrant for defendant's automobile	Vacuum sweepings from defendant's 1951 Pontiac	Search warrant invalid because issued by New Hampshire AG acting as justice of the peace rather than by neutral and detached magistrate	Invalid SIVA; invalid automobile; invalid plain view	Relying on *Johnson v. United States*, 333 U.S. 10 (1948), law enforcement officers cannot be neutral and detached for purposes of issuing warrants. If officer, pursuant to initial valid intrusion, inadvertently discovers evidence in plain view, it may be admitted at trial. Pt. I, lacking neutrality; IIA, invalid SIVA; IIB, invalid auto; IIC, invalid plain view; III, valid consent. New Hampshire Supreme Court reversed; remanded. (5-4; Stewart, J., DOC; Harlan, J., concurs; Burger, C.J., Black, & White, JJ., c/p, d/p.)

Case Name	Charge on Arrest	Authority for Arrest	Articles Seized	Warrant Clause	Exceptions to Warrant Clause	Decision
United States v. Harris, 403 U.S. 573 (1971)	Possessing non-tax-paid liquor	Federal tax investigator and local constable executing search warrant discovered contraband; possessory offense committed in presence of officers	Jugs of whiskey upon which no federal tax had been paid	Search warrant	None	Distinguishing *Spinelli v. United States*, 393 U.S. 410 (1969), here there was substantial basis for crediting hearsay of unnamed informant—the accusation was a statement against penal interest of informant—and officers had personal knowledge of defendant's prior bootlegging activities. CCA reversed. (5-4; Burger, C.J., DOC; Black & Blackmun, JJ., concur; Harlan, Douglas, Brennan, & Marshall, JJ., dissent.)
Papachristou v. City of Jacksonville, 405 U.S. 156 (1972)	Violating Jacksonville, Florida vagrancy ordinance, "prowling by auto"	Defendants engaged in interracial dating, standing in a driveway; defendant had a poor reputation and "no good reason for being on the street"	Persons of the defendants	No warrant	Ordinance unconstitutional as applied	Jacksonville ordinance struck down as void for vagueness because it fails to give person of ordinary intelligence fair notice that contemplated conduct is forbidden; Amd. IV violated because too much discretion is placed in police hands by permitting arbitrary arrests without PC. Florida District Court of Appeal reversed. (7-0; Douglas, J., DOC; Powell & Rehnquist, JJ., took no part.)
United States v. Biswell, 406 U.S. 311 (1972)	Violating firearms laws by dealing in firearms without paying special occupation tax	Indictment pursuant to inspection under Gun Control Act of 1968: Alcohol, Tobacco and Firearms (ATF) agent discovered two rifles in defendant pawnbroker's storeroom	Two sawed-off rifles	No warrant	Regulatory inspection of business premises limited in time, place, and scope under valid statutory authority such as Gun Control Act of 1968, 18 U.S.C. § 923(g)	Distinguishing *Colonnade Catering Corp. v. United States*, 397 U.S. 72 (1970), unannounced, warrantless regulatory searches of firearms dealers is credible deterrent, furthering urgent federal interest authorized by statute. CCA reversed. (8-1; White, J., DOC; Blackmun, J., concurs; Douglas, J., dissents.)
Adams v. Williams, 407 U.S. 143 (1972)	Illegal possession of handgun, possession of heroin	Known informant tipped off patrol officer in high crime area that defendant was armed and holding heroin; during *Terry* stop, defendant rolled down car window, officer seized gun concealed in defendant's waistband	Loaded revolver and heroin from defendant's person; heroin, another	No warrant	RAS for *Terry* stop and evidence from defendant's person; SIVA for evidence from car	Relying on *Terry v. Ohio*, 392 U.S. 1 (1968), under the circumstances of the case, informant's hearsay plus officer's corroboration was sufficient RAS for stop and frisk and, after gun discovered, PC for arrest. CCA reversed. (6-3; Rehnquist, J., DOC; Douglas, Marshall, & Brennan, JJ., dissent.)

Case Name	Charge on Arrest	Authority for Arrest	Articles Seized	Warrant Clause	Exceptions to Warrant Clause	Decision
United States v. United States District Court for Eastern District of Michigan, 407 U.S. 297 (1972)	Review of government's writ of mandamus to set aside USDC order to disclose fruits of surveillance	Writ of mandamus arose in context of trial of 3 defendants charged with conspiracy to destroy government property	handgun, machete from defendant's car Conversations obtained via electronic surveillance of domestic subversives without prior judicial approval	No warrant	Improper reliance on 18 U.S.C. § 2511(3) as allowing President to conduct warrantless domestic security surveillance	Addressing question left open in *Katz v. United States*, 389 U.S. 347 (1967), to satisfy Amd. IV, prior judicial approval is required to authorize electronic surveillance in situations involving domestic aspects of national security; executive branch approval fails "neutral and detached" test. CCA affirmed. (8-0; Powell, J., DOC; Burger, C.J., White, J., c/j; Douglas, J., concurs; Rehnquist, J., took no part.)
Shadwick v. City of Tampa, 407 U.S. 345 (1972)	Impaired driving	Arrest warrant issued by clerk of municipal court	Person of the defendant	Arrest warrant	None	Provided they are neutral, detached, and capable of determining PC, municipal court clerks may be designated magistrates and authorized by city charter to issue warrants for city ordinance violations. Florida Supreme Court affirmed. (9-0; Powell, J., DOC.)
Combs v. United States, 408 U.S. 224 (1972)	Receiving, possessing, and concealing 26 cases of tax-paid whisky stolen from interstate shipment	Indictment	26 cases of whisky, identified as stolen from railroad shipment, in shed on father's farm; defendants not present at execution of warrant	Search warrant subject of challenge by defendant on direct appeal that affidavit failed to meet test of *Aguilar v. Texas*, 378 U.S. 108 (1964)	None	Declining to overrule *Jones v. United States*, 362 U.S. 257 (1960), CCA's judgment, that defendant lacks standing to challenge search warrant executed on his father's farm, is vacated and remanded for fact finding under *DeForte* doctrine (*Mancusi v. DeForte*, 392 U.S. 364 (1968)) (9-0; per curiam; Douglas, J., c/j.)
United States v. Dionisio, 410 U.S. 1 (1973)	Civil contempt for refusing to furnish voice exemplars to grand jury	Refusing to obey USDC order, following a hearing, to produce voice exemplars to the grand jury	Person of the defendant	Grand jury subpoena	None	Distinguishing *Davis v. Mississippi*, 394 U.S. 721 (1969), compelled appearance before grand jury is not an unreasonable seizure; under *Katz v. United States*, 389 U.S. 347 (1967), no LEP in what is exposed to the public—here, defendant's voice. CCA reversed; remanded. (6-3; Stewart, J., DOC; Brennan, J., c/p, d/p; Douglas & Marshall, JJ., dissent.)

Case Name	Charge on Arrest	Authority for Arrest	Articles Seized	Warrant Clause	Exceptions to Warrant Clause	Decision
United States v. Mara, 410 U.S. 19 (1973)	Civil contempt for refusing to furnish handwriting and printing exemplars to grand jury	Refusing to obey USDC order to produce handwriting and printing exemplars for grand jury	Person of the defendant	Grand jury subpoena	None	Relying on *United States v. Dionisio*, 410 U.S. 1 (1973), grand jury subpoena is not seizure for Amd. IV purposes; no LEP in physical characteristics exposed to public—here, handwriting. CCA reversed; remanded. (6-3; Stewart, J., DOC; Douglas, Brennan, & Marshall, JJ., dissent.)
Brown v. United States, 411 U.S. 223 (1973)	Transporting and conspiring to transport stolen goods in interstate commerce	Officers observed merchandise from warehouse being loaded onto truck; defendants were followed, stopped, arrested	Store merchandise, including clothing and household goods	Search warrant, defective	None	Where defendants have no LEP in premises or goods seized and no automatic standing rule applies, defendants lack standing to contest admission of evidence. CCA affirmed. (9-0; Burger, C.J., DOC.)
Schneckloth v. Bustamonte, 412 U.S. 218 (1973)	Possessing a check with intent to defraud	Fruits of crime uncovered during consent search of car pursuant to traffic violation stop	Three checks stolen from a car wash	No warrant	Consent (1st party)	Using Amd. V voluntary confession analysis as template for Amd. IV voluntary consent to search, "voluntariness" of consent is determined by TOC; proof of knowledge of right to refuse is not prerequisite. CCA reversed. (6-3; Stewart, J., DOC; Blackmun, Powell, & Rehnquist, JJ., Burger, C.J., concur; Douglas, Brennan, & Marshall, JJ., dissent.)
Cupp v. Murphy, 412 U.S. 291 (1973)	Second-degree murder	Defendant came to station house voluntarily; police took fingernail scrapings, which yielded incriminating evidence, over his protest, and subsequently made arrest	Fingernail scrapings	No warrant	SIVA	Distinguishing *Davis v. Mississippi*, 394 U.S. 721 (1969), when there is PC for detention, limited intrusion to obtain evanescent evidence in fingernail scrapings acceptable as *Chimel v. California*, 395 U.S. 752 (1969) search. CCA reversed. (7-2; Stewart, J., DOC; White, Marshall, Blackmun, Powell, & Rehnquist, JJ., Burger, C.J., concur; Douglas & Brennan, JJ., d/p.)

Case Name	Charge on Arrest	Authority for Arrest	Articles Seized	Warrant Clause	Exceptions to Warrant Clause	Decision
Almeida-Sanchez v. United States, 413 U.S. 266 (1973)	Knowingly receiving, concealing, and facilitating transportation and concealment of illegally imported marijuana	Defendant's car stopped on east-west highway entirely within U.S., 25 miles north of border, by roving border patrol, which conducted thorough search	Marijuana	No warrant	Immigration and Naturalization Act § 287(a)(3) unconstitutional as applied	A warrantless automobile search that takes place absent PC, RAS, auto exception, or consent, and that takes place neither at the border nor its functional equivalent, is unreasonable under Amd. IV. CCA reversed. (5-4; Stewart, J., DOC; Powell, J., concurs; White, Blackmun, & Rehnquist, JJ., Burger, C.J., dissent.)
Cady v. Dombrowski, 413 U.S. 433 (1973)	Drunken driving, first-degree murder charge	Police observed defendant, driver in one-car crash, as drunk; search of vehicle produced evidence of violent crime; defendant directed police to body	From Dodge: back and front seats, bloody sock, bloody rear floor mat, briefcase, front floor mat; from trunk of Thunderbird: police nightstick and uniform trousers, slacks, floor mat, towel, all bloody	Search warrants issued for both cars; articles seized from 1967 Thunderbird before warrant issued	Search for purpose of ensuring public safety not unreasonable	Where officer follows standard procedure to protect public from revolver believed to be in trunk of car held under police custody, intrusion into vehicle was not unreasonable simply because warrant had not yet been obtained. CCA reversed. (5-4; Rehnquist, J., DOC; Brennan, Douglas, Stewart, & Marshall, JJ., dissent.)
United States v. Robinson, 414 U.S. 218 (1973)	Operating car without valid license, possession and facilitation of concealment of heroin	During investigation, officer had previously run a check on defendant's operator's permit; results of check provided reason to believe defendant's driving was a traffic violation	14 gelatin capsules of heroin in a cigarette pack seized during patdown	No warrant	SIVA	Under Amd. IV, a full body search is reasonable incident to arrest based on PC; SIVA is not limited to merely a *Terry*-type frisk. (*Terry v. Ohio*, 392 U.S. 1 (1968)). CCA reversed. (6-3; Rehnquist, J., DOC; Marshall, Douglas, & Brennan, JJ., dissent.)
Gustafson v. Florida, 414 U.S. 260 (1973)	Operating car without valid license, unlawful possession of marijuana	Officer observed automobile driving erratically, stopped car, and asked defendant for his operator's license; defendant arrested for failure to have license in his possession	Marijuana	No warrant	SIVA	Relying on *United States v. Robinson*, *supra*, lawful arrest gives police authority to search. SIVA is an exception to the warrant clause and reasonable under Amd. IV. Florida Supreme Court affirmed. (6-3; Rehnquist, J., DOC; Powell & Stewart, JJ., concur; Marshall, Douglas, & Brennan, JJ., dissent.)

Case Name	Charge on Arrest	Authority for Arrest	Articles Seized	Warrant Clause	Exceptions to Warrant Clause	Decision
United States v. Calandra, 414 U.S. 338 (1974)	Defendant refused to answer questions before grand jury investigating loansharking	Police executed search warrant at defendant's place of business for evidence of gambling activities; officer seized evidence of possible loansharking	Promissory notes, company books and records, stock certificates, and address books	Search warrant particularizing gambling parapherna-lia invalid due to insufficient PC; subpoena issued for grand jury testimony	Grand jury proceeding inapplicable	Amd. IV exclusionary rule does not apply to fruits or derivative use of illegal searches and seizures in context of grand jury proceeding; grand jury questions involve no independent invasion and work no new Amd. IV wrong. CCA reversed. (6-3; Powell, J., DOC; Brennan, Douglas, Marshall, dissent.)
United States v. Matlock, 415 U.S. 164 (1974)	Robbery of a federally insured bank	Defendant, suspect in bank robberies, was arrested at 9:30 a.m. outside a house rented by his girlfriend's mother, where he shared the east bedroom	$4,995 cash found in a diaper bag seized from the only closet in the east bedroom	No warrant	Consent (3d party)	Consent for warrantless search may be obtained from 3d party with common authority over or other sufficient relationship to the pre-mises; no automatic rule against receiving hearsay evidence in suppression hearings. CCA reversed. (6-3; White, J., DOC; Douglas, Brennan, Marshall, dissent.)
United States v. Edwards, 415 U.S. 800 (1974)	Attempted breaking and entering of United States Post Office	Crime committed in the presence of officers; defendant apprehended while attempting to enter window of post office after 11:00 p.m.	Defendant's clothing taken from him in jail and found to contain paint chips matching those on the post office window sill	No warrant	SIVA	Relying on *United States v. Robinson*, 414 U.S. 427 (1973), and *Abel v. United States*, 362 U.S. 217 (1960), 10-hour delay between custodial arrest and warrantless seizure of defendant's clothing is reasonable; possessions subject to search at time and place of detention may be searched and seized without warrant even after time lapse. CCA reversed. (5-4; White, J., DOC; Stewart, Douglas, Brennan, & Marshall, JJ., dissent.)
Cardwell v. Lewis, 417 U.S. 583 (1974)	First-degree murder	Arrest warrant; in addition to PC for arrest, police had PC to believe defendant's car was used in commission of the crime	Defendant's car, paint scrapings from car, and tire tread identifi-cation	No warrant	None	Relying on *Chambers v. Maroney*, 399 U.S. 42 (1970), examination of vehicle's exterior based on PC is reasonable and invades no LEP which the requirement of a warrant was meant to protect. CCA reversed. (5-4; Blackmun, J., AJC; Powell, J., c/j; Stewart, Douglas, Brennan, & Marshall, JJ., dissent.)

Case Name	Charge on Arrest	Authority for Arrest	Articles Seized	Warrant Clause	Exceptions to Warrant Clause	Decision
Gerstein v. Pugh, 420 U.S. 103 (1975)	Class action brought under 42 U.S.C. § 1983 against Dade County officials claiming constitutional right to PC hearing for pretrial detention	Under Florida law, person charged by information could be detained solely on the decision of the prosecutor	Persons of the accused	No arrest warrant; warrantless arrest of persons charged by information	Argument that the prosecutor's decision to file information is itself a determination of PC rejected	Amd. IV requires timely judicial determination of PC as prerequisite to detention; such hearing need not be adversarial and is not prerequisite to prosecution by information. CCA affirmed in part, reversed in part. (5-4; Powell, J., DOC; Stewart, Brennan, Douglas, & Marshall, JJ., dissent.)
United States v. Peltier, 422 U.S. 531 (1975)	PWID marijuana	Four months prior to *Almeida-Sanchez* decision, defendant's car stopped by roving border patrol 70 air miles from Mexican border and searched without PC or RAS	Three garbage bags containing 270 pounds of marijuana seized from trunk of defendant's car	No warrant	Good faith reliance by border patrol on Immigration and Nationality Act § 287(a)(3)	Using *Stovall v. Denno*, 388 U.S. 293 (1967), analysis, since purpose of exclusionary rule is deterrence, *Almeida-Sanchez v. United States*, 413 U.S. 266 (1972), should be applied only prospectively—not where agents acted in reliance on long-supported federal statute. CCA reversed. (5-4; Rehnquist, J., DOC; Stewart, Douglas, Brennan, & Marshall, JJ., dissent.)
Brown v. Illinois, 422 U.S. 590 (1975)	Murder	Victim's brother named defendant as an acquaintance of the victim; police broke into defendant's apartment, searched it, arrested defendant when he returned home	Incriminating statements made by defendant, subsequent to receiving *Miranda* warnings, during his illegal detention	No warrant	*Miranda v. Arizona*, 384 U.S. 43 (1966), exception rejected	Interpreting *Wong Sun v. United States*, 371 U.S. 471 (1963), *Miranda* warnings, standing alone, are insufficient to purge taint of illegal arrest. 3 factors for dissipation: temporal proximity of arrest and confession, intervening circum-stances, flagrancy of police miscon-duct. Illinois Supreme Court reversed. (7-2; Blackmun, J., DOC; White, J., c/j; Powell & Rehnquist, JJ., c/p.)
United States v. Brignoni-Ponce, 422 U.S. 873 (1975)	Knowingly transport-ing illegal immigrants	Border patrol officers stopped defendant's car because all 3 occupants looked to be of Mexican descent; questioning revealed 2 passengers were illegal aliens	Testimony of and about the 2 passengers	No warrant	Immigration and Nationality Act §§ 287(a)(1), 287(a)(3) unconstitutional as applied	Random stops are unreasonable; except at a border or its functional equivalent, all stops must be supported by RAS (Mexican ancestry alone is insufficient to support RAS). CCA affirmed. (9-0; Powell, J., DOC; Rehnquist, J., concurs; Douglas, J., c/j.)

Case Name	Charge on Arrest	Authority for Arrest	Articles Seized	Warrant Clause	Exceptions to Warrant Clause	Decision
United States v. Ortiz, 422 U.S. 891 (1975)	Knowingly transporting illegal aliens	Defendant's car stopped at San Clemente, CA, checkpoint; routine immigration search revealed 3 aliens in the trunk	Testimony by and about the 3 aliens in the trunk	No warrant	None	Following *Almeida-Sanchez v. United States*, 413 U.S. 266 (1973), border patrol officers may not conduct vehicle searches without consent or PC at traffic checkpoints removed from border or its equivalent. CCA affirmed. (9-0; Powell, J., DOC; Rehnquist, J., concurs; White & Blackmun, JJ., Burger, C.J., c/j.)
Bowen v. United States, 422 U.S. 916 (1975)	Smuggling and transporting smuggled marijuana, possession of depressant and stimulant drugs	Defendant's camper pickup stopped at border patrol checkpoint 36 miles from Mexican border; when camper was opened to search for aliens, officer smelled and then found marijuana	356 pounds of marijuana, benzedrine tablets	No warrant	Good faith reliance on Ninth Circuit precedents prior to *Almeida-Sanchez*	Relying on *Peltier v. United States*, 422 U.S. 531 (1975), non-retroactivity of *Almeida-Sanchez* applies also to its extension to searches at traffic checkpoints. CCA affirmed. (5-4; Powell, J., DOC; Douglas, Brennan, Marshall, & Stewart, JJ., dissent.)
Texas v. White, 423 U.S. 67 (1975)	Knowingly attempting to pass as true a forged instrument in writing	Officers received tip that man fitting defendant's description tried to pass fraudulent checks; minutes later, officers apprehended defendant at drive-in window of bank attempting to pass fraudulent checks	Four checks, corresponding to those defendant attempted to pass at first bank, seized from defendant's car after officers drove car to station house	No warrant	Automobile	Relying on *Chambers v. Maroney*, 399 U.S. 42 (1970), where PC exists to search car at scene, PC still obtained shortly thereafter at the station house. Texas Court of Criminal Appeals reversed. (7-2; per curiam; Marshall & Brennan, JJ., dissent.)
United States v. Watson, 423 U.S. 411 (1976)	Possession of stolen mail	Informant of known reliability assisted postal inspectors in stolen credit card sting operation; defendant arrested when informant indicated he held stolen credit cards	Two stolen credit cards found under floor mat of defendant's car	No warrant	Consent for car search; 39 CFR § 232.5 (a)(3), 18 U.S.C. § 3061(a)(3), give postal officers power to make warrantless arrests upon PC	Federal law enforcement officers may make warrantless public space arrests based on PC that suspect has committed a felony but might find it prudent to seek warrant where practicable. CCA reversed. (6-2; White, J., DOC; Powell, J., concurs; Stewart, J. c/j; Marshall & Brennan, JJ., dissent; Stevens, J., took no part.)

Case Name	Charge on Arrest	Authority for Arrest	Articles Seized	Warrant Clause	Exceptions to Warrant Clause	Decision
United States v. Miller, 425 U.S. 435 (1976) Limited by *Carpenter v. United States* (2018).	Possession of unregistered still, carrying out distillery business without giving bond and with intent to defraud government of whiskey tax, possessing whiskey on which no tax had been paid, conspiring to defraud U.S. of tax monies	Indictment	Microfilm bank records of defendant's transactions at two banks obtained by ATF agents using grand jury subpoena duces tecum	No warrant; grand jury subpoenas duces tecum served on two banks	Bank business records inapplicable	No LEP in negotiable instruments since they are open to the public through their use in commercial transactions; subpoenaed materials were bank's business records, not defendant's, nor does Bank Secrecy Act, as applied, violate Amd. IV. CCA reversed; remanded. (7-2; Powell, J., DOC; Brennan & Marshall, JJ., dissent.)
United States v. Santana, 427 U.S. 38 (1976)	PWID heroin	Undercover narcotics officers used marked money to make heroin buy; target of sting told officers defendant had the marked money, and officers confronted defendant	Marked "buy" money, heroin	No warrant	Exigent circumstances (hot pursuit)	Relying on *United States v. Watson*, 423 U.S. 411 (1976), police may make warrantless arrest in public place upon PC; "hot pursuit" exception (*Warden v. Hayden*, 387 U.S. 294 (1967)) allows police to seize defendant after she retreats into vestibule of her home. CCA reversed. (7-2; Rehnquist, J., DOC; White, Stevens, & Stewart, JJ., concur; Brennan & Marshall, JJ., dissent.)
Andresen v. Maryland, 427 U.S. 463 (1976)	Fraudulent misappropriation by a fiduciary, false pretenses	Information in part, indictment in part	2%-3% of files from defendant's law office and less than 5% of files from his real estate development corporation	Search warrant (n.9 dismisses defendant's argument that affidavits failed to establish PC because informant's reliability was not established and information was stale)	None	Search of a business office pursuant to warrant and seizure of documents entered into evidence does not violate Amd. V proscription against self-incrimination; provided investigators reasonably believe that additional evidence seized may be used to show motive or plan, that seizure is not unreasonable under Amd. IV. Court of Special Appeals of Maryland affirmed. (7-2; Blackmun, J., DOC; Brennan & Marshall, JJ., dissent.)

Case Name	Charge on Arrest	Authority for Arrest	Articles Seized	Warrant Clause	Exceptions to Warrant Clause	Decision
South Dakota v. Opperman, 428 U.S. 364 (1976)	Possession of marijuana	Defendant's illegally parked car was towed to police impound-ment lot where standard inventory search was conducted and contraband found	Marijuana seized from glove compartment of defendant's im-pounded car	No warrant	Inventory search exception created	Warrantless inventory searches conducted under established police procedures do not require PC and are reasonable under Amd. IV as long as they are not pretextual. Supreme Court of South Dakota reversed. (5-4; Burger, C.J., DOC; Powell, J., concurs; Marshall, Brennan, Stewart, & White, JJ., dissent.)
United States v. Janis, 428 U.S. 433 (1976)	Civil tax suit based on IRS assessment of unreported wagering income as recorded in seized documents	Officers executing defective search warrant, in good faith, discovered wagering records and cash; informed IRS	$4,940 cash and wagering records	Search warrant ruled defective under *Spinelli v. United States*, 393 U.S. 410 (1969); subsequent tax assessment based on FOPT quashed	Civil tax proceeding inapplicable	Exclusionary rule does not extend to forbid use in civil proceeding by or against U.S. of evidence seized in good faith (but unconstitutionally) by state criminal law enforcement agents. CCA reversed. (5-3; Blackmun, J., DOC; Brennan, Marshall, & Stewart, JJ., dissent; Stevens, J., took no part.)
Stone v. Powell, 428 U.S. 465 (1976)	Vagrancy, second-degree murder (Powell); first-degree murder (Rice) (consolidated cases)	Crime of vagrancy committed in the presence of officers (Powell); possession of explosive material in investigation of dynamite explosion death of police officer (Rice)	.38 caliber revolver with six spent cartridges (Powell); dynamite, blasting caps, materials used in constructing explosive device, clothes (Rice)	No search warrant (Powell); search warrant (Rice)	SIVA (Powell); none (Rice)	Where state prisoner receives full and fair hearing of Amd. IV claim in the state court, he may not be granted federal habeas corpus relief on ground that evidence introduced was obtained in unconstitutional search or seizure. CCA reversed. (6-3; Powell, J., DOC; Burger, C.J., concurs; Brennan, Marshall, & White, JJ., dissent.)
United States v. Martinez-Fuerte, 428 U.S. 543 (1976)	Illegally transporting aliens	Driving through border patrol checkpoint with passengers who, upon routine questioning, admit to being illegal aliens	Testimony by and about the illegal aliens	No warrant	Border search; 8 U.S.C. § 1357(a), 8 CFR § 287.1 authorize inspection of vehicles and questioning of suspected aliens	Stops for brief questioning at permanent border checkpoint are reasonable under Amd. IV and need not be supported by warrant; further detention requires PC, consent, or warrant. CCA reversed. (6-2; Powell, J., DOC; Brennan & Marshall, JJ., dissent.)

Case Name	Charge on Arrest	Authority for Arrest	Articles Seized	Warrant Clause	Exceptions to Warrant Clause	Decision
Connally v. Georgia, 429 U.S. 245 (1977)	Possession of marijuana	Officers executing search warrant found marijuana in defendant's house: possessory offense committed in the presence of officers	Marijuana	Search warrant issued by nonsalaried justice of the peace who earned $5 fee for each issuance of a warrant and no fee for denial	None	Applying *Tumey v. Ohio*, 273 U.S. 510 (1927), statutory scheme where unsalaried justice is paid for issuing warrant but receives nothing for denial subjects defendant to court officer with substantial personal pecuniary interest and violates Amd. IV. Georgia Supreme Court judgment vacated; remanded. (9-0; per curiam.)
G.M. Leasing Corp. v. United States, 429 U.S. 338 (1977)	Suit brought against the government asserting claim of wrongful levy and seeking return of seized automobiles, suppression of evidence from seized documents, and damages from IRS agents	IRS levy and seizure of corporate assets to satisfy individual tax liability of corporation's general manager, pursuant to 26 U.S.C. §§ 6331, 7701	Automobiles, documents, corporate business records	No warrant	None	No per se exception to warrant clause for tax collection; warrantless search of offices where there is LEP is unreasonable; seizure of cars parked in open areas does not intrude on privacy interest. CCA affirmed in part, reversed in part. (9-0; Blackmun, J., DOC; Burger, C.J., concurs.)
United States v. Ramsey, 431 U.S. 606 (1977)	Narcotics violations	Pursuant to 19 U.S.C. § 482, Customs Inspector at NYC Post Office opened suspiciously bulky envelopes from Thailand; found heroin. DEA resealed envelopes and mailed under surveillance; defendant arrested	Heroin, buffering agents used to cut heroin for street sale, $1,100 cash, 2 pistols	No warrant (DEA obtained search warrant after receiving envelopes, but n.4 declares that the warrant issued post-opening is not significant)	19 U.S.C. § 482 (airmail border search)	Citing *Boyd v. United States*, 116 U.S. 616 (1886), and *Carroll v. United States*, 267 U.S. 132 (1925), warrantless border searches without PC are reasonable under Amd. IV. CCA reversed. (6-3; Rehnquist, J., DOC; Powell, J., concurs; Stevens, Brennan, & Marshall, JJ., dissent.)

Case Name	Charge on Arrest	Authority for Arrest	Articles Seized	Warrant Clause	Exceptions to Warrant Clause	Decision
United States v. Chadwick, 433 U.S. 1 (1977) (OR: *California v. Acevedo*, 500 U.S. 565 (1991))	PWID marijuana, conspiracy PWID	Amtrak officials in San Diego noticed powder leaking from defendant's footlocker and alerted federal authorities. In Boston, agents met defendants with detector dogs. Dogs signalled at footlocker; arrest made when footlocker placed in trunk of defendant's car	Marijuana seized from 200-pound double-locked footlocker opened by agents at the Boston federal building	No warrant	Invalid SIVA, invalid automobile exception; luggage exception rejected	Reaffirming *Katz v. United States*, 389 U.S. 347 (1967), defendant has LEP in contents of footlocker; absent exigent circumstances, warrantless search of footlocker under dominion and control of federal authorities is per se unreasonable. CCA affirmed. (7-2; Burger, C.J., DOC; Brennan, J., concurs; Blackmun & Rehnquist, JJ., dissent.)
Pennsylvania v. Mimms, 434 U.S. 106 (1977)	Carrying a concealed weapon and unlawfully carrying a firearm without a license	Officers on patrol stopped car to issue summons for expired tags; when defendant was ordered out of car, police noticed bulge in sport coat; frisk produced loaded .38 caliber revolver	.38 caliber revolver containing five rounds of ammunition; person of defendant	No warrant	"...reasonableness depends on a balance between the public interest and the individual's right to personal security free from arbitrary interference by law officers"	Once a car is lawfully detained for traffic violation, ordering driver to get out does not constitute an unreasonable seizure; under *Terry v. Ohio*, 392 U.S. 1 (1968), bulge in jacket is sufficient RAS for frisk. Pennsylvania Supreme Court reversed. (6-3; per curiam; Marshall, Stevens, & Brennan, JJ., dissent.)
United States v. Ceccolini, 435 U.S. 268 (1978)	Perjury	Local police officer "tarrying" behind counter of flower shop saw envelope with policy slips and was told it belonged to defendant; 4 months later, defendant denied, in front of a grand jury, that he had taken policy bets	Testimony of flower shop employee; envelope with policy slips	No warrant	FOPT dissipated; live witness exception rejected	Considerations relating to principles of exclusionary rule must play a factor in attenuation analysis; here, degree of attenuation between officer's search and the testimony was sufficient to dissipate the taint of the illegality. Where search is unintentional, no deterrent effect is served by excluding testimony. CCA reversed. (6-2; Rehnquist, J., DOC; Burger, C.J., c/j; Brennan & Marshall, JJ., dissent; Blackmun, J., took no part.)

Case Name	Charge on Arrest	Authority for Arrest	Articles Seized	Warrant Clause	Exceptions to Warrant Clause	Decision
Marshall v. Barlow's, Inc., 436 U.S. 307 (1978)	Suit brought to obtain injunctive relief against warrantless inspection of business premises pursuant to OSHA § 8(a), which authorizes inspection of any employment facility in the Act's jurisdiction	Reliance on OSHA § 8(a)	NA	No warrant	OSHA § 8(a) unconstitutional as applied	Relying on *Camara v Municipal Court*, 387 U.S. 523 (1967), and *See v. City of Seattle*, 387 U.S. 541 (1967), warrantless administrative searches may be permitted in "closely regulated" industries, but such searches of commercial premises are generally unreasonable; warrantless inspection pursuant to OSHA § 8(a) violates Amd. IV. USDC affirmed. (5-3; White, J., DOC; Stevens, Blackmun, & Rehnquist, JJ., dissent; Brennan took no part.)
Michigan v. Tyler, 436 U.S. 499 (1978)	Conspiracy to burn real property	Fire chief removed evidence from smouldering embers of furniture store blaze; weeks later arson investigators repeatedly entered premises to gather evidence	Two containers of flammable liquid, samples of carpet and stairwell with burn marks, fuse	No warrant	None	After a fire has been extinguished and firefighters have left the premises, further official entries—detached from initial exigency—to investigate the cause of the fire require consent or warrant. Michigan Supreme Court affirmed. (7-1; Stewart, J., DOC; Stevens, J., c/p, c/j; White & Marshall, JJ., c/p, d/p; Rehnquist, J., dissents; Brennan, J., took no part.)
Zurcher v. Stanford Daily, 436 U.S. 547 (1978)	Suit brought seeking declaratory and injunctive relief under 42 U.S.C. § 1983	NA	NA	Search warrant, particularizing negatives, films, and pictures of demonstrators who assaulted officers during seizure of university offices	None	Under Amd. IV, the state is not prevented from issuing a warrant to search for evidence simply because the possessor of the place is a 3d-party student newspaper not suspected of criminal involvement; critical element is PC that "things" are located where search is to be conducted. CCA reversed. (5-3; White, J., DOC; Powell, J., concurs; Stewart, Marshall, & Stevens, JJ., dissent; Brennan, J., took no part.)

Case Name	Charge on Arrest	Authority for Arrest	Articles Seized	Warrant Clause	Exceptions to Warrant Clause	Decision
Mincey v. Arizona, 437 U.S. 385 (1978)	Murder, assault, narcotics offenses	Defendant agreed to sell heroin to undercover officer; officer, accompanied by plainclothes policemen, returned to defendant's apartment, went into back bedroom, and was killed in gunfight	200 to 300 objects gathered during 4-day search of apartment, including guns, bullets, shell casings, drugs, narcotics paraphernalia; statements made by defendant while in hospital ICU	No warrant	Murder scene exception struck down: (1) search not justified on ground no constitutionally protected privacy right invaded; (2) not justified on ground that possible homicide presents emergency; (3) offense itself did not create exigent circumstances; (4)protection not afforded to resident where homicide occurs	Arizona's murder scene exception struck down; seriousness of offense under investigation does not create exigent circumstances to justify warrantless search. Further, defendant's statements made during 4-hour interrogation in ICU were involuntary, thus violative of due process. Arizona Supreme Court reversed. (8-1; Stewart, J., DOC; Marshall & Brennan, JJ., concur; Rehnquist, J., c/p, d/p.)
Franks v. Delaware, 438 U.S. 154 (1978)	Rape, kidnapping, burglary	Absent *Miranda v. Arizona*, 384 U.S. 436 (1966), warnings, defendant awaiting bail hearing made inculpatory statement to youth officer	White thermal undershirt, knit hat, dark pants, leather jacket, single-blade knife	Search warrant supported by perjured affidavit	None	Where defendant makes substantial preliminary showing that false statement necessary to finding of PC perjuriously or with reckless disregard was included in affidavit, a hearing must be held at defendant's request; if shown by preponderance and PC is no longer established, the warrant is voided. Supreme Court of Delaware reversed; remanded. (7-2; Blackmun, J., DOC; Rehnquist, J., Burger, C.J., dissent.)
Rakas v. Illinois, 439 U.S. 128 (1978)	Armed robbery	Officer received radio bulletin of robbery of a store with description of getaway car and stopped car that fit description; car was searched	Sawed-off rifle (from under front passenger seat), box of rifle shells (from locked glove compartment)	No warrant	Burden on defendants to demonstrate standing to object to the search; not done here	Further limiting *Jones v. United States*, 362 U.S. 257 (1960), automatic standing doctrine, persons who assert neither property nor possessory interest in area searched or property seized and who fail to show LEP in area have not demonstrated standing to challenge an illegal search. Illinois Appellate Court affirmed. (5-4; Rehnquist, J., DOC; Powell, J., Burger, C.J., concur; White, Brennan, Marshall, & Stevens, JJ., dissent.)

Case Name	Charge on Arrest	Authority for Arrest	Articles Seized	Warrant Clause	Exceptions to Warrant Clause	Decision
Michigan v. Doran, 439 U.S. 282 (1978)	Receiving and concealing stolen property in Michigan, theft of motor vehicle, theft by embezzlement in Arizona	Habeas corpus attack on validity of extradition warrant	Person of defendant detained as fugitive, truck with California plates driven from Arizona to Michigan	Arrest warrant issued and extradition ordered by governor of Michigan (Michigan); arrest warrant (Arizona)	Extradition Clause, U.S. Constitution, Art. IV, § 2, cl.2	Under extradition clause, once governor of asylum state acts on requisition for extradition based on demanding state's judicial determination that PC exists, asylum state may make no further judicial inquiry on that issue. Michigan Supreme Court reversed; remanded. (9-0; Burger, C.J., DOC; Blackmun, Brennan, & Marshall, JJ., c/j.)
Delaware v. Prouse, 440 U.S. 648 (1979)	Possession of marijuana	Officer made random stop of car in which respondent was passenger to check license and registration; he smelled marijuana smoke and seized marijuana in plain view	Marijuana	No warrant	None	Absent PC or RAS that driver is unlicensed, car unregistered, or vehicle and occupants otherwise in violation of law, stopping a car to check license and registration is unreasonable under Amd. IV. Delaware Supreme Court affirmed. (8-1; White, J., DOC; Blackmun & Powell, JJ., concur; Rehnquist, J., dissents.)
United States v. Caceres, 440 U.S. 741 (1979)	Bribing an IRS agent	Indictment	Incriminating statements made by defendant to IRS agent seized by electronic monitoring; bribe money	No warrant	Consent of IRS agent; good faith effort to comply with IRS's authorization procedures for electronic monitoring	Because neither constitution nor statute requires IRS to adopt particular rules for monitoring or recording conversations, violations of internal agency regulations concerning electronic monitoring fall outside the purview of Amd. IV. CCA reversed. (7-2; Stevens, J., DOC; Marshall &, Brennan, JJ., dissent.)
Dunaway v. New York, 442 U.S. 200 (1979)	Attempted robbery and felony murder	Incriminating statements were made by defendant during custodial interrogation after he had received *Miranda* warnings	Statements and sketches made by defendant during custodial interrogation	No warrant	Voluntariness exception rejected	Relying on *Brown v. Illinois*, 422 U.S. 590 (1975), and *Terry v. Ohio*, 392 U.S. 1 (1968), arrests or seizures of equivalent intrusiveness absent PC violate Amd. IV; test for attenuation reviews temporal proximity of arrest and confession, intervening circumstances, purpose and flagrancy of official misconduct. New York Supreme Court, Appellate Division, reversed. (7-2; Brennan, J., DOC; White, J., c/j; Stevens, J., concurs; Rehnquist, J., Burger, C.J., dissent.)

Case Name	Charge on Arrest	Authority for Arrest	Articles Seized	Warrant Clause	Exceptions to Warrant Clause	Decision
Lo-Ji Sales, Inc. v. New York, 442 U.S. 319 (1979)	Second-degree obscenity	Undercover investigator bought 2 films from adult book store and used them for determination of PC for warrant; subsequent search party raid resulted in 3-count information	Coin-operated film projectors, 23 films from coin-operated projectors, 397 magazines, 431 reels of film	Search warrant with "things to be seized" particularity portion left blank in order to be filled in by town justice during the raid	None	Open-ended warrants, to be completed as the search is conducted, are violative of Amd. IV; where town justice functions as adjunct law enforcement officer, he cannot also serve as neutral and detached magistrate. New York Supreme Court, Appellate Division reversed. (9-0; Burger, C.J., DOC.)
Torres v. Puerto Rico, 442 U.S. 465 (1979)	Possession of one ounce of marijuana in violation of CSA of Puerto Rico, Public Law No. 22	Defendant at San Juan airport forced to submit to luggage search by officer pursuant to the act	One ounce of marijuana, wooden pipe with marijuana residue	No warrant	Controlled Substances Act of Puerto Rico authorized luggage searches of anyone entering Puerto Rico from the U.S.	Amd. IV applies to Commonwealth of Puerto Rico; CSA of Puerto Rico is unconstitutional as applied because it does not require PC for search and seizure. Supreme Court of Puerto Rico reversed. (9-0; Burger, C.J., DOC; Brennan, Stewart, Marshall, & Blackmun, JJ., c/j.)
Smith v. Maryland, 442 U.S. 735 (1979) Limited by *Carpenter v. United States* (2018).	Robbery	After robbery, victim received phone calls from robber; police traced license plate to defendant's home and placed pen register on his home phone, which revealed call placed to victim's home	Phone book with page containing mark beside victim's name obtained from defendant's home; record of calls placed from defendant's home phone obtained via pen register	Search warrant	None	Distinguishing *Katz v. United States*, 389 U.S. 47 (1967), on the ground that pen registers do not acquire the contents of a conversation, defendant has no LEP in the telephone numbers he dialed; installation of pen register at phone company headquarters is not a search under Amd. IV and requires no warrant. Maryland Court of Appeals affirmed. (5-3; Blackmun, J., DOC; Stewart, Brennan, & Marshall, JJ., dissent; Powell, J., took no part.)
Arkansas v. Sanders, 442 U.S. 753 (1979) (OR: *California v. Acevedo*, 500 U.S. 565(1991))	PWID marijuana	Police received tip from informant of known reliability that defendant would arrive at airport with green suitcase containing marijuana; after defendant arrived and placed suitcase in taxi, police stopped cab and opened trunk and suitcase	9.3 pounds of marijuana packaged in 10 plastic bags seized from green suitcase in trunk of taxicab	No warrant	Invalid extension of *Carroll* automobile exception to personal luggage within lawfully stopped vehicle	Amd. IV applies to personal luggage taken from an automobile; absent exigent circumstances or consent, police must obtain warrant before searching luggage taken from automobile properly stopped and searched for contraband. Arkansas Supreme Court affirmed. (7-2; Powell, J., DOC; Burger, C.J., Stevens, J., c/j; Blackmun & Rehnquist, JJ., dissent.)

Case Name	Charge on Arrest	Authority for Arrest	Articles Seized	Warrant Clause	Exceptions to Warrant Clause	Decision
Michigan v. DeFillippo, 443 U.S. 31 (1979)	Violation of a Detroit failure to identify ordinance (struck down on interlocutory appeal as void for vagueness), possession of marijuana and phencyclidine (PCP) subsequent to custodial search	Officer investigating intoxicated persons in an alley asked defendant for ID; defendant refused, was arrested pursuant to state statute, and was searched	Person of the defendant, marijuana, PCP	No warrant	SIVA	Arrest made in good faith reliance on ordinance subsequently declared unconstitutional is valid where officers had PC to believe suspect was committing an offense; search incident to that arrest is likewise valid and no purpose served by exclusionary rule under the circumstances. Michigan Court of Appeals reversed. (6-3; Burger, C.J., DOC; Blackmun, J., concurs; Brennan, Marshall, & Stevens, JJ., dissent.)
Brown v. Texas, 443 U.S. 47 (1979)	Violation of Texas "failure to identify" statute	Officers saw defendant in an alley in a high drug trafficking area; defendant refused to identify himself	Person of the defendant	No warrant	None	When a stop is not based on objective criteria for suspecting misconduct, the individual's right to personal security and privacy outweighs public interest in crime prevention; under Amd. IV, such a seizure—absent PC or RAS—is unreasonable. El Paso County Court reversed. (9-0; Burger, C.J., DOC.)
Ybarra v. Illinois, 444 U.S. 85 (1979)	Possession of heroin	Illinois statute allowed officers executing a warrant in a tavern to search "any person in the place at the time" for weapons or items in warrant; officers frisked defendant and felt objects in cigarette pack	Heroin	Search warrant for tavern and bartender	None	Relying on *Di Re v. United States*, 332 U.S. 581 (1948), warrantless search must be supported by PC and *Terry* frisk for weapons by RAS; Illinois statute allowing searches without PC violates Amd. IV. Illinois Appellate Court reversed. (6-3; Stewart, J., DOC; Burger, C.J., Blackmun & Rehnquist, JJ., dissent.)
Massachusetts v. Meehan, 445 U.S. 39 (1980)	Murder	During custodial interrogation, defendant's explanation of blood on his sneakers contradicted by independent interviewee	Confession, dungarees worn on the night of the murder, undershorts, sneakers	Search warrant for dungarees	None	Dismissed as improvidently granted; judgment of Supreme Judicial Court of Massachusetts stands: warrant based on involuntary confession and *Miranda v. Arizona,* 384 U.S. 436 (1966), violation is invalid; evidence seized pursuant to it must be suppressed. (9-0; per curiam.)

Case Name	Charge on Arrest	Authority for Arrest	Articles Seized	Warrant Clause	Exceptions to Warrant Clause	Decision
United States v. Crews, 445 U.S. 463 (1980)	Armed robbery	Robbery suspect picked up, ostensibly as a truant, and photographed; defendant was identified from photo and again in court-ordered lineup; defendant indicted	Photograph of the defendant taken during his detention as a suspected truant	No warrant	None	Distinguishing *Davis v. Mississippi*, 394 U.S. 721 (1969), and explaining *Wong Sun v. United States*, 371 U.S. 471 (1963), photo taken during illegal arrest is FOPT and must be suppressed; however, in-court identification premised on information antedating illegal arrest is untainted by Amd. IV violation. D.C. Court of Appeals reversed. (8-0; Brennan, J., DOC; Powell & Blackmun, JJ., c/p; White & Rehnquist, JJ., Burger, C.J., c/j; Marshall, J., took no part.)
Payton v. New York, 445 U.S. 573 (1980)	Murder (Payton); armed robbery and narcotics possession (Riddick) (consolidated cases)	Two-day investigation yielded sufficient evidence for PC to make arrest of defendant Payton; victim identifications yielded sufficient PC to arrest defendant Riddick	.30 caliber shell casing in plain view in defendant's Bronx apartment (Payton); narcotics and paraphernalia seized from defendant's Queens home (Riddick)	No warrant	State statute authorizing police to enter any premise to make felony arrest found unconstitutional; neither consent nor exigent circumstances argued below	Absent consent or exigent circumstances, a warrantless sanctuary seizure is unreasonable; NY statute struck down; under Amd. IV, an arrest warrant founded on PC carries limited authority to enter dwelling where suspect lives when there is reason to believe he is within. New York Court of Appeals reversed. (6-3; Stevens, J., DOC; Blackmun, J., concurs; White & Rehnquist, JJ., Burger, C.J., dissent.)
United States v. Mendenhall, 446 U.S. 544 (1980)	PWID heroin	Defendant, who fit drug courier profile, was stopped by DEA agents, consented to accompany them, consented to body search, handed packages from her underwear to officer, and was arrested	Heroin	No warrant	Consent (1st party)	A person is "seized" for Amd. IV purposes when, in view of all the circumstances, a reasonable person would not believe that she was free to leave; issue turns on whether defendant acted voluntarily, and factors include: threatening presence of officers, display of weapons, physical touching, tone of voice. CCA reversed. (5-4; Stewart, J., DOC; Powell & Blackmun, JJ., Burger, C.J., c/p, c/j; White, Brennan, Marshall, & Stevens, JJ., dissent.)

Case Name	Charge on Arrest	Authority for Arrest	Articles Seized	Warrant Clause	Exceptions to Warrant Clause	Decision
United States v. Havens, 446 U.S. 620 (1980)	Importing, conspiring to import, and possessing cocaine	Defendant cleared customs in Miami airport but was later implicated by his partner, who was detected carrying cocaine sewn into makeshift pockets of a T-shirt, as an accomplice	T-shirt, seized from defendant's luggage and holes in which matched pieces sewn into partner's T-shirt	No warrant	None	While T-shirt illegally seized from defendant's luggage was suppressed pre-trial, illegally seized evidence may be used in rebuttal to impeach defendant's perjurious testimony on cross-examination (relying on *Walder v. United States*, 347 U.S. 62 (1954), *Harris v. New York*, 401 U.S. 222 (1971), and *Oregon v. Hass,* 420 U.S. 714 (1975)). CCA reversed; remanded. (5-4; White, J., DOC; Brennan, Marshall, Stewart, & Stevens, JJ., dissent.)
Walter v. United States, 447 U.S. 649 (1980)	Obscenity charges for interstate shipment of 5 packages of 8mm film depicting homosexual activities	Shipment mistakenly delivered to 3d party rather than intended recipient; 3d party opened package and called FBI who took and viewed films without a warrant; indictment followed	12 large sealed boxes containing 871 boxes of 8mm film depicting homosexual activities	No warrant	None	Projection of films expanded private party's search and is characterized as separate search; despite description on package, viewing of films by FBI agents absent warrant, consent, or exigent circumstances was unreasonable invasion of owner's LEP. Question left open whether FBI would need warrant if 3d party viewed films first. CCA reversed. (PL; Stevens, J., AJC; Marshall, J., c/j; White & Brennan, JJ., c/p, c/j; Blackmun, Powell, & Rehnquist, JJ., Burger, C.J., dissent.)
United States v. Payner, 447 U.S. 727 (1980)	Falsifying federal income tax return by knowingly denying maintenance of foreign bank account	Indictment handed down pursuant to IRS sting investigation of American banking activities in the Bahamas	Loan guarantee agreement pledging funds from defendant's Bahamian bank account as security for $100,000 loan (among 400 documents from bank VP's briefcase photographed by investigators for IRS)	No warrant	Defendant lacks standing to move to suppress loan guarantee as fruit of illegal search and seizure of Bahamian bank VP's briefcase	Relying on *Rakas v. Illinois,* 439 U.S. 128 (1978), and *United States v. Miller,* 425 U.S. 435 (1976), defendant has no LEP in bank records and no 3d party standing to object to search of Bahamian bank VP's briefcase; *Rakas*'s denial of 3d party standing extends to supervisory power of federal courts, as well as under Amd. IV. CCA reversed. (6-3; Powell, J., DOC; Burger, C.J., concurs; Marshall, Brennan, & Blackmun, JJ., dissent.)

Case Name	Charge on Arrest	Authority for Arrest	Articles Seized	Warrant Clause	Exceptions to Warrant Clause	Decision
United States v. Salvucci, 448 U.S. 83 (1980)	Unlawful possession of stolen mail	Indictment	12 checks seized by Massachusetts police executing warrant to search co-defendant's mother's house	Search warrant for house of co-defendant's mother	Defendants do not have standing merely because they are in possession of the seized good; on remand they may demonstrate standing	Overruling the *Jones v. United States*, 362 U.S. 257 (1960), automatic standing rule and applying *Rakas v. Illinois*, 439 U.S. 128 (1978), standing turns on whether one has LEP in area searched. Question whether *Simmons v. United States*, 390 U.S. 377 (1968), use immunity extends to impeachment is left open, but n.9 declares that *Simmons* use immunity does not attach to perjured testimony at suppression hearing. CCA reversed. (7-2; Rehnquist, J., DOC; Marshall & Brennan, JJ., dissent.)
Rawlings v. Kentucky, 448 U.S. 98 (1980)	PWID various controlled substances	During in-house execution of arrest warrant, officers smelled and saw marijuana, held guests 45 minutes, and secured search warrant; when guest complied with officer's request to empty her handbag, defendant claimed ownership of contraband within	1,800 LSD tablets and other controlled substances from guest's purse; $4,500 cash, knife (from person of defendant); post-*Miranda* admission of ownership of the drugs	Search warrant for house; arrest warrant for owner of house	SIVA for money and knife; no standing to object to drugs; illegal seizure, 45-minute detention sufficiently attenuated to purge admission of taint	Applying principle of *Rakas v. Illinois*, 439 U.S. 128 (1978), articulated in *Salvucci, supra*, defendant has no LEP in guest's purse; applying 5-part attenuation analysis of *Brown v. Illinois*, 422 U.S. 590 (1975), *Miranda v. Arizona*, 384 U.S. 436 (1966), warnings and courtesy of officers during 45-minute illegal detention weigh heavily for concluding statement was voluntary. Supreme Court of Kentucky affirmed. (7-2; Rehnquist, J., DOC; Blackmun, J., concurs; White & Stewart, JJ., c/p; Marshall & Brennan, JJ., dissent.)
Reid v. Georgia, 448 U.S. 438 (1980)	Possession of cocaine	Defendant, who fit drug courier profile, was approached outside airport building by DEA agent and agreed to return for luggage and body search; in concourse, he fled, discarding shoulder bag	Cocaine, found in discarded shoulder bag	No warrant	None	Relying on *Terry v. Ohio*, 392 U.S. 1 (1968), Amd. IV searches and seizures—including seizures of only brief detention—are prohibited unless supported by objective justification; an agent acting on mere hunch cannot support a seizure. Judgment of Georgia Court of Appeals vacated; remanded. (8-1; per curiam; Powell & Blackmun, JJ., Burger, C.J., concur; Rehnquist, J., dissents.)

Case Name	Charge on Arrest	Authority for Arrest	Articles Seized	Warrant Clause	Exceptions to Warrant Clause	Decision
Colorado v. Bannister, 449 U.S. 1 (1980)	Theft of motor vehicle parts	Officer stopped speeding car to issue traffic summons; saw items in open glove compartment that were reported stolen on radio dispatch; made arrest	Chrome lug nuts, lug wrenches	No warrant	Plain view, automobile	Relying on *Chambers v. Maroney*, 399 U.S. 42 (1970), PC that contents of validly stopped car offend the law permits warrantless seizure. Judgment of Supreme Court of Colorado vacated; remanded. (9-0; per curiam.)
United States v. Cortez, 449 U.S. 411 (1981)	Transporting illegal aliens	Two-month border patrol investigation of illegal alien smuggling route culminated in stake-out of deserted highway where officers predicted an alien pickup would occur; only one suspect vehicle appeared within the proper time frame; officers pulled over that vehicle, found illegal aliens in camper	Six illegal aliens, sneakers of passenger with Chevron design on soles	No warrant	Consent (1st party)	Relying on *United States v. Brignoni-Ponce*, 422 U.S. 873 (1975), test of reasonableness of border patrol stop is whether, based on TOC, experienced border patrol officers could reasonably surmise particular vehicle stopped was engaged in criminal activity. CCA reversed. (9-0; Burger, C.J., DOC; Marshall & Stewart, JJ., c/j.)
Steagald v. United States, 451 U.S. 204 (1981)	PWID cocaine	Pursuant to arrest warrant for federal fugitive, DEA agents entered defendant's home to search for fugitive; agents did not find fugitive but found what appeared to be cocaine; 2d search uncovered incriminating evidence, and 3d search—under warrant—uncovered cocaine	43 pounds of cocaine	Arrest warrant for 3d party who did not have proprietary interest in house and was not present; agents secured search warrant only for 3d search of defendant's house	None; neither consent nor exigent circumstances argued below	Distinction made between arrest warrants, which protect against unreasonable seizure, and search warrants, which protect the privacy interest of the place searched; addressing question left open in *Payton v. New York*, 445 U.S. 573 (1980), absent consent or exigent circumstances, a search warrant is required to search the home of a 3d party when executing an arrest warrant. CCA reversed (7-2; Marshall, J., DOC; Burger, C.J., c/j; Rehnquist & White, JJ., dissent.)

Case Name	Charge on Arrest	Authority for Arrest	Articles Seized	Warrant Clause	Exceptions to Warrant Clause	Decision
Donovan v. Dewey, 452 U.S. 594 (1980)	Suit by Secretary of Labor to enjoin mine owner from refusing to allow inspection	Federal inspector sought access to Wankesha Lime and Stone Co. to determine whether 25 health and safety violations had been corrected	Wankesha Lime and Stone Co. president, Dewey, refused to allow the inspector to proceed without a search warrant	No warrant	Mine Safety and Health Act of 1977, 30 U.S.C. § 813(a)	Warrantless inspections under Mine Safety and Health Act are reasonable for Amd. IV purposes due to expressly articulated standards and procedures reflecting substantial federal interest in heavily regulated industry. USDC summary judgment reversed. (8-1; Marshall, J., DOC; Stevens & Rehnquist, JJ., concur; Stewart, J., dissents.)
Michigan v. Summers, 452 U.S. 692 (1981)	Possession of heroin	Officers arrived at defendant's house to execute search warrant for narcotics, saw him leaving, and detained him while conducting a search; after police found narcotics and determined defendant was homeowner, he was arrested	Envelope containing 8.5 grams of heroin seized from defendant's pocket pursuant to custodial search	Search warrant for the building	SIVA	Distinguishing *Dunaway v. New York*, 442 U.S. 200 (1979), search warrant for contraband, founded on PC, implicitly carries limited authority to detain occupants of premises while search is conducted. Michigan Supreme Court reversed. (6-3; Stevens, J., DOC; Stewart, Brennan, & Marshall, JJ., dissent.)
Robbins v. California, 453 U.S. 420 (1981) (OR: *United States v. Ross*, 456 U.S. 798 (1982))	Possession of marijuana, possession of marijuana for sale and transportation	California Highway Patrol officers observed defendant driving erratically, pulled him over, smelled marijuana smoke, and proceeded to search the car	Two bricks of marijuana wrapped in opaque green plastic, seized from recessed luggage compartment in station wagon; marijuana and paraphernalia seized from passenger compartment	No warrant	None	Explaining n.13 of *Arkansas v. Sanders*, 442 U.S. 753 (1979), absent consent or SIVA, opening closed containers in an automobile requires a warrant unless their very nature renders their contents the equivalent of being in plain view. California Court of Appeal reversed. (6-3; Stewart, J., AJC; Burger, C.J., Powell, J., c/j; Blackmun, Rehnquist, & Stevens, JJ., dissent.)

Case Name	Charge on Arrest	Authority for Arrest	Articles Seized	Warrant Clause	Exceptions to Warrant Clause	Decision
New York v. Belton, 453 U.S. 454 (1981) (Modified by *Arizona v. Gant*, 129 S. Ct. 1710 (2009))	Possession of controlled substance	New York state trooper pulled over car travelling at excessive speed; officer smelled marijuana and saw envelope marked "supergold"; none of car's occupants was owner; all placed under arrest	Marijuana in envelope marked "supergold," cocaine seized from pocket of defendant's jacket found in passenger compartment	No warrant	SIVA	Applying *Chimel v. California*, 395 U.S. 752 (1969), to automobiles, "bright-line" rule is created: with PC, interior of passenger compartment and all containers therein comprise "the area within the immediate control of the arrestee." Scope of SIVA does not extend to contents of the trunk, n.4. New York Court of Appeals reversed. (6-3; Stewart, J., DOC; Rehnquist, J., concurs, Stevens, J., c/j; Brennan, White, & Marshall, JJ., dissent.)
Washington v. Chrisman, 455 U.S. 1 (1982)	Possession of marijuana and possession of LSD	University police saw Overdahl, who appeared to be underage, carrying liquor; because liquor was contraband on university grounds, Overdahl was arrested, asked for ID, and went with officer to get ID from his room, where officer saw marijuana on a table; student and defendant gave consent to search room	Marijuana, paraphernalia, LSD	No warrant	Plain view for marijuana; consent (1st party) for LSD and marijuana seized pursuant to room search	In a quasi-sanctuary case, officer, incident to valid arrest, had right to be beside arrestee at all times. Thus, officer's presence in dorm room being valid, incriminating evidence discovered on table is classic instance of plain view exception. Supreme Court of Washington reversed. (6-3; Burger, C.J., DOC; White, Brennan, & Marshall, JJ., dissent.)
United States v. Ross, 456 U.S. 798 (1982)	Illegal possession of a firearm, PWID heroin	Acting on tip from reliable informant that defendant was selling drugs out of his car, police pulled car over; officers found a bullet on the seat, a pistol in glove compartment, and made the arrest	Paper bag containing heroin; zippered pouch containing $3,200, seized when officer conducted inventory search	No warrant	Automobile	Overruling *Robbins v. United States*, 453 U.S. 420 (1981), and reaffirming *Carroll v. United States*, 267 U.S. 132 (1925), no LEP in vehicle containing contraband; scope of warrantless vehicle search is defined by object of search and places in which there is PC to believe it may be found, including containers therein. CCA reversed. (6-3; Stevens, J., DOC; Blackmun & Powell, JJ., concur; White, Marshall, & Brennan, JJ., dissent.)

Case Name	Charge on Arrest	Authority for Arrest	Articles Seized	Warrant Clause	Exceptions to Warrant Clause	Decision
United States v. Johnson, 457 U.S. 537 (1982)	Attempting to negotiate a misdelivered U.S. Treasury check	Secret Service agents informed of defendant's check cashing scheme waited for him at his home; agents were admitted, searched premises, read defendant his rights and questioned him; defendant admitted involvement and was arrested	Written statement by defendant admitting his involvement with the scheme, oral admissions made to agents by defendant	No warrant	None	Distinguishing *United States v. Peltier,* 422 U.S. 531 (1975), decision construing Amd. IV is applied retroactively to all convictions not final when decision is rendered; thus, *Payton v. New York*, 445 U.S. 573 (1980), decision construing Amd. IV is applied retroactively to all convictions not final when decision is rendered; thus, *Payton* applies retrospectively to all cases pending direct appeal except where clearly controlled by existing retroactivity precedents. CCA affirmed. (5-4; Blackmun, J., DOC; Brennan, J., concurs; White, Rehnquist, & O'Connor, JJ., Burger, C.J., dissent.)
Taylor v. Alabama, 457 U.S. 687 (1982)	Robbery	Conducting manhunt for robbers, police acted on uncorroborated tip from informant of unknown reliability and arrested defendant	Waiver of rights form and signed confession executed by defendant during his illegal arrest	No warrant	None	Relying on *Brown v. Illinois,* 442 U.S. 590 (1975), and *Dunaway v. New York*, 422 U.S. 200 (1979), where defendant is arrested without PC, his confession is fruit of illegal arrest. *Miranda v. Arizona*, 384 U.S. 436 (1966), warnings may satisfy Amd. V voluntariness requirement but do not purge taint for Amd. IV purposes. Alabama Supreme Court reversed. (5-4; Marshall, J., DOC; O'Connor, Powell, & Rehnquist, JJ., Burger, C.J., dissent.)
Michigan v. Thomas, 458 U.S. 259 (1982)	Possession of open intoxicants, possession of controlled substances, carrying a concealed weapon	Defendant's car was stopped for traffic infraction and officers saw open can of malt liquor on floor; defendant, riding as passenger, was arrested and the car impounded	Inventory search of auto produced marijuana from glove compartment, loaded .38 caliber revolver	No warrant	Automobile after impoundment	Relying on *Chambers v. Maroney*, 399 U.S. 42 (1970), *Ross v. United States*, 456 U.S. 798 (1982), and *Texas v. White*, 423 U.S. 67 (1975), PC to believe automobile stopped on the road contains contraband allows warrantless search of vehicle even after impounding. Michigan Court of Appeals reversed. (7-2; per curiam; Brennan & Marshall, JJ., would set for argument.)

Case Name	Charge on Arrest	Authority for Arrest	Articles Seized	Warrant Clause	Exceptions to Warrant Clause	Decision
United States v. Knotts, 460 U.S. 276 (1983)	Conspiracy to manufacture controlled substances including methamphetamine in violation of 21 U.S.C. § 846	Police placed beeper in chemical container purchased by defendant and used it to track him; police pursued defendant to his cabin, where a search pursuant to warrant was conducted and drug lab discovered	$10,000 worth of laboratory equipment, formulae for amphetamines and methamphetamines, chemicals to produce amphetamines	Search warrant for cabin	None	Relying on *Katz v. United States*, 389 U.S. 347 (1967), and *Smith v. Maryland*, 442 U.S. 735 (1979), governmental surveillance with beeper is limited to public areas where there is no LEP; beeper monitoring does not violate Amd. IV when it reveals no information that could not have been obtained by visual surveillance. Constitutionality of beeper installation left open. CCA reversed. (9-0; Rehnquist, J., DOC; Blackmun, Stevens, Brennan, & Marshall, JJ., c/j.)
Florida v. Royer, 460 U.S. 491 (1983)	Possession of marijuana	Narcotics officers approached defendant, who fit drug courier profile, on the airport concourse and requested identification; officers kept ID and escorted defendant to a room; marijuana was found in his luggage	Marijuana	No warrant	Sufficient RAS for stop, but detention became illegal	Distinguishing *United States v. Mendenhall*, 446 U.S. 544 (1980), while there was RAS for initial encounter, detention in the room was equivalent to arrest; since PC did not attach until defendant's luggage was opened, detention was illegal and tainted any "consent" he may have given to open his luggage. Florida District Court of Appeal affirmed. (PL; White, J., AJC; Powell, J., concurs; Brennan, J., c/j; Blackmun, Rehnquist, & O'Connor, JJ., Burger, C.J., dissent.)
Texas v. Brown, 460 U.S. 730 (1983)	Driving without a license, possession of heroin; record not clear as to precise time of arrest	Officer at routine driver's license checkpoint stopped defendant's car and saw defendant take tied green balloon out of pocket; when defendant opened glove compartment, officer observed white powder, vials, and balloons; defendant could not produce license	Balloon containing heroin; plastic bags containing green leafy substance and jar of milk sugar seized pursuant to on-the-scene inventory of defendant's car	No warrant	Plain view	Plain view seizures are presumptively reasonable as long as there is PC; PC for contraband does not demand that belief be correct or more likely true than false. "Immediately apparent" language in *Coolidge v. New Hampshire,* 403 U.S. 443 (1971), is relaxed to PC. Texas Court of Criminal Appeals reversed; case remanded. (PL; Rehnquist, J., AJC; White, J., concurs; Powell, Blackmun, Stevens, Brennan, & Marshall, JJ., c/j.)

Case Name	Charge on Arrest	Authority for Arrest	Articles Seized	Warrant Clause	Exceptions to Warrant Clause	Decision
Illinois v. Gates, 462 U.S. 213 (1983)	Violation of Illinois drug laws	Police corroborated defendants' modus operandi as detailed in anonymous letter, then executed search warrant for defendants' automobile and house	350 pounds of marijuana seized from trunk of car; contraband seized from house included marijuana and weapons	Search warrant held invalid by Illinois courts because letter failed to satisfy 2-prong *Aguilar/Spinelli* test for PC sufficiency of affidavits	None	Two-prong *Aguilar v. Texas*, 378 U.S. 108 (1964)/*Spinelli v. United States*, 393 U.S. 410 (1969), test overruled in favor of a "totality-of-the-circumstances" analysis for establishing PC to issue warrant. Illinois Supreme Court reversed. (6-3; Rehnquist, J., DOC; White, J., c/j; Brennan, Marshall, & Stevens, JJ., dissent.)
Haring v. Prosise, 462 U.S. 306 (1983)	Possession of controlled substance resulted in guilty plea to one count of manufacturing phencyclidine (PCP)	Suit brought under 42 U.S.C. § 1983 for police search absent warrant and subsequent search excessive in scope	Devices and chemicals used to manufacture PCP, receipts for chemicals, written formula for PCP, 2 buckets containing traces of PCP	Search warrant	NA	42 U.S.C. § 1983 action to redress alleged Amd. IV violation is not barred by defendant's state court conviction entered following guilty plea: collateral estoppel would not be invoked under VA law, Amd. IV claims are not waived by pleading guilty in state court, and justification for denial of habeas review following guilty plea is inappropriate under § 1983. CCA affirmed. (9-0; Marshall, J., DOC.)
United States v. Villamonte-Marquez, 462 U.S. 579 (1983)	Conspiring to import marijuana, conspiring PWID and PWID marijuana	U.S. Customs officer and state police officer boarded sailboat to inspect documentation pursuant to 19 U.S.C. § 1581(a); they smelled marijuana, observed burlap-wrapped bales, and arrested defendants	5,800 pounds of marijuana	No warrant	19 U.S.C. § 1581(a)	Distinguishing *United States v. Brignoni-Ponce*, 422 U.S. 873 (1975), and *United States v. Martinez-Fuerte*, 428 U.S. 543 (1976), suspicionless boarding of boat pursuant to § 1581(a) is reasonable; government interest in deterring or apprehending smugglers outweighs limited intrusion on privacy. CCA reversed. (6-3; Rehnquist, J., DOC; Brennan, Marshall, & Stevens, JJ., dissent.)
Florida v. Casal, 462 U.S. 637 (1983)	Possession of marijuana	Marine patrol officers stopped a vessel to check its registration certificate; when officer was permitted aboard to help find registration, captain admitted the ship was loaded with marijuana	Several bales of marijuana	No warrant	None	Grant of cert. dismissed as improvidently granted because the state court relied on IASG—article I, § 12 of Florida Constitution—in affirming suppression of evidence. Ruling, that search was unreasonable under Florida law because no PC, stands. (9-0; per curiam; Burger, C.J., concurs.)

Case Name	Charge on Arrest	Authority for Arrest	Articles Seized	Warrant Clause	Exceptions to Warrant Clause	Decision
Illinois v. Lafayette, 462 U.S. 640 (1983)	Disturbing the peace, possession of amphetamines	Officer responded to complaint at local movie theater and arrested defendant for disturbing the peace; during booking, inventory of defendant's bag revealed amphetamine tablets	Ten amphetamine tablets	No warrant	Inventory	Relying on *South Dakota v. Opperman*, 428 U.S. 364 (1976), it is not unreasonable, as routine procedure incident to incarceration, for police to search any container or article in possession of arrestee in accordance with established inventory procedures. Illinois Appellate Court reversed; remanded. (9-0; Burger, C.J., DOC; Marshall & Brennan, JJ., concur.)
United States v. Place, 462 U.S. 696 (1983)	PWID cocaine	Defendant aroused suspicion at Miami airport; DEA agents met him at NY airport and he refused to consent to search of his bags; Friday, dogs sniffed and reacted to 1 bag; search warrant issued Monday	1,125 grams of cocaine	Search warrant issued Monday morning for luggage seized and held since Friday afternoon	Sufficient RAS for stop, but detention became illegal	While personal luggage may be subject to a *Terry v. Ohio*, 392 U.S. 1 (1968), stop based on less than PC, the duration of defendant's detention (90 minutes) exceeded the bounds of a *Terry* stop, constituting a seizure unsupported by PC. CCA affirmed. (9-0; O'Connor, J., DOC; Brennan, Marshall, & Blackmun, JJ., c/j.)
Illinois v. Andreas, 463 U.S. 765 (1983)	Possession of marijuana	Customs inspectors at Chicago airport found marijuana in package shipped from Calcutta; DEA agent resealed and delivered it. Before officers could get a search warrant, agents arrested defendant as he exited his apartment with the package	Marijuana, found when police opened resealed container at station house	No warrant	Legitimate authority of customs officials to inspect packages arriving from foreign countries	Perfect controlled deliveries of contraband are nearly impossible. Absent substantial likelihood that contents have been changed, no LEP remains in contents of a container once officers have opened it under lawful authority and found contents illegal. Appellate Court of Illinois reversed; remanded. (7-2; Burger, C.J., DOC; Brennan & Marshall, JJ., dissent.)

Case Name	Charge on Arrest	Authority for Arrest	Articles Seized	Warrant Clause	Exceptions to Warrant Clause	Decision
Michigan v. Long, 463 U.S. 1032 (1983)	Possession of marijuana	Officers stopped to investigate disabled car, noticed hunting knife on floor of car, and subjected defendant to patdown search; officer shined flashlight into car, which led him to find marijuana and arrest defendant	75 pounds of marijuana in trunk	No warrant	*New York v. Belton*, 453 U.S. 454 (1981), applies to *Terry* stops	Applying *Terry v. Ohio*, 392 U.S 1 (1968), search of passenger compartment of a car is reasonable when it is for weapons and predicated on officer's concern for his safety. New standard for reviewing cases from state courts: absent plain statement that decision rests on IASG, Supreme Court will presume jurisdiction. Michigan Supreme Court reversed; remanded for trunk seizure. (6-3; O'Connor, J., DOC; Blackmun, J., c/p, d/p; Brennan, Marshall, & Stevens, JJ., dissent.)
Michigan v. Clifford, 464 U.S. 287 (1984)	Arson	Evidence seized during search	Three empty fuel cans, electric Crock-Pot, timer and attached cord; testimony of investigators	Neither administrative nor search warrant	Plain view for only 1 fuel can	Where homeowners have LEP in fire-damaged residence after police leave scene, post-fire search must be conducted pursuant to warrant, consent, or exigency; administrative warrant will suffice for search reasonably limited in scope. Michigan Court of Appeals affirmed on all but 1 can. (PL; Powell, J., AJC; Stevens, J., c/j; Burger, C.J., Rehnquist, Blackmun, & O'Connor, JJ., dissent.)
Donovan v. Lone Steer, Inc., 464 U.S. 408 (1984)	Challenge to Fair Labor Standards Act 29 U.S.C. §§ 9, 11 investigatory procedure, which authorizes an investigation regarding wages, hours and other employment conditions	NA	Requested production for inspection of payroll records	Subpoena duces tecum	No exception for records requested under FLSA where subpoena is served in public lobby of motel/restaurant	Entry into public lobby to serve subpoena is not type of governmental act forbidden by Amd. IV; reasonableness of subpoena may be questioned, but defenses available do not include the right to insist on judicial warrant as condition precedent to otherwise valid subpoena. District Court reversed. (9-0; Rehnquist, J., DOC.)

Case Name	Charge on Arrest	Authority for Arrest	Articles Seized	Warrant Clause	Exceptions to Warrant Clause	Decision
United States v. Jacobsen, 466 U.S. 109 (1984)	PWID illegal substance	Pursuant to discovery of contraband during search of package sent by carrier, warrant was obtained to search the place where the package was sent	Cocaine	No warrant to search contents of package	"As if" plain view, based on private party's description of package contents	Invasion of defendant's privacy by private parties does not violate Amd. IV. Invasions by DEA agents are evaluated by degree to which they exceed scope of original private-party search and reasonableness of agent's conduct. CCA reversed. (7-2; Stevens, J., DOC; White, J., c/p, c/j; Brennan & Marshall, JJ., dissent.)
Oliver v. United States/ Maine v. Thornton, 466 U.S. 170 (1984)	Manufacturing controlled substance in violation of CSA (Oliver); unlawfully furnishing scheduled drugs in violation of Maine statute (Thornton) (consolidated cases)	Pursuant to officers' discovery of marijuana growing on defendants' property, defendants were arrested and indicted	Marijuana	No search warrant (*Oliver*); no search warrant for initial search (*Thornton*)	"Open fields" doctrine (*Hester v. United States*, 265 U.S. 57 (1924))	Relying on Hester's "open fields" doctrine, government intrusion upon the "open fields" is not an unreasonable search proscribed by Amd. IV. No LEP for activities conducted out of doors except immediately around the home. CCA affirmed (*Oliver*). Maine Supreme Judicial Court reversed (*Thornton*). (6-3; Powell, J., DOC; White, J., c/p, c/j; Marshall, Brennan, & Stevens, JJ., dissent.)
INS v. Delgado, 466 U.S. 210 (1984)	Challenge of "factory surveys" of workforce conducted in search for illegal aliens, seeking declaratory and injunctive relief under 42 U.S.C. § 1983	NA	NA	"Factory survey" carried out pursuant to 2 warrants issued on showing of PC that illegal aliens were employed in the factory	Third "factory survey" conducted with employer's consent	Where INS activity involves merely asking individuals employed in a factory from 1 to 3 questions regarding their citizenship, questioning does not result in detention or seizure of workforce under Amd. IV unless circumstances of the encounter are so intimidating that a reasonable person would not believe himself free to leave if he did not respond. CCA reversed. (7-2; Rehnquist J., DOC; Stevens & Powell, JJ., concur; Brennan & Marshall, JJ., c/p, d/p.)

Case Name	Charge on Arrest	Authority for Arrest	Articles Seized	Warrant Clause	Exceptions to Warrant Clause	Decision
Florida v. Meyers, 466 U.S. 380 (1984)	Sexual battery	Arrest pursuant to happenings in motel bathroom which occurred at approximately 4:40 a.m.	Second search of automobile produced a long strip of cloth that corroborated victim's version of events that took place in the motel bathroom earlier that morning	No warrant	Automobile after impoundment	Relying on *Michigan v. Thomas*, 458 U.S. 259 (1982), and *Chambers v. Maroney*, 399 U.S. 42 (1970), warrantless second search of automobile held in police custody is not invalid despite prior inventory search; justification to search a car based on PC to believe there is evidence of crime inside does not disappear once vehicle is immobilized and impounded. Florida District Court of Appeal reversed; remanded. (6-3; per curiam; Stevens, J. (dissent on IASG rationale), Brennan, & Marshall, JJ., dissent.)
Massachusetts v. Upton, 466 U.S. 727 (1984)	Burglary, RSP, and related crimes	Discovery of stolen property in motor home parked on defendant's property led to arrest	Jewelry, silver, gold, and other stolen items	Search warrant	None	Reaffirming *Illinois v. Gates,* 462 U.S. 213 (1983), PC requirement for issuance of warrant is based on TOC analysis of facts presented to a magistrate; magistrate's decision to issue a warrant must be reviewed deferentially rather than by de novo standard. Supreme Judicial Court of Massachusetts reversed; remanded. (7-2; per curiam; Stevens, J., c/j (challenges Supreme Court of MA on PC issue); Brennan & Marshall, JJ., dissent.)
Welsh v. Wisconsin, 466 U.S. 740 (1984)	DUI in violation of state statute (non-criminal violation for first offense)	Officers, believing defendant had been driving while intoxicated, entered his home to make arrest	Defendant	No warrant	Insufficient exigent circumstances to justify warrantless home entry	Under *Payton v. New York*, 445 U.S. 573 (1980), warrantless home entries are presumed unreasonable; when determining whether exigency exists that justifies entry for arrest, gravity of underlying offense is of primary consideration—entry should rarely be sanctioned if PC to believe only minor offense was committed. Wisconsin Supreme Court order vacated; remanded. (6-3; Brennan, J., DOC; Blackmun, J., concurs; Burger, C.J., would DIG; White & Rehnquist, JJ., dissent.)

Case Name	Charge on Arrest	Authority for Arrest	Articles Seized	Warrant Clause	Exceptions to Warrant Clause	Decision
Florida v. Rodriguez, 469 U.S. 1 (1984)	PWID cocaine	Defendant and companions aroused officer's suspicions at airport; after brief exchange, defendant consented to search of his luggage; cocaine was found and defendant was arrested	Cocaine	No warrant	Sufficient RAS, detention legal	Brief detainment for questioning in an airport public space—seizure for Amd. IV purposes—may be justified without showing of PC if there exists RAS on the officer's part that a person has committed or is about to commit a crime; government need not prove that defendant consenting to a search knew he had the right to deny consent. Florida Court of Appeal reversed; remanded. (6-3; per curiam; Marshall, Stevens, & Brennan, JJ., dissent.)
Nix v. Williams, 467 U.S. 431 (1984)	Federal habeas corpus review of retrial	Warrant issued for defendant's arrest based on information gathered regarding the disappearance of 10-year-old girl	Evidence of child's body, articles and photographs of child's clothing; defendant's statement taken but not offered as evidence because of absent counsel interrogation	Arrest warrant	Ultimate or inevitable discovery applicable to Amd. IV, V, and VI, assistance of counsel clause	If government proves by preponderance of evidence that information inevitably would have been discovered by lawful means, exclusion of that evidence adds nothing to integrity or fairness of proceedings, and evidence should be admitted; no obligation on prosecution to show absence of police bad faith. CCA reversed; remanded. (7-2; Burger, C.J., DOC; White, J., concurs; Stevens, J., c/j; Brennan & Marshall, JJ., dissent.)
Hudson v. Palmer, 468 U.S. 517 (1984)	Destroying state property, under prison disciplinary procedures; action brought under 42 U.S.C. § 1983 challenging official's conduct in a penal institution as violative of inmate's rights	NA	Ripped pillow case	NA	None	Inmate has no LEP in his prison cell entitling him to Amd. IV protection against unreasonable searches; intentional destruction of property during "shakedown" in cell does not violate due process as long as meaningful and adequate state remedies are available. CCA reversed in part, affirmed in part. (5-4; Burger, C.J., DOC; Brennan, Marshall, Blackmun, & Stevens, JJ., c/p, d/p; O'Connor, J., concurs.)

Case Name	Charge on Arrest	Authority for Arrest	Articles Seized	Warrant Clause	Exceptions to Warrant Clause	Decision
United States v. Karo, 468 U.S. 705 (1984)	Various cocaine-related offenses including conspiracy PWID	Police monitored beeper installed in can of ether during transportation; when they suspected the ether was currently being used to extract cocaine, they conducted a search pursuant to a warrant and made arrests	Cocaine, laboratory equipment	No warrant for installation of electronic "beeper"; search warrant for house	None	Expanding *United States v. Knotts*, 460 U.S. 276 (1983), no Amd. IV interest of buyer is infringed when beeper is installed in container with seller's consent, then tranferred to uninformed buyer, provided beeper conveys no information intended to be kept private and does not interfere with possessory interests in meaningful way; monitoring beeper in residence violates rights of those with LEP in premises. CCA reversed. (6-3; White, J., DOC; Rehnquist & O'Connor, JJ., c/p, c/j; Brennan, Marshall, & Stevens, JJ., c/p, d/p.)
Segura v. United States, 468 U.S. 796 (1984)	Cocaine-related charges including conspiring to distribute, distributing, and PWID	Authorization from Assistant U.S. Attorney based on admissions of co-defendants	Cocaine, ammunition, $50,000 cash, records of narcotics transactions	Search warrant	Independent source	No violation of right to be free from unreasonable seizures when officers secure premises to maintain status quo while other officers proceed to obtain a valid search warrant; where information used to obtain warrant comes from sources unrelated to initial illegality, evidence need not be excluded as FOPT. CCA affirmed. (5-4; Burger, C.J., AJC; White, Powell, Rehnquist, & O'Connor, JJ., j/p; Stevens, Brennan, Marshall, & Blackmun, JJ., dissent.)
United States v. Leon, 468 U.S. 897 (1984)	Conspiracy PWID and a variety of substantive counts	Based on evidence discovered by police during search with facially valid search warrant, defendants indicted	Large quantities of drugs	Search warrant, invalidly issued because affidavit was insufficient to establish PC	Good faith warrant exception	If officers act in reliance on warrant issued by neutral and detached magistrate but subsequently found unsupported by PC, "good faith" exception allows government to use evidence obtained in reliance on such warrant; reliance must be objectively reasonable (suppress if: misleading affidavit or lack of neutral and detached magistrate, if warrant based on affidavit lacking in indicia of PC, or if warrant is facially deficient). CCA reversed. (6-3; White, J., DOC; Blackmun, J., concurs; Brennan, Marshall, & Stevens, JJ., dissent.)

Case Name	Charge on Arrest	Authority for Arrest	Articles Seized	Warrant Clause	Exceptions to Warrant Clause	Decision
Massachusetts v. Sheppard, 468 U.S. 981 (1984)	First-degree murder	Based on evidence gathered during investigation, arrest warrant issued for defendant and search warrant for premises	Incriminating evidence including bloodstained articles of clothing, wire matching that on victim's body, woman's hairpiece identified as the victim's	Search warrant invalidly issued because it did not incorporate affidavit information and did not particularly describe items to be seized	Good faith warrant exception	Applying *United States v. Leon*, 468 U.S. 897 (1984), provided officers reasonably believe search was authorized by valid warrant and assuming there exists an objectively reasonable basis for this mistaken belief, the exclusionary rule will not serve deterrent function and should not be applied. Supreme Judicial Court of Massachusetts reversed; remanded. (7-2; White, J., DOC; Stevens, J., c/j; Brennan & Marshall, JJ., dissent.)
INS v. Lopez-Mendoza, 468 U.S. 1032 (1984)	Illegal entry into the country under 8 U.S.C. § 1251	INS investigators, responding to tip, visited Lopez-Mendoza and Sandoval-Sanchez at their places of employment; after questioning, both were arrested and deportation proceedings followed	NA	No warrant	Civil deportation proceeding inapplicable	Exclusionary rule is not applied in civil deportation hearings held by INS. Under *United States v. Janis*, 428 U.S. 433 (1976), likely social benefits of applying rule are weighed against likely social costs; in deportation proceedings, the costs outweigh benefits. CCA reversed. (PL; O'Connor, J., AJC; Brennan, White (dissent based on FOPT rationale), Marshall & Stevens, JJ., dissent.)
Thompson v. Louisiana, 469 U.S. 17 (1984)	Second-degree murder	Following warrantless investigatory search of homicide and attempted suicide scene, defendant was indicted for murder of her husband	Pistol, torn-up note, suicide letter	No warrant	None	Reaffirming *Mincey v. Arizona*, 437 U.S. 385 (1978), there exists no "murder scene" exception; even if homicide investigators have PC to search defendant's home, such a warrantless search intrudes significantly on defendant's privacy and is invalid under Amd. IV. Louisiana Supreme Court reversed. (9-0; per curiam.)

Case Name	Charge on Arrest	Authority for Arrest	Articles Seized	Warrant Clause	Exceptions to Warrant Clause	Decision
United States v. Hensley, 469 U.S. 221 (1985)	Convicted felon in possession of firearms	Based on "wanted bulletin" issued by another department, police stopped defendant's car; gun in plain view gave officers PC to search car, and additional weapons found during search gave officers PC for arrest	Handguns	No warrant	Sufficient RAS ("wanted bulletin")	Where police make a *Terry*-type stop in objective reliance on a "wanted" bulletin, evidence uncovered is admissible if bulletin issued on basis of RAS that "wanted" person committed an offense, and provided the stop is not significantly more intrusive than would have been permitted issuing police. CCA reversed; remanded. (9-0; O'Connor, J., DOC; Brennan, J., concurs.)
New Jersey v. T.L.O., 469 U.S 325 (1985)	Delinquency charges brought against defendant in juvenile court	Defendant was discovered smoking in the lavatory in violation of a school rule; school official questioned her and found evidence of drug dealing in her purse; she was then taken to police headquarters	Cigarettes, marijuana, pipe, plastic bags, cash, and papers implicating defendant in drug dealing	No warrant	Sufficient RAS	Public school officials act as state representatives when carrying out searches and other disciplinary functions pursuant to school policy; legality of a search of a student depends not on PC but on reasonableness of the search under all circumstances—balancing need to search against invasion the search entails. New Jersey Supreme Court reversed. (6-3; White, J., DOC; Brennan, Marshall, & Stevens, JJ., j/p, c/p, d/p; Powell & O'Connor, JJ., concur; Blackmun, J., c/j.)
United States v. Johns, 469 U.S. 478 (1985)	Conspiracy to possess and PWID (in violation of 21 U.S.C. §§ 841, 846)	Pursuant to investigation, customs officers observed rendezvous between pickup trucks and small planes and had PC to believe packages in trucks and trucks themselves contained contraband; truck drivers and pilots were arrested	Marijuana	No warrant	Automobile exception	Relying on *United States v. Ross*, 456 U.S. 798 (1982), where officers have PC to search lawfully stopped vehicle, they also may search containers that might conceal the object of the search; subsequent warrantless search of containers is not unreasonable merely because it occurs 3 days after containers are removed from vehicles. CCA reversed; remanded. (7-2; O'Connor, J., DOC; Brennan & Marshall, JJ., dissent.)

Case Name	Charge on Arrest	Authority for Arrest	Articles Seized	Warrant Clause	Exceptions to Warrant Clause	Decision
United States v. Sharpe, 470 U.S. 675 (1985)	PWID of controlled substance in violation of 21 U.S.C. § 841 and 18 U.S.C. § 2	DEA agent's suspicions were aroused by heavily loaded truck and car traveling in tandem on known drug trafficking route; after making investigative stop, agent placed defendant under arrest	Truck containing bales of marijuana	No warrant	Sufficient RAS, detention legal	Under *Terry v.Ohio,* 392 U.S. 1 (1968), evaluation of investigatory stop requires dual inquiry: whether police action was justified at inception and whether stop was reasonably related in scope to circumstances justifying initial interference; police must pursue investigation in diligent and reasonable manner likely to confirm or dispel suspicions quickly. CCA reversed; remanded. (7-2; Burger, C.J., DOC; Black-mun, J., concurs; Marshall, J., c/j; Brennan & Stevens, JJ., dissent.)
Winston v. Lee, 470 U.S. 753 (1985)	Attempted robbery, malicious wounding, 2 counts of using a firearm in the commission of a felony; action brought under 42 U.S.C. § 1983 to enjoin state court's order compelling surgery to remove a bullet from defendant's chest	Following shooting, victim was taken to hospital emergency room; when defendant arrived for treatment of gunshot wound, victim identified defendant as his assailant	NA	NA	None	Compelled surgical intrusion of person's body implicates such significant expectations of privacy that it may be deemed unreasonable under Amd. IV even if likely to produce evidence. Under *Schmerber v. California*, 384 U.S. 757 (1966), factors to consider include: extent to which surgery threatens safety or health; extent of intrusion; community interest in determining guilt or innocence. CCA affirmed. (9-0; Brennan, J., DOC; Burger, C.J., concurs; Blackmun & Rehnquist, JJ., c/j.)
Hayes v. Florida, 470 U.S. 811 (1985)	Burglary and sexual battery under Florida law	Defendant taken by officers to station house for fingerprinting without consent, PC, or judicial authorization; police determined that prints matched those left at scene of crime and arrested defendant	Defendant's fingerprints	No warrant	Fingerprint exception again rejected	Reaffirming *Davis v. Mississippi*, 394 U.S. 721 (1969), where police transport suspect to police station for fingerprinting absent consent, PC, or prior judicial authorization, that investigatory detention violates Amd. IV. Florida District Court of Appeal reversed. (8-0; White, J., DOC; Brennan, Marshall, & Blackmun, JJ., concur; Powell, J., took no part.)

Case Name	Charge on Arrest	Authority for Arrest	Articles Seized	Warrant Clause	Exceptions to Warrant Clause	Decision
Tennessee v. Garner, 471 U.S. 1 (1985)	Action brought challenging constitutionality of state statute and seeking damages under 42 U.S.C. § 1983	Acting under authority of TN statute, officer shot and killed suspect as, after being ordered to halt, suspect fled over backyard fence of house he was suspected of burglarizing	Defendant's person	No warrant	None	Apprehending a suspect by use of deadly force is seizure subject to Amd. IV reasonableness requirement. Unless officer has PC to believe suspect poses significant threat of death or serious physical injury to officer or others, it is unreasonable to prevent escape by use of deadly force. CCA affirmed. (6-3; White, J., DOC; O'Connor & Rehnquist, JJ., Burger, C.J., dissent.)
Oklahoma v. Castleberry, 471 U.S. 146 (1985)	PWID narcotics	Information supplied by informant was corroborated by officers in every detail except the actual presence of narcotics; drugs discovered pursuant to officer's warrantless search of containers in defendant's automobile	Cocaine and other narcotics	No warrant	Automobile	Following *United States v. Chadwick*, 433 U.S. 1 (1977), and *Arkansas v. Sanders*, 442 U.S. 753 (1979), where officer only has PC to believe there is contraband in a specific container in car, he must detain container and delay search until warrant is obtained; under *United States v. Ross*, 456 U.S. 798 (1982), if officer has PC to believe there is contraband somewhere in the car, he may search entire car, including any containers found within. Court of Criminal Appeals of Oklahoma affirmed. (8-0; per curiam; Powell, J., took no part.)
California v. Carney, 471 U.S. 386 (1985)	Possession of marijuana for sale	A youth confirmed that motor home was being used to exchange drugs for sex; youth then knocked on the door and when defendant answered, police entered, saw marijuana, and took defendant into custody	Motor home containing marijuana, plastic bags, scale	No warrant	Automobile exception, applicable to motor home	Warrantless search of motor home falls within the automobile exception under *Carroll v. United States*, 267 U.S. 132 (1925); where agents have PC to enter and search, and vehicle is found in nonresidential lot, automobile exception is justified by ready mobility and reduced expectation of privacy in vehicle. California Supreme Court reversed; remanded. (6-3; Burger, C.J., DOC; Stevens, Brennan, & Marshall, JJ., dissent.)

Case Name	Charge on Arrest	Authority for Arrest	Articles Seized	Warrant Clause	Exceptions to Warrant Clause	Decision
Maryland v. Macon, 472 U.S. 463 (1985)	Distribution of obscene materials in violation of Maryland statute	Detectives concluded that 2 magazines purchased from an adult bookstore by undercover officer were obscene; detectives returned to store and arrested defendant	Two allegedly obscene magazines, marked $50 bill used to make purchase	No warrant	None	Undercover officer's entry into adult bookstore and examination of publications offered for sale does not constitute search, nor does purchase of allegedly obscene matter constitute a seizure; absent search or seizure, Amd. IV does not apply. Maryland Court of Special Appeals reversed. (7-2; O'Connor, J., DOC; Brennan & Marshall, JJ., dissent.)
United States v. Montoya de Hernandez, 473 U.S. 531 (1985)	PWID, unlawful importation of cocaine	Suspected of being an alimentary canal smuggler ("balloon swallower"), defendant was detained by customs officials at the border; a rectal exam resulted in obtaining evidence	88 balloons containing cocaine	No warrant; court order, obtained after 16 hours of detention, authorized a pregnancy test, X-ray, and rectal exam	Sufficient RAS, detention legal	Detaining traveler at border beyond the scope of routine customs search is justified if customs agents, considering facts surrounding traveler, have RAS that traveler is engaged in alimentary canal smuggling; detention to dispel or verify suspicion may not be unreasonable. CCA reversed. (7-2; Rehnquist, J., DOC; Stevens, J., c/j; Brennan & Marshall, JJ., dissent.)
Lanier v. South Carolina, 474 U.S. 25 (1985)	Armed robbery	Defendant contends that his confession should have been suppressed as product of illegal arrest	Defendant's confession	No warrant	None	Reaffirming *Taylor v. Alabama*, 457 U.S. 687 (1982), *Dunaway v. New York*, 442 U.S. 200 (1979), and *Brown v. Illinois*, 422 U.S. 590 (1975), the fact that a confession may be "voluntary" for Amd. V purposes (*Miranda* warnings read and understood) is not, by itself, sufficient to purge the taint of an illegal arrest. Judgment of South Carolina Court of Appeals vacated; case remanded. (9-0; per curiam; O'Connor & Rehnquist, JJ., c/j.)

Case Name	Charge on Arrest	Authority for Arrest	Articles Seized	Warrant Clause	Exceptions to Warrant Clause	Decision
New York v. Class, 475 U.S. 106 (1986)	Criminal possession of a weapon under state statute, traffic violations	After stopping defendant for 2 traffic violations, officer reached into defendant's car to move papers that covered the vehicle identification number (VIN); officer saw a gun under the driver's seat and made arrest	Gun	No warrant	None	Because of VIN's role in regulation of automobiles and requirement that VIN appear in plain view, defendant has no LEP in VIN; state court decision not based on IASG. New York Court of Appeals reversed; remanded. (5-4; O'Connor J., DOC; Brennan, Marshall, & Stevens, JJ., j/p, c/p, d/p; Powell, J., Burger, C.J., concur; White & Stevens, JJ., dissent.)
Malley v. Briggs, 475 U.S. 335 (1986)	Damages action under 42 U.S.C. § 1983; officer allegedly caused plaintiff's unconstitutional arrest because affidavit for warrant failed to establish PC	Based on information intercepted pursuant to court-authorized wiretap, officer prepared complaint and supporting affidavits and arrest warrants issued	NA	Arrest warrant	None	Where action is brought under 42 U.S.C. § 1983, defendant officer who allegedly caused unconstitutional arrest is awarded qualified immunity under objective reasonableness standard (*United States v. Leon*, 468 U.S. 897 (1984); immunity is granted if reasonably competent officers could disagree whether or not warrant should issue. CCA affirmed. (7-2; White, J., DOC; Powell & Rehnquist, JJ., c/p, d/p.)
United States v. Quinn, 475 U.S. 791 (1986)	Importation and possession of cocaine	Fish and game officials saw marijuana debris when aboard boat; federal officials intercepted the vessel and pumped out holds	Marijuana	No warrant	None	Dismissed as improvidently granted. CCA concluded that defendant's status as boat's owner and co-venturer with boat's operator, together with possessory interest in contraband discovered aboard, gave him standing. (7-2; per curiam; Burger, C.J., Blackmun, J., dissent.)
New York v. P.J. Video, Inc., 475 U.S. 868 (1986)	Six counts of obscenity under New York penal law	Investigator viewed movies rented from defendant's store and prepared affidavits summarizing the theme and conduct depicted in each	13 videocassette movies	Search warrant	None	Applications for warrants authorizing seizure of materials protected by Amd. I are evaluated under the same standard of PC used to review warrant applications generally; no "higher" standard is required. New York Court of Appeals reversed; remanded. (6-3; Rehnquist, J., DOC; Marshall, Brennan, & Stevens, JJ., dissent.)

Case Name	Charge on Arrest	Authority for Arrest	Articles Seized	Warrant Clause	Exceptions to Warrant Clause	Decision
California v. Ciraolo, 476 U.S. 207 (1986)	Felonious cultivating of marijuana	Following anonymous tip, officers flew over defendant's house and identified marijuana growing in the yard; a warrant was issued and executed and defendant arrested	73 marijuana plants	Search warrant obtained after flyover	None	Defendant may manifest his subjective intent to maintain privacy, but officers' naked-eye observation of defendant's curtilage from an aircraft lawfully operating at an altitude of 1000 feet violates no LEP; Amd. IV does not require police to obtain warrant for flyover. California Court of Appeal reversed. (5-4; Burger, C.J., DOC; Powell, Brennan, Marshall, & Blackmun, JJ., dissent.)
Dow Chemical v. United States, 476 U.S. 227 (1986)	Action brought alleging EPA's aerial observation was a violation of Amd. IV and beyond EPA's statutory investigative authority under 42 U.S.C. §§ 7413-7414	NA	Aerial photographs	No warrant	None	EPA's taking aerial photographs—for regulatory purposes—of an industrial plant complex from lawfully navigable airspace is not a search prohibited by Amd. IV; open areas of complex are more comparable to "open fields" than to curtilage of dwelling for surveillance purposes. CCA affirmed. (5-4; Burger, C.J., DOC; Brennan, Marshall, Blackmun, & Powell, JJ., j/p, c/p, d/p.)
Colorado v. Bertine, 479 U.S. 367 (1987)	DUI, PWID cocaine, unlawful possession of methaqualone	Defendant arrested for driving under the influence of alcohol	Controlled substances, cocaine paraphernalia, cash	No warrant	Inventory	Relying on *South Dakota v. Opperman*, 428 U.S. 364 (1976), and *Illinois v. Lafayette*, 462 U.S. 640 (1983), police officers may—absent a warrant based on PC—open closed containers while conducting a routine inventory search of impounded vehicle; evidence obtained from such containers is admissible. Colorado Supreme Court reversed. (7-2; Rehnquist, C.J., DOC; Blackmun, Powell, & O'Connor, JJ., concur; Marshall & Brennan, JJ., dissent.)

Case Name	Charge on Arrest	Authority for Arrest	Articles Seized	Warrant Clause	Exceptions to Warrant Clause	Decision
Maryland v. Garrison, 480 U.S. 79 (1987)	Violation of Maryland's CSA	Evidence found during search of defendant's mistakenly described apartment pursuant to search warrant	Heroin, cash, drug paraphernalia	Search warrant	None	Discovery of facts illustrating that warrant was unnecessarily broad does not retroactively invalidate warrant; search is assessed according to validity of the warrant (whether supported by PC and describing place to search and things to seize) and its execution (whether officers knew or should have known of mistaken description). Maryland Court of Appeals reversed; remanded (6-3; Stevens, J., DOC; Blackmun, Brennan, & Marshall, JJ., dissent.)
United States v. Dunn, 480 U.S. 294 (1987)	Conspiring to manufacture and manufacturing phenylacetone and amphetamine, PWID in violation of 21 U.S.C. § 846	Based on DEA agent's observation and investigation, warrant was issued for defendant's ranch; officers executed the warrant, seized evidence, and arrested defendant	Chemicals and laboratory equipment, amphetamines	No warrant for initial entry, search warrant for subsequent search	None	Four factors are useful in analyzing whether area near a barn is within ranch home's curtilage for Amd. IV protection: proximity to home, whether within enclosure surrounding home, how area is used, steps taken to protect from observation. Even LEP in barn does not prevent officers from peering in. CCA reversed. (7-2; White, J., DOC; Scalia, J., j/p, c/p; Brennan & Marshall, JJ., dissent.)
Arizona v. Hicks, 480 U.S. 321 (1987)	Armed robbery	Following shooting, officers entered defendant's apartment looking for shooter, victims, weapons; one officer moved and inspected stereo parts which he suspected—and confirmed—were stolen	Stocking cap mask, stereo turntable, 3 weapons, including a sawed-off rifle	No warrant	Invalid plain view	Exigent circumstances may legitimate entry of dwelling place, but under *Mincey v. Arizona*, 437 U.S. 385 (1978), a subsequent warrantless search is limited by exigencies that justified its initiation; absent PC, search conducted separately is unconstitutional. Court of Appeals of Arizona affirmed. (6-3; Scalia, J., DOC; White, J., concurs; Rehnquist, C.J., O'Connor & Powell, JJ., dissent.)

Case Name	Charge on Arrest	Authority for Arrest	Articles Seized	Warrant Clause	Exceptions to Warrant Clause	Decision
Illinois v. Krull, 480 U.S. 340 (1987)	Various criminal violations of Illinois Vehicle Code	Officer conducted warrantless inspection of vehicles in defendant's wrecking yard pursuant to Illinois Vehicle Code; after he determined that several vehicles were stolen, defendants were arrested	Four vehicles	No warrant	Good-faith exception applicable to reliance on state statute subsequently found unconstitutional	Applying *United States v. Leon*, 468 U.S. 897 (1984), approach, a good-faith exception to the exclusionary rule is recognized when officers act in objectively reasonable reliance on statute that authorizes warrantless administrative searches but is subsequently found unconstitutional. Supreme Court of Illinois reversed; remanded. (5-4; Blackmun, J., DOC; Marshall, O'Connor, Brennan, & Stevens, JJ., dissent.)
O'Connor v. Ortega, 480 U.S. 709 (1987)	Action filed by defendant, a state hospital employee, under 42 U.S.C. § 1983 alleging search of his office violated Amd. IV	NA	Personal items from desk and file cabinets in defendant's office	Arrest warrant	None	Under *Colonnade Catering Corp. v. United States*, 397 U.S. 72 (1970), and *United States v. Biswell*, 406 U.S. 311 (1972), owner of commercial premises in "closely regulated" industry has reduced expectation of privacy; warrantless inspection may be reasonable if: substantial government interest, necessary for furthering regulatory scheme, existence of adequate substitute for warrant. NY Court of Appeals reversed. (6-3; Blackmun, J., DOC; Brennan, Marshall, & O'Connor, JJ., dissent.)
New York v. Burger, 482 U.S. 691 (1987)	Possession of stolen property, unregistered operation as vehicle dismantler	Officers conducted inspection of defendant's junkyard pursuant to NY statute; when officers determined defendant was in possession of stolen vehicles and parts, he was arrested	Two automobiles reported stolen; statements made by defendant to officers	No warrant	Administrative inspection of closely regulated business pursuant to statute	Government employer's intrusions on constitutionally protected privacy interests enjoyed by public employees for noninvestigatory work-related purposes as well as investigation of work-related misconduct are judged by a reasonableness standard under the circumstances. CCA reversed; remanded. (5-4; O'Connor, J., AJC; Scalia c/j; Blackmun, Brennan, Marshall, & Stevens, JJ., dissent.)

Case Name	Charge on Arrest	Authority for Arrest	Articles Seized	Warrant Clause	Exceptions to Warrant Clause	Decision
California v. Rooney, 483 U.S. 307 (1987)	Bookmaking and associated crimes	Warrant issued on basis of at least 5 elements (including trash bag contents) establishing PC; incriminating evidence was seized during search of apartment with warrant and defendant was arrested	Evidence indicating defendant was conducting illegal bookmaking operation	Search warrant	None	Cert. granted to decide whether defendant retained expectation of privacy in trash bag placed in communal bin of multiunit apartment complex; but because Court reviews only judgments, and issue was neither subject of judgment nor properly presented, writ is DIG. (6-3; per curiam; Marshall, J., c/j; White & Powell, JJ., Rehnquist, C.J., dissent.)
Anderson v. Creighton, 483 U.S. 635 (1987)	Claim asserted under *Bivens* against FBI agents for money damages	FBI agent, along with other state and federal officers, conducted warrantless search of Creighton family home; bank robbery suspect not found	Bank robbery suspect, who police believed might be found in the home, was not there	No warrant	None	FBI agent is entitled to summary judgment on qualified immunity grounds if he establishes, as a matter of law, objective reasonableness of action; he must show that reasonable officer would have believed search comported with Amd. IV even though it did not. CCA's judgment vacated. (6-3; Scalia, J., DOC; Stevens, Brennan, & Marshall, JJ., dissent.)
Griffin v. Wisconsin, 483 U.S. 868 (1987)	Possession of a firearm by a convicted felon	Probationer's home was searched by officers pursuant to state statute authorizing such searches when there are reasonable grounds and supervisor's approval	Handgun	No warrant	None	Search of probationer's home may be reasonable under Amd. IV if conducted pursuant to valid state regulations; "special needs" of state probation system may justify searches based on less than usual warrant and PC requirements in order to intervene before probationer damages himself or society. Wisconsin Supreme Court affirmed. (5-4; Scalia, J., DOC; Blackmun, Marshall, Brennan, & Stevens, JJ., dissent.)

Case Name	Charge on Arrest	Authority for Arrest	Articles Seized	Warrant Clause	Exceptions to Warrant Clause	Decision
California v. Greenwood, 486 U.S. 35 (1988)	Felony narcotics charges	Items indicative of narcotics were found when investigators searched through defendant's trash bags; based on items found in rubbish, search warrant for defendant's house was issued and executed	Cocaine, hashish, evidence of narcotics trafficking	Search warrant	None	Amd. IV does not prohibit warrantless search and seizure of trash left for collection outside curtilage of home; where garbage is deposited in an area suited for public inspection, society recognizes no LEP in the rubbish—any claim of Amd. IV protection is defeated. California Court of Appeal reversed; remanded. (6-2; White, J., DOC; Brennan & Marshall, JJ., dissent; Kennedy, J., took no part.)
Michigan v. Chesternut, 486 U.S. 567 (1988)	Knowingly and intentionally possessing heroin, codeine, and diazepam in violation of Michigan law	Officers in cruiser followed defendant and observed him discard packets of pills; an officer identified the pills as codeine and defendant was arrested	Heroin, hypodermic needle, packets of pills containing codeine	No warrant	Whether flight constitutes RAS not reached	Under *United States v. Mendenhall*, 446 U.S. 544 (1980), objective reasonable person standard is used to determine whether police conduct amounts to seizure; investigatory pursuit amounts to seizure only when it communicates to a reasonable person that he cannot ignore police and go about his business. Here, pursuit did not constitute seizure; question whether defendant's fleeing constitutes RAS for seizure not reached. Michigan Court of Appeals reversed; remanded. (9-0; Blackmun, J., DOC; Kennedy & Scalia, JJ., concur.)
Murray/Carter v. United States, 487 U.S. 533 (1988)	Conspiring PWID	Defendants were observed driving in and out of a warehouse; both vehicles and warehouse were found to contain marijuana	270 bales of marijuana, notebooks listing drug customers	No warrant for initial entry; search warrant for re-entry	Independent source	Independent source doctrine applies not only to evidence acquired for the first time during independent lawful search but also to information and tangible evidence initially discovered during unlawful search and later obtained pursuant to valid warrant but wholly independent of initial illegal entry. CCA judgment vacated; remanded. (4-3; Scalia, J., DOC; Marshall, Stevens, & O'Connor, JJ., dissent; Brennan & Kennedy, JJ., took no part.)

Case Name	Charge on Arrest	Authority for Arrest	Articles Seized	Warrant Clause	Exceptions to Warrant Clause	Decision
Florida v. Riley, 488 U.S. 445 (1989), rehearing denied, 490 U.S. 1014	Possession of marijuana under Florida law	Tipped off by anonymous informant, police viewed and identified marijuana from a helicopter; based on these observations, warrant was issued	Marijuana plants	No warrant for flyover observation; warrant for search	None	Relying on *California v. Ciraolo*, 476 U.S. 207 (1986), defendant cannot reasonably expect that greenhouse within home's curtilage is free from examination where the public can legally fly helicopters through public airways and observe contents; Amd. IV does not require police to secure warrant to view what is visible to the naked eye. Supreme Court of Florida reversed. (PL; White, J., AJC; O'Connor, J., c/j; Brennan, Marshall, Stevens, & Blackmun, JJ., dissent.)
Brower v. County of Inyo, 489 U.S. 593 (1989)	Action brought under 42 U.S.C. § 1983 claiming that defendants, in establishing a roadblock, effected an unreasonable seizure in violation of Amd. IV	NA	Plaintiff's decedent, killed when the stolen car he had been driving to elude police crashed into a police roadblock	NA	None	Where defendants, under color of law, seek to make stop by means of a roadblock—designed to stop by physical impact if no voluntary compliance is forthcoming—and succeed in so doing, their actions constitute a seizure under Amd. IV; seizure alone is not enough for § 1983 liability; it must also be unreasonable. CCA reversed; remanded. (9-0; Scalia, J., DOC; Stevens, Brennan, Marshall, & Blackmun, JJ., c/j.)
Skinner v. Railway Labor Executives' Association, 489 U.S. 602 (1989)	Suit brought seeking to enjoin the Federal Railroad Administration's regulations under 42 U.S.C. § 1983 as a violation of Amd. IV	Federal Railroad Admin. promulgated regulations governing drug and alchohol testing of railroad employees following certain major train accidents or for employees who violate certain safety rules	Blood, breath, urine samples	NA	None	Federal regulations authorizing drug and alcohol testing of private railroad employees implicate Amd. IV; since collection and analysis of blood, breath, and urine samples are searches, testing must be reasonable. Where government interests present "special needs," they may outweigh privacy expectations and justify intrusions absent warrant or individualized suspicion. Judgment of CCA reversed. (7-2; Kennedy, J., DOC; Stevens, J., j/p, c/p, c/j; Brennan & Marshall, JJ., dissent.)

Case Name	Charge on Arrest	Authority for Arrest	Articles Seized	Warrant Clause	Exceptions to Warrant Clause	Decision
National Treasury Employees Union v. Von Raab, 489 U.S. 656 (1989)	Suit brought on behalf of Customs Service employees who seek covered positions, alleging that the Customs Service drug testing program violates Amd. IV and seeking injunction and declaratory judgment	Customs Service drug testing program analyzed urine samples of employees who applied for promotion to positions involving interdiction of illegal drugs, carrying firearms, or handling classified materials	Urine sample	NA	None	Suspicionless drug screening through urinalysis of employees applying for promotion to positions that involve interdiction of illegal drugs or require carrying a firearm is reasonable under Amd. IV; government interests in safeguarding international borders outweigh privacy interests. CCA affirmed in part and vacated in part. (5-4; Kennedy, J., DOC; Marshall, Brennan, Scalia, & Stevens, JJ., dissent.)
United States v. Sokolow, 490 U.S. 1 (1989)	PWID in violation of 21 U.S.C. § 841(a)(1)	Travel schedule and demeanor led DEA agents to approach, stop, and escort defendant to office at the airport; detector dog alerted on defendant's bag and defendant was arrested	1,063 grams of cocaine, other evidence seized from luggage	No warrant for initial stop	Sufficient RAS; detention legal	Under *Terry v. Ohio*, 392 U.S. 1 (1968), police can stop and briefly detain an individual for investigative purposes if officers have RAS, based on TOC, that criminal activity may be afoot, even if officers lack PC. CCA reversed; remanded. (7-2; Rehnquist, C.J., DOC; Marshall & Brennan, JJ., dissent.)
Graham v. Connor, 490 U.S. 386 (1989)	Suit filed under 42 U.S.C. § 1983 alleging that defendants used excessive force in making investigatory stop, in violation of Amd. XIV	Petitioner, a diabetic, entered store to buy juice to counteract insulin reaction and exited when line was too long; when officers stopped him, they refused to treat his condition and he sustained injuries	Petitioner's person	NA	None	Claim that law enforcement officers used excessive force while making an arrest, investigatory stop, or seizure of a person is properly analyzed under Amd. IV objective reasonableness standard, rather than due process; reasonableness is evaluated under given circumstances. Judgment of CCA vacated; remanded. (9-0; Rehnquist, C.J., DOC; Blackmun, Brennan, & Marshall, JJ., c/p, c/j.)

Case Name	Charge on Arrest	Authority for Arrest	Articles Seized	Warrant Clause	Exceptions to Warrant Clause	Decision
Fort Wayne Books, Inc. v. Indiana, 489 U.S. 46 (1989)	NA	Owners of two adult bookstores civilly charged with state RICO statute violation by repeatedly violating state laws proscribing distribution of obscene books and materials; in RICO complaint, state sought forfeiture of all property used or intended for use in, derived from, or realized through alleged racketeering activity; pursuant to state law, state also filed separate petition for immediate seizure of all property subject to forfeiture as set out in complaints; seizure petition supported by affidavit of police officer recounting criminal convictions involving bookstores and describing other books and materials for sale at bookstores believed to be obscene; after ex parte hearing on seizure petition, court concluded PC existed to conclude that bookstore was violating state RICO law and ordered immediate seizure of real and personal property comprising bookstores; bookstores padlocked and contents of stores seized and removed by police	Real and personal property comprising adult bookstores	No warrant	NA	General rule under Amd. IV is that all contraband, instrumentalities, and evidence of crimes may be seized on PC and, in certain circumstances, even without warrant; general rule does not apply when dealing with materials presumptively protected by Amd. I; pretrial seizure of expressive materials can only be made pursuant to procedure focusing on question of obscenity; while single copy of book or film may be seized and retained as evidence based on finding of PC, neither books nor films can be completely removed from circulation until court has made determination of obscenity after full adversarial hearing; pretrial seizure here unconstitutional. Indiana Supreme Court reversed; remanded. (5-4; White, J., DOC; Blackmun, J., concurs; O'Connor, J., c/p, d/p; Stevens, Brennan, & Marshall, JJ., d/p in first case, c/p, d/p, second case.)

Case Name	Charge on Arrest	Authority for Arrest	Articles Seized	Warrant Clause	Exceptions to Warrant Clause	Decision
James v. Illinois, 493 U.S. 307 (1990)	Murder, attempted murder	Based on eyewitness accounts, police took defendant into custody and proceeded to question him about his hairstyle; subsequently, he was indicted	Illegally obtained statements regarding defendant's hair color and style	No warrant	*Havens* expansion rejected	Balancing approach recognized in *Walder v. United States*, 347 U.S. 62 (1954) and *United States v. Havens*, 446 U.S. 620 (1980), which justifies expanding impeachment exception to permit prosecutor's use of illegally obtained evidence to impeach defendant's testimony, does not justify expanding the class of impeachable witnesses. Illinois State Supreme Court reversed; remanded. (5-4; Brennan, J., DOC; Kennedy, O'Connor, & Scalia, JJ., Rehnquist, C.J., dissent.)
United States v. Verdugo-Urquidez, 494 U.S. 259 (1990)	Various narcotics-related offenses	Arrest warrant	Documents including a tally sheet believed to reflect quantities of marijuana smuggled into U.S.	Arrest warrant; no search warrant for defendant's property located in Mexico	Defendant not one of the "people" within the meaning of Amd. IV	Based on plain language, history, and precedent, Amd. IV does not apply to search and seizure by U.S. agents of property owned by nonresident alien and located in a foreign country; such restrictions must be imposed politically. CCA reversed. (6-3; Rehnquist, C.J., DOC; Kennedy, J., concurs; Stevens, J., c/j; Brennan, Marshall, & Blackmun, JJ., dissent.)
Maryland v. Buie, 494 U.S. 325 (1990)	Robbery with a deadly weapon, using a handgun in the commission of a felony	Arrest warrants issued for defendant and his suspected accomplice	Red running suit	Arrest warrant	SIVA "protective sweep" based on RAS, *not* PC	Amd. IV permits a limited protective sweep in conjunction with sanctuary arrest where arresting officer possesses RAS that area harbors dangerous 3d parties; sweep entails cursory inspection of areas where a person might be found. Judgment of Court of Appeals of Maryland vacated; remanded. (7-2; White, J., DOC; Stevens & Kennedy, JJ., concur; Brennan & Marshall, JJ., dissent.)

Case Name	Charge on Arrest	Authority for Arrest	Articles Seized	Warrant Clause	Exceptions to Warrant Clause	Decision
Smith v. Ohio, 494 U.S. 541 (1990)	Drug abuse (felony in Ohio)	Officers approached defendant, retrieved a brown bag that he had thrown onto hood of his car, open the bag, and discovered drug paraphernalia	Drug paraphernalia including scales, weighing pan, and paper used to package cocaine	No warrant	Invalid SIVA	SIVA exception permits police to search lawfully arrested person and areas within his immediate control; it does not allow police, absent warrant or PC, to search any citizens provided an arrest immediately follows; incident search may not precede arrest and serve as justification. Ohio Supreme Court reversed. (8-1; per curiam; Marshall, J., dissents.)
Florida v. Wells, 495 U.S. 1 (1990)	DUI, possession of a controlled substance	Trooper stopped defendant for speeding, smelled alcohol, and made arrest	Marijuana (found in locked suitcase in trunk of defendant's impounded vehicle)	No warrant	Invalid inventory search	Absent police policy with respect to opening closed containers during inventory search, such search is not sufficiently regulated; evidence found pursuant to it is properly suppressed. Florida State Supreme Court affirmed. (9-0; Rehnquist, C.J., DOC; Brennan, Marshall, Blackmun, & Stevens, JJ., c/j.)
New York v. Harris, 495 U.S. 14 (1990)	Second-degree murder	With PC to believe defendant committed murder, officers made warrantless entry of defendant's home, read his *Miranda* rights, obtained admission of guilt, and arrested him	Three statements: admission of guilt, written inculpatory statement, videotaped interview	No warrant	None	Where police have PC for arrest but lack warrant, the state may use statement made by suspect outside his home even if statement is taken after arrest in violation of *Payton v. New York*, 445 U.S. 573 (1980); such statement is not product of illegal entry, nor would its suppression serve purpose of *Payton* rule—evidence gathered during sanctuary arrest being already excluded. NY Court of Appeals reversed. (5-4; White, J., DOC; Marshall, Brennan, Blackmun, & Stevens, JJ., dissent.)

Case Name	Charge on Arrest	Authority for Arrest	Articles Seized	Warrant Clause	Exceptions to Warrant Clause	Decision
Minnesota v. Olson, 495 U.S. 91 (1990)	First-degree murder, armed robbery, second-degree assault	Following armed robbery, a "probable cause" bulletin was issued for defendant; police surrounded the house where defendant was staying, then entered and found him in a closet	Defendant's inculpatory statement, made at police headquarters following his arrest	No warrant	Invalid exigent circumstances	Where police arrest suspect following warrantless, nonconsensual entry into house where he is overnight guest, his Amd. IV rights are violated; status as overnight guest is alone sufficient to show LEP in host's home. MN court held there were no exigent circumstances to justify warrantless entry; Minnesota Supreme Court affirmed. (7-2; White, J., DOC; Stevens & Kennedy, JJ., concur; Rehnquist, C.J., Blackmun, J., dissent.)
Horton v. California, 496 U.S. 128 (1990)	Armed robbery	Search of sanctuary pursuant to warrant and seizure of incriminating evidence	Two stun guns, Uzi machine gun, .38 caliber revolver, handcuff key, items of clothing identified by victim	Search warrant authorized search for proceeds of robbery; stun guns were not listed	Inadvertence prong of plain view no longer necessary in sanctuary seizure	Overruling in part *Coolidge v. New Hampshire*, 403 U.S. 443 (1971), Amd. IV does not prohibit warrantless seizure of incriminating evidence found in plain view even though its discovery is not inadvertent; while inadvertence is characteristic of plain view seizures, it is not necessary. California Court of Appeal affirmed. (7-2; Stevens, J., DOC; Brennan & Marshall, JJ., dissent.)
Alabama v. White, 496 U.S. 325 (1990)	Possession of marijuana, possession of cocaine	Based on telephone tip, police stopped defendant's vehicle; during consensual search of the car, officers found marijuana and arrested defendant	Marijuana, cocaine	No warrant	Sufficient RAS (anonymous tip)	Under TOC (*Illinois v. Gates*, 462 U.S. 213 (1983)) anonymous tip corroborated by independent police work may show sufficient indicia of reliability to furnish reasonable suspicion (*Terry v. Ohio*, 392 U.S. 1 (1968)) that individual is engaged in criminal activity and to justify an investigatory stop. Court of Criminal Appeals of Alabama reversed; remanded. (6-3; White, J., DOC; Stevens, Brennan, & Marshall, JJ., dissent.)

Case Name	Charge on Arrest	Authority for Arrest	Articles Seized	Warrant Clause	Exceptions to Warrant Clause	Decision
Michigan Dep't of State Police v. Sitz, 496 U.S. 444 (1990)	Plaintiffs filed complaint seeking declaratory and injunctive relief from potential subjection to state's sobriety checkpoints	MI state police department established highway sobriety checkpoint program; guidelines governed operation, site selection, publicity; during operation 126 cars passed through, 2 drivers arrested for DUI	NA	NA	None	Seizure occurs when vehicle is stopped at highway sobriety checkpoint; *United States v. Martinez-Fuerte*, 428 U.S. 543 (1976), balancing test applies to determining reasonableness of seizure and constitutionality of checkpoint program. Where intrusion on motorists, state interest in preventing drunk driving, and effectiveness of program weigh in favor, Amd. IV is not violated. Michigan Court of Appeals reversed; remanded. (6-3; Rehnquist, C.J. DOC; Blackmun, J., c/j: Brennan, Marshall, & Stevens, JJ., dissent.)
Illinois v. Rodriquez, 497 U.S. 177 (1990)	PWID controlled substance	With consent and assistance of former housemate, police gained entry to defendant's apartment where they found defendant and incriminating evidence	Drug paraphernalia, cocaine	No warrant	Consent (3d party)	Warrantless entry of house is valid when based on consent of 3d party who police, at time of entry, have objectively reasonable basis to believe possesses common authority over premises, but who in fact does not. Illinois Appellate Court reversed; remanded. (6-3; Scalia, J., DOC; Marshall, Brennan, & Stevens, JJ., dissent.)
California v. Hodari D., 499 U.S. 621 (1991)	Possession of cocaine, violation of probation curfew restriction, brought against defendant in juvenile proceeding	Police cruising in unmarked car saw youths run away from small red car; defendant was pursued by officer on foot, ordered to stop, tossed rock of crack cocaine, and was tackled by officer	Crack cocaine	No warrant	Evidence abandoned before seizure	A seizure does not occur where its subject does not yield to show of police authority; where defendant does not comply with order to stop, he is not seized until he is physically tackled. Contraband abandoned before tackle is not fruit of a seizure. California Court of Appeal reversed; remanded. (7-2; Scalia, J., DOC; Stevens & Marshall, JJ., dissent.)

Case Name	Charge on Arrest	Authority for Arrest	Articles Seized	Warrant Clause	Exceptions to Warrant Clause	Decision
County of Riverside v. McLaughlin, 500 U.S. 44 (1991)	Defendant brought class action seeking injunctive and declaratory judgment under 42 U.S.C. § 1983 and challenging the way county of Riverside provides PC determination for warrantless arrests	Riverside County combines judicial determinations of PC for warrantless arrests with arraignment procedures which, under county policy, must be held within 2 working days of arrest	NA	NA	None	Relying on *Gerstein v. Pugh*, 420 U.S. 103 (1975), a prompt—not immediate—judicial determination of PC is required as prerequisite to pre-trial detention following warrantless arrest; a jurisdiction that provides determination of PC, either separately or combined with other pre-trial hearings, within 48 hours of arrest will generally comply. Judgment of CCA vacated; remanded. (5-4; O'Connor, J., DOC; Marshall, Blackmun, Stevens, & Scalia, JJ., dissent.)
Florida v. Jimeno, 500 U.S. 248 (1991)	PWID cocaine, traffic infraction	After stopping defendant for traffic violation, officer requested and received permission to search the car; officer saw brown paper bag on passenger's side floor and found cocaine inside	Cocaine	No warrant	Consent (1st party)	Where criminal suspect gives officers permission to search his car, officers may open closed containers found within as long as it is objectively reasonable for officer to believe the scope of consent would include a particular container. Florida Supreme Court reversed; remanded. (7-2; Rehnquist, C.J., DOC; Marshall & Stevens, JJ., dissent.)
California v. Acevedo, 500 U.S. 565 (1991)	PWID marijuana	Police saw defendant enter a house and reappear with a bag corresponding in size to package of marijuana police knew was inside; after watching defendant place bag in the trunk and begin to drive away, police made stop and opened trunk and bag	Marijuana	No warrant	Automobile	Amd. IV does not require police to obtain a warrant to open a container in a vehicle simply because they lack PC to search the entire car; relying on *Carroll v. United States*, 267 U.S. 132 (1925), police may search an automobile and containers within it where they have PC to believe evidence is contained. *United States v. Chadwick*, 433 U.S. 1 (1977) and *Arkansas v. Sanders*, 442 U.S. 753 (1979), overruled. California Court of Appeal reversed; remanded. (6-3; Blackmun, J., DOC; Scalia, J., c/j; White, Stevens, & Marshall, JJ., dissent.)

Case Name	Charge on Arrest	Authority for Arrest	Articles Seized	Warrant Clause	Exceptions to Warrant Clause	Decision
Florida v. Bostick, 501 U.S. 429 (1991)	Trafficking in cocaine	Officers boarded defendant's bus and, without RAS, requested permission to search his bags; he consented and officers found cocaine	Cocaine	No warrant	Consent (1st party)	When determining whether police encounter on a bus necessarily constitutes a seizure, inquire "whether a reasonable person would feel free to decline the officer's requests or otherwise terminate the encounter"; all surrounding circumstances must be considered. Florida Supreme Court reversed; remanded. (6-3; O'Connor, J., DOC; Marshall, Blackmun, & Stevens, JJ., dissent.)
Soldal v. Cook County, 506 U.S. 56 (1992)	NA	Soldal lived in trailer home in mobile home park; prior to hearing on eviction notice, forcibly evicted by mobile home park owner; Cook County deputies accompanied persons who readied trailer for removal and removed it; deputies kept Soldal from interfering with removal of trailer and, after talking to a district attorney, refused Soldal's request for trespass complaint; eviction subsequently found to be unlawful and trailer returned in damaged state; action brought under 42 U.S.C. § 1983 alleging violation of Amds. IV and XIV	Trailer home	No warrant	NA	Amd. IV is applicable to states under Amd. XIV; seizure exists under Amd. IV when some meaningful interference with person's possessory interests in property occurs; right of person to retreat into own home is at core of Amd. IV, which protects both property and privacy; reason for law enforcement seizure or entry onto property is wholly irrelevant to determination whether Amd. IV applies; intrusion on security from governmental interference is determining consideration; reasonableness is ultimate standard under Amd. IV and determination of such requires balancing of governmental and private interests; facts here establish seizure under Amd. IV. CCA reversed; remanded. (9-0; White, J., DOC.)

Case Name	Charge on Arrest	Authority for Arrest	Articles Seized	Warrant Clause	Exceptions to Warrant Clause	Decision
United States v. James Daniel Good Real Property, 510 U.S. 43 (1993)	Narcotics charges	Police executed search warrant of owner's home and found 89 pounds of marijuana; owner pled guilty to state drug charge and sentenced to one year in jail, five years probation, and $1,000 fine; owner also required to forfeit to state $3,187 in case found in home; over four years after owner pled guilty, federal government sought forfeiture of home; seizure warrant issued after ex parte hearing; home seized without prior notice or adversarial hearing; owner filed claim for property and challenged seizure of home	Real property (home)	Civil seizure warrant	NA	While Amd. IV imposes restrictions on civil forfeiture seizures, it is not sole source of constitutional protection afforded owners in forfeiture cases; here seizure implicated both Amds. IV and V; question is whether either constitutional provision violated; therefore, here, even assuming Amd. IV satisfied, Court must determine whether seizure satisfied requirements of Due Process Clause. CCA reversed; remanded. (5-4; Kennedy, J., DOC; Rehnquist, C.J., Scalia & O'Connor, JJ., c/p, d/p; O'Connor & Thomas, JJ., c/p, d/p.)
United States v. Padilla, 508 U.S. 77 (1993)	PWID cocaine, conspiracy to distribute	Co-conspirator was arrested after police found 560 pounds of cocaine in his automobile; he cooperated with police and controlled delivery of cocaine ultimately led police to defendants	Cocaine	No warrant	Co-conspirator exception rejected	Analysis of Amd. IV search and seizure claims is governed by expectations of privacy and property interest; motion to suppress due to Amd. IV violation can be successfully made only by those individuals whose rights were violated and not those who are merely harmed by introduction of evidence; while neither co-conspirators nor co-defendants have been given special standing under federal Constitution, participants in criminal conspiracy may have, under facts of individual case, expectation of privacy or property interest; lower court's co-conspirator exception is contrary to Amd. IV principles and is invalid. CCA reversed, remanded to determine whether reasonable expectation of privacy or property existed. (9-0; per curiam.)

Case Name	Charge on Arrest	Authority for Arrest	Articles Seized	Warrant Clause	Exceptions to Warrant Clause	Decision
Minnesota v. Dickerson, 508 U.S. 366 (1993)	Possession of controlled substance	Defendant took evasive action to avoid police when exiting building known for cocaine traffic; defendant stopped and subjected to pat-down; while pat-down revealed no weapon, officer felt object that, when squeezed and manipulated through defendant's clothing, led officer to believe object was crack cocaine; defendant arrested.	Crack cocaine	No warrant	Plain view	Police may seize contraband detected through sense of touch during protective pat-down permitted by *Terry* provided incriminating nature of contraband is immediately discernable upon pat-down; where, as here, nature of material is not apparent until officer manipulates contents of pocket by squeezing and sliding contents, search exceeds legal bounds of *Terry. v. Ohio*, 392 U.S. 1 (1968). Minnesota Supreme Court affirmed. (9-0 Parts I and II; White, J., DOC; Scalia, J., c/j; 6-3 Parts III and IV; White, J., DOC; Scalia, J., c/j; Rehnquist, C.J., Blackmun, & Thomas, JJ., c/p, d/p.)
Albright v. Oliver, 510 U.S. 266 (1994)	Unspecified drug charge	Albright turned himself in after learning warrant issued for his arrest; warrant later dismissed for failure to state offense under state law; Albright brought civil rights action under 42 U.S.C. § 1983 claiming Amd. XIV provided right to be free from criminal prosecution except upon PC	Defendant's person	Arrest warrant	NA	Albright's claim that arrest not supported by PC should be judged under Amd. IV rather than substantive due process; Amd. IV exclusionary rule applicable to states under Amd. XIV; where one particular constitutional amendment provides specific constitutional protection or guidance, it, rather than more general notion of substantive due process, must be framework for analyzing claim; Amd. IV specifically addresses or considers pretrial deprivations of liberty; while Court expressed no opinion as to whether claim would succeed under Amd. IV, it held substantive due process afforded Albright no relief. CCA affirmed. (7-2; Rehnquist, C.J., DOC; Scalia & Ginsburg, JJ., c/j; Kennedy & Thomas, JJ., c/j; Souter, J., c/j; Stevens & Blackmun, JJ., dissent.)

Case Name	Charge on Arrest	Authority for Arrest	Articles Seized	Warrant Clause	Exceptions to Warrant Clause	Decision
Powell v. Nevada, 511 U.S. 79 (1994)	Felony child abuse and first-degree murder	Defendant arrested for felony child abuse; on that afternoon, arresting officer prepared sworn declaration describing cause for and circumstances of arrest; PC hearing held four days later and magistrate found PC to hold defendant for preliminary hearing; on same day as PC hearing, defendant made incriminating statements to police that were later used against him at trial; 10 days after arrest defendant made his first appearance before magistrate and by that time, since victim had died of her injuries, defendant had been additionally charged with murder	Defendant's person	Arrest warrant	NA	*Griffith v. Kentucky*, 479 U.S. 314 (1987), provides that new rule for conduct of criminal prosecu-tions is to be applied retroactively to all state and federal cases pending on direct review or not yet final; inasmuch as defendant's conviction was not final when *County of Riverside v. McLaughlin,* 500 U.S. 44 (1991), was issued, defendant is entitled, under *Griffin*, to rely on *McLaughlin*; here delay exceeding 48 hours in having PC determination by magistrate presumptively violated Amd. IV as set out in *McLaughlin*; *McLaughlin* did not resolve issue of remedy for delay in PC determination; failure to timely conduct PC determination does not necessarily mean that defendant must be released or obtain other relief. Nevada Supreme Court reversed and remanded for determination of appropriate remedy. (7-2; Ginsburg, J., DOC; Thomas, J., & Rehnquist, C.J., dissent.)

Case Name	Charge on Arrest	Authority for Arrest	Articles Seized	Warrant Clause	Exceptions to Warrant Clause	Decision
Arizona v. Evans, 514 U.S. 1 (1995)	Possession of marijuana	During routine traffic stop, computer check on defendant indicated that there was outstanding arrest warrant for him; as he was being handcuffed, he dropped marijuana cigarette; subsequent search of automobile revealed bag of marijuana; it was later discovered that arrest warrant had been quashed prior to arrest but this information had not been transmitted by clerk of court to law enforcement	Marijuana	Arrest warrant	Good faith	Exclusionary rule historically intended to deter police misconduct; analysis of *United States v. Leon*, 468 U.S. 897 (1984), supports categorical exception to rule for clerical errors of court employees; seizure here did not violate Amd. IV because officer acted objectively reasonably when relied on computer record of arrest warrant. Supreme Court of Arizona reversed; remanded. (7-2; Rehnquist, C.J., DOC; Souter & Beyer, JJ., c/j; O'Connor, Souter & Beyer, JJ., c/j; Ginsburg & Stevens, JJ., dissent; Stevens, J., dissent.)
Wilson v. Arkansas, 514 U.S. 927 (1995)	Delivery of marijuana, delivery of methamphetamine, possession of drug paraphernalia, possession of marijuana	Defendant sold marijuana and methamphetamine to informant; subsequently, police obtained warrant to search defendant's home. When police arrived, door was open; police opened unlocked screen door, identified themselves, and proceeded to search home; police found defendant attempting to flush quantity of marijuana in toilet and made arrest.	Marijuana, methamphetamine, Valium, paraphernalia, gun, ammunition	Warrant authorized search of home and arrest of defendant and another	None	Common-law knock-and-announce principle is part of Amd. IV reasonableness inquiry; officer's unannounced entry might violate individual's Amd. IV rights unless such entry serves countervailing law enforcement interests, such as prevention of destruction of evidence or considerations of safety; determination of what is relevant countervailing factor is left to lower courts. Arkansas Supreme Court reversed; remanded to make determination of reasonableness. (9-0; Thomas, J., DOC.)

Case Name	Charge on Arrest	Authority for Arrest	Articles Seized	Warrant Clause	Exceptions to Warrant Clause	Decision
Vernonia School District 47J v. Acton, 515 U.S. 646 (1995)	Teachers and school administrators observed sharp increase in drug use among students; school athletes were found to be among leaders of school drug culture and this caused particular concern due to increased risk of sports-related injury; after district offered classes, speakers and presentations to deter drug use by students, school board approved drug-testing program for students participating in interscholastic athletics; program required consent of students and parents to pre-season testing and random testing during season; respondent refused to consent to testing and was denied opportunity to play on school team; declaratory and injunctive action brought by his parents alleging policy violated Amd. IV	NA	NA	NA	Special Needs	Amd. XIV extends Amd. IV protection against unreasonable searches and seizures to action by state officers, including school officials; state-compelled collection and testing of urine constitutes search subject to Amd. IV; ultimate measure of constitutionality of governmental search is reasonableness; determination of reasonableness of search is made by balancing intrusion on individual's Amd. IV interests against promotion of legitimate governmental interests; where search undertaken by police to discover evidence of criminal wrongdoing, reasonableness generally requires that warrant based on PC be obtained; warrant not required to establish reasonableness of all government searches and, when warrant not required, PC not always required; search not supported by PC can be constitutional when special needs, beyond normal need for law enforcement, make warrant and PC requirement impracticable; special needs have been found to justify suspicionless drug testing of railroad employees involved in train accidents, random drug testing of federal customs agents who carry arms or are involved in drug interdiction, and checkpoints for illegal immigrants, contraband, and drunk drivers; Amd. IV does not protect all subjective expectations of privacy but only those society recognizes as legitimate, and determination of what expectations are legitimate varies with context and individual's legal relationship with government; determination of reasonableness does not require least intrusive search practicable under

Case Name	Charge on Arrest	Authority for Arrest	Articles Seized	Warrant Clause	Exceptions to Warrant Clause	Decision
Vernonia School District 47J v. Acton (continued)						(continued) circumstances; drug-testing policy here is reasonable and constitutional because school athletes have reduced expectation of privacy, privacy interests compromised by process of obtaining sample under policy in this case is negligible, and government interest here is important enough to justify search. CCA vacated and remanded. (6-3; Scalia, J., DOC.; Ginsburg, J., c/j; O'Connor, Stevens, & Souter, JJ., dissent.)
Ornelas v. United States, 517 U.S. 690 (1996)	Possession of cocaine with intent to distribute	Officer conducting drug-interdiction surveillance saw older-model Oldsmobile with California tags in motel parking lot; because of officer's knowledge that older-model General Motors cars are favorite of drug couriers because it is easy to hide things in them and California is source state for drugs, information requested on car's registration; one of names provided to officer matched name of person registered at motel; computer search of federal database of known and suspected drug traffickers revealed both persons' names; when defendants left motel room and got in car, police approached and inquired about contraband and obtained consent to search car; panel above	Two kilograms of cocaine	No warrant	RAS, automobile	Reasonable suspicion is particularized and objective basis for suspecting person stopped is engaged in criminal activity; PC to search exists where known facts and circumstances are sufficient to warrant reasonably prudent person to believe that contraband or evidence of crime will be found; as compared to finely tuned standards of proof beyond reasonable doubt and proof by preponderance of evidence, reasonable suspicion and PC are fluid concepts that take substantive content from particular context in which they are being assessed; principal factors in determination of reasonable suspicion or PC will be events that lead up to stop or search and, then, determination of whether those events, viewed from standpoint of objectively reasonable police officer, add up to reasonable suspicion or PC; as general matter, determinations of reasonable suspicion and PC to make warrantless search should be reviewed de novo on appeal, with reviewing court taking care to review

Case Name	Charge on Arrest	Authority for Arrest	Articles Seized	Warrant Clause	Exceptions to Warrant Clause	Decision
Ornelas v. United States (continued)		armrest found to be loose and drugs found when panel removed				(continued) findings of fact only for clear error and giving due weight to inferences drawn from facts by trial judges and police officers. CCA reversed and case remanded for review of district court's determinations in light of opinion. (8-1; Rehnquist, C.J., DOC; Scalia, J., dissent.)
Whren v. United States, 517 U.S. 806 (1996)	Various, unspecified federal drug charges	Patrolling in high drug area, police observed suspicious behavior; after turning around, officers saw truck turn without signaling and drive away at unreasonable speed; police stopped truck to warn driver of traffic violations; bags of drugs seen in defendant's hands	Crack cocaine	No warrant	Automobile	Temporary detention of individuals during automobile stop, regardless of length or limited purpose of detention, is seizure under Amd. IV and is subject to constitutional mandate that it not be unreasonable; decision to stop automobile is generally reasonable when there exists PC to believe that traffic violation has occurred; subjective intentions of police play no role in ordinary PC analysis under Amd. IV; temporary detention of motorist upon PC to believe he has violated traffic laws does not violate Amd. IV, even if reasonable officer would not have stopped motorist absent some other legal objective. CCA affirmed. (9-0; Scalia, J., DOC.)
Pennsylvania v. Labron, 518 U.S. 938 (1996)	Delivery of controlled substance, criminal conspiracy	Two cases: in first case, police witnessed series of drug transactions on street; they arrested Labron and searched car from which drugs produced for sales; in second case, informant met with Kilgore and bought drugs; police then arrested Kilgore and searched automobile to and from which Kilgore was seen walking	Cocaine from both automobiles	No warrant	Automobile	If automobile is readily mobile and PC exists to believe it contains contraband, Amd. IV permits police to search without warrant; warrantless searches of vehicles here did not violate Amd. IV because they were supported by PC inasmuch as police saw Labron put drugs into automobile and police saw Kilgore act as if there were drugs in automobile. Pennsylvania Supreme Court reversed; remanded. (7-2; per curiam; Stevens & Ginsburg, JJ., dissent.)

Case Name	Charge on Arrest	Authority for Arrest	Articles Seized	Warrant Clause	Exceptions to Warrant Clause	Decision
Ohio v. Robinette, 519 U.S. 33 (1996)	Possession of controlled substance	After stopping defendant for traffic violation, officer asked and was granted permission to search vehicle; during search, pill and marijuana found	Marijuana, pill (MDMA)	No warrant	Automobile, consent (1st party)	Subjective intentions of police play no role in ordinary PC analysis under Amd. IV; touchstone of Amd. IV is reasonableness; Amd. IV does not require that lawfully seized defendant be advised that he is "free to go" before his consent to search is recognized as voluntary; constitutional test for valid consent to search is that consent be voluntary, and determination of voluntariness is question of fact to be made from all circumstances. Ohio Supreme Court reversed; remanded. (8-1; Rehnquist, C.J., DOC; Ginsburg, J., c/j; Stevens, J., dissent.)
Chandler v. Miller, 520 U.S. 305 (1997)	Petitioners were candidates for elected office in Georgia who brought action challenging constitutionality of state statute requiring them to submit to and pass drug test to qualify for elected office	NA	Urine sample	No warrant	Special needs not applicable	Amd. IV restraint against unreasonable searches and seizures generally prohibits government officials from conducting search or seizure absent individualized suspicion; searches conducted without individualized suspicion are sometimes warranted where special needs, beyond normal need for law enforcement, exist; when such special needs are alleged to exist, courts must carry out context-specific inquiry and closely examine competing private and public interests offered by parties; despite absence of individualized suspicion, search may be reasonable when privacy interests implicated by search are minimal and when important government interest advanced by intrusion would be jeopardized by requirement of individualized suspicion; instant case distinguishable from prior special needs cases in that Georgia failed to carry its burden to show that proffered special need for drug testing of

Case Name	Charge on Arrest	Authority for Arrest	Articles Seized	Warrant Clause	Exceptions to Warrant Clause	Decision
Chandler v. Miller (continued)						(continued) candidates for elected office was substantial; because need for drug testing of candidates in instant case is symbolic rather than special, public safety genuinely not in jeopardy and suspicionless search violates Amd. IV; where risk to public safety is substantial and real, blanket suspicionless searches attuned to risk may be classified as reasonable; opinion explicitly not encompass medical examinations designed to certify candidate's general health, financial disclosure requirements for candidates, and drug testing in private sector. CCA reversed. (8-1; Ginsburg, J., DOC; Rehnquist, C.J., dissent.)
Maryland v. Wilson, 519 U.S. 408 (1997)	PWID cocaine	Police observed automobile speeding and, after activating lights and signaling for automobile to pull over, saw passengers in automobile turn to look at police car and duck down several times; automobile stopped and defendant, who was passenger, was ordered out of car; when defendant exited, cocaine fell to ground	Cocaine	No warrant	Automobile	Police making routine traffic stop may order passengers out of car pending completion of stop and any evidence found as result is admissible; since vehicle has already been legally stopped, any additional inconvenience to passengers is allowable and minimal if done in interest of safety. Maryland Court of Appeals reversed and remanded. (7-2; Rehnquist, C.J., DOC; Stevens & Kennedy, JJ., dissent; Kennedy, J., dissent.)

Case Name	Charge on Arrest	Authority for Arrest	Articles Seized	Warrant Clause	Exceptions to Warrant Clause	Decision
Richards v. Wisconsin, 520 U.S. 385 (1997)	PWID cocaine	Based on investigation that revealed defendant dealing drugs from motel rooms, police requested search warrant to search motel room for drugs and paraphernalia; police requested "no knock" warrant but magistrate struck those provisions from warrant before it was issued; dressed as maintenance man, officer knocked on defendant's motel room door; defendant opened door, which was still secured with chain lock, but slammed it shut upon seeing uniformed officer; after waiting two or three seconds, police kicked in door as they identified themselves as police officers; defendant was caught trying to escape through window; search of motel room revealed cash and cocaine hidden in bathroom ceiling	Money, cocaine	Search warrant	None	Amd. IV prohibits blanket exception to knock-and-announce rule for drug cases; in order to justify "no knock" entry, police must have reasonable suspicion that announcing presence would expose either themselves or others to danger, would be futile under circumstances, or would inhibit proper investigation of crime; here, officers had reasonable suspicion that defendant might destroy evidence if given opportunity to do so and, therefore, "no knock" entry did not violate Amd. IV. Wisconsin Court of Appeals affirmed. (9-0; Stevens, J., DOC.)

Case Name	Charge on Arrest	Authority for Arrest	Articles Seized	Warrant Clause	Exceptions to Warrant Clause	Decision
United States v. Ramirez, 523 U.S. 65 (1998)	Felon in possession of firearms	Shelby escaped from custody; informant reported sighting of person resembling Shelby at defendant's residence confirmed by officer; police requested and received "no knock" warrant to search residence where person resembling Shelby had been seen; in executing warrant, police simultaneously identified themselves and broke window through which they pointed gun; defendant responded by firing shots into ceiling; defendant then surrendered	Gun	"No knock" warrant for premises where escapee had been seen	"No knock" entry under exigent circumstances	To justify "no knock" warrant, police must have reasonable suspicion that knocking and announcing presence, under particular circumstances, would be dangerous or futile or inhibit effective investigation of crime, such as through destruction of evidence; Amd. IV does not hold officers to higher standard when "no knock" entry results in destruction of property; officers executing search warrant did not violate Amd. IV when they broke garage window during course of "no knock" entry into defendant's residence. CCA reversed; remanded. (9-0; Rehnquist, C.J., DOC.)
County of Sacramento v. Lewis, 523 U.S. 833 (1998)	Police responding to call saw motorcycle, on which there were two individuals, approaching them at high speed; although individuals on motorcycle had nothing to do with police call, police signaled them to stop; instead of stopping, driver maneuvered motorcycle between police cars and then sped off; police began high-speed pursuit; motorcycle tipped over and patrol car skidded into passenger, who died at scene; parents of deceased filed action	NA	None	NA	NA	Amd. IV covers only searches and seizures, neither of which is present in instant case; police pursuit in attempting to seize person is not itself seizure within meaning of Amd. IV; neither governmentally desired and/or caused termination of individual's freedom of movement is seizure within meaning of Amd. IV unless there is governmental termination of freedom of movement through intentionally applied means. CCA reversed. (9-0; Souter, J., DOC; Rehnquist, C.J., c/j; Kennedy & O'Connor, JJ., c/j; Breyer, J., c/j; Stevens, J., c/j; Scalia & Thomas, JJ., c/j.)

Case Name	Charge on Arrest	Authority for Arrest	Articles Seized	Warrant Clause	Exceptions to Warrant Clause	Decision
County of Sacramento v. Lewis (continued)	(continued) under 42 U.S.C. § 1983 alleging deprivation of passenger's substantive due process rights to life					
Minnesota v. Carter, 525 U.S. 83 (1998)	Aiding and abetting, conspiracy to commit controlled substance crime.	Following up on tip, officer looked through window and observed people in apartment packaging white powder into bags; when defendants left apartment, they were stopped and police saw handgun on floor of automobile; defendants arrested and search of automobile revealed cocaine, pagers, and scales; police later searched apartment and seized more drugs	Car, gun, cocaine, scales, pagers	Search warrant for later search of apartment	None	Ability of individuals to claim protection of Amd. IV depends on whether individuals have legitimate expectation of privacy in invaded space; expectation of privacy in property used for commercial purposes is different from and less than that in residential property; defendants in another's home for short time solely for purpose of packaging drugs had no legitimate expectation of privacy in home and, therefore, any search that may have occurred did not violate their Amd. IV rights. Minnesota Supreme Court reversed; remanded. (6-3; Rehnquist, C.J., DOC; Scalia & Thomas, JJ., c/j; Kennedy, J., c/j; Breyer, J., c/j; Ginsburg, Stevens, & Souter, JJ., dissent.)

Case Name	Charge on Arrest	Authority for Arrest	Articles Seized	Warrant Clause	Exceptions to Warrant Clause	Decision
Knowles v. Iowa, 525 U.S. 113 (1998)	Possession of controlled substance, keeping controlled substance in automobile	Police stopped defendant for speeding and issued citation rather than placing defendant under arrest; officer then conducted full search of automobile pursuant to state statute that had been interpreted by state appellate court as allowing search when only citation issued; bag of marijuana and pipe found under driver seat	Marijuana and pipe	None	Search incident to arrest not applicable	Two historical rationales for search incident to arrest exception recognized in *United States v. Robinson*, 414 U.S. 218 (1973): (1) need to disarm suspect to take him into custody and (2) need to preserve evidence for later use at trial; while there is concern for officer safety in routine traffic stop, it does not *by itself* justify greater intrusion attending full field-type search; inasmuch as no further evidence of offense of speeding was to be found on defendant's person or in passenger compartment of automobile, there was no need to search automobile to preserve evidence; bright-line rule developed in *Robinson* will not be extended to situation present here where not same level of concern for officer safety and no concern for destruction or loss of evidence. Iowa Supreme Court reversed and remanded. (9-0; Rehnquist, C.J., DOC.)
Maryland v. Dyson, 527 U.S. 465 (1999)	Conspiracy to possess cocaine with intent to distribute	Police received information from CI that defendant had gone to New York to buy drugs and would return to Maryland in specified car later that day with large amount of cocaine; police corroborated tip; when defendant drove specified car into county, he was stopped and car searched; 23 grams of cocaine found in bag in trunk of car	23 grams of cocaine and duffle bag	No warrant	PC, automobile	Amd. IV generally requires police to secure SW before conducting search; there is exception to this requirement for searches of automobiles if automobile is readily mobile and PC exists to believe it contains contraband; there is no separate exigency requirement for automobile exception; as lower court found abundant PC that automobile contained contraband, this finding alone satisfied automobile exception to Amd. IV. Maryland Court of Special Appeals reversed. (7-2; Per curiam, DOC; Breyer & Stevens, JJ., dissent.)

Case Name	Charge on Arrest	Authority for Arrest	Articles Seized	Warrant Clause	Exceptions to Warrant Clause	Decision
Wyoming v. Houghton, 526 U.S. 295 (1999)	Felony possession of controlled substance	During traffic stop, officer noticed needle in plain sight on driver's person; defendant, who was passenger, was asked to step out of car; police search of defendant's purse and car revealed drug paraphernalia	Syringes, methamphetamine, paraphernalia	No warrant	PC, automobile	Police officers, having PC to believe car contains contraband, may inspect passenger's belongings found in car that are capable of concealing object of search. Wyoming Supreme Court reversed. (6-3; Scalia, J., DOC; Breyer, J., c/j; Stevens, Souter, & Ginsburg, JJ., dissent.)
Florida v. White, 526 U.S. 559 (1999)	Possession of cocaine	Police observed defendant using car to deliver cocaine; when defendant arrested on unrelated charge, police legally seized car under state forfeiture law due to its use to transport cocaine; cocaine discovered in car	Car, cocaine	No warrant	Automobile as forfeitable contraband	Amd. IV does not require police to obtain warrant before seizing automobile from public place when there is probable cause to believe it is forfeitable contraband under state statute. Florida Supreme Court reversed and remanded. (7-2; Thomas, J., DOC; Souter & Breyer, JJ., c/j; Stevens & Ginsburg, JJ., dissent.)
Hanlon v. Berger, 525 U.S. 808 (1999)	Ranch owners brought *Bivens* action against federal agents and reporters and photographers of CNN alleging that search of property, which was taped by CNN, violated owners' Amd. IV rights	NA	NA	NA	None	Police violate Amd. IV rights of homeowners by allowing members of media to accompany them during execution of warrant in home; because law on this issue was not clearly established prior to date of this decision, police entitled to defense of qualfied immunity. CCA reversed; remanded. (8-1-1; per curiam; Stevens, J., c/p, d/p.)
Wilson v. Layne, 526 U.S. 603 (1999)	Federal and state law enforcement officers, accompanied by representatives of media, went to petitioners' home to execute arrest warrant; media photographer took photographs in home and reporter present when officer talked to	NA	NA	NA	None	Absent warrant or exigent circumstances, police cannot enter home to make arrest; arrest warrant founded on PC implicitly carries with it limited authority to enter dwelling in which suspect lives when there is reason to believe suspect is within; while not every action taken by police while inside dwelling must be explicitly authorized by wording of warrant,

Case Name	Charge on Arrest	Authority for Arrest	Articles Seized	Warrant Clause	Exceptions to Warrant Clause	Decision
Wilson v. Layne (continued)	(continued) petitioner; none of photographs taken by media were published; after officers ascertained person for whom warrant was issued was not present in home, police and media representatives left; homeowners brought action under 42 U.S.C. § 1983 and *Bivens* against officers alleging that officers' actions in bringing media representatives into their home to observe and record attempted execution of warrant violated their Amd. IV rights					(continued) Amd. IV requires that they be related to objectives of authorized intrusion; Amd. IV violated when police bring members of media or other third parties into home during execution of warrant when presence of third parties in home is not for purpose of assisting in execution of warrant; inasmuch as media's presence in this case not reasonably related to objective of arrest warrant, which was arrest of Wilson, it violated owners' Amd. IV right; officers entitled to qualified immunity and shielded from civil damages because this Amd. IV right of owners was not clearly established at time of incident. CCA affirmed. (8-1-1; Rehnquist, C.J., DOC; Stevens, J., c/p, d/p.)
Flippo v. West Virginia, 528 U.S. 11 (1999)	Murder	Responding to call for assistance from defendant, police found his wife dead; police secured crime scene for processing; officers found, opened, and searched briefcase at scene; inside briefcase were photographs that provided sufficient motive to charge defendant with murder.	Photographs, negatives	No warrant	Murder scene exception rejected	Reiterating holding in *Mincey v. Arizona*, 437 U.S. 385, Court held there is no murder scene exception to warrant clause of Amd. IV that would allow warrantless searches of everything found within crime scene once it is secured. West Virginia Supreme Court of Appeals reversed; remanded. (9-0; per curiam.)

Case Name	Charge on Arrest	Authority for Arrest	Articles Seized	Warrant Clause	Exceptions to Warrant Clause	Decision
Illinois v. Wardlow, 528 U.S. 119 (2000)	Unlawful use of weapon by felon	Suspect fled when he saw police vehicles; police chased, caught him, patted him down, and discovered gun	Gun	No warrant	Sufficient RAS	Unprovoked flight upon sighting of police in area of high drug trafficking is enough to create RAS of criminal behavior and sufficient justification for protective pat-down. Illinois Supreme Court reversed; remanded. (5-4; Rehnquist, C.J., DOC; Stevens, Souter, Ginsburg, & Breyer, JJ., c/p, d/p.)
Florida v. J.L., 529 U.S. 266 (2000)	Carrying concealed firearm without license, possessing firearm under age of 18	Police received anonymous tip that young black male wearing plaid shirt at bus stop carrying gun; police approached defendant, who matched description, and other youths at bus stop and, based on tip alone, searched them; gun was found on defendant	Gun	No warrant	Insufficient RAS (anonymous tip)	Anonymous tip that person carrying gun is not, without more, sufficient justification for police to stop and frisk that person; without any predictive features, tip lacks sufficient reliability to provide RAS. Supreme Court of Florida affirmed. (9-0; Ginsburg, J., DOC; Kennedy, J., & Rehnquist, C.J., c/j.)
Bond v. United States, 529 U.S. 334 (2000)	Conspiracy to possess, PWID methamphetamine	After stopping bus to check for illegal aliens, border patrol agent proceeded to squeeze and feel passenger bags placed in overhead compartments; upon feeling hard brick-shaped object in defendant's bag, agent asked for and received consent to search; methamphetamine found in bag	Methamphetamine	No warrant	None	Law enforcement officer's search of bag, by squeezing and physical manipulation, that defendant carried onto cross-country bus and placed in rack directly above him violated Amd. IV protection because defendant had reasonable expectation that another person would not feel bag in exploratory manner. CCA reversed. (7-2; Rehnquist, C.J., DOC; Breyer & Scalia, JJ., dissent.)

Case Name	Charge on Arrest	Authority for Arrest	Articles Seized	Warrant Clause	Exceptions to Warrant Clause	Decision
Indianapolis v. Edmond, 531 U.S. 32 (2000)	Action filed by defendants, on behalf of all persons stopped at checkpoint or who were subject to being stopped at narcotics checkpoints, under 42 U.S.C. § 1983 alleging roadblocks violated Amd. IV and state constitution	Police set up roadblocks at which predetermined number of vehicles were stopped, license and registration documentation examined, drivers observed for signs of impairment, open view examination of vehicle from outside conducted, and outside of vehicle subjected to examination by narcotics dog	NA	No warrant	Special needs not applicable	Roadblock program violates Amd. IV because primary purpose was to advance general interest in crime or narcotics control; checkpoints intended to detect general crime must be satisfied by some quantum of individualized suspicion; prior holdings addressing sobriety and border checkpoints not affected by this decision. CCA affirmed. (6-3; O'Connor, J. DOC; Rehnquist, C.J., Thomas & Scalia, JJ., dissent; Thomas, J., dissent.)
Illinois v. McArthur, 531 U.S. 326 (2001)	Misdemeanor charges of possession of marijuana and drug paraphernalia	Based on information provided by defendant's wife, one officer went to get search warrant for home while other officer, securing residence, refused to allow defendant in home unaccompanied for almost two hours until search warrant was issued; when search warrant executed, marijuana and drug paraphernalia found	Marijuana and drug paraphernalia	Search warrant	None	Officer's refusal to allow defendant to enter home for almost two hours while another officer obtained search warrant was reasonable restriction and not in violation of Amd. IV because police had PC to believe home contained evidence of jailable offense and contraband—drugs—and reason to believe defendant would destroy drugs before search warrant arrived. Appellate Court of Illinois reversed; remanded. (8-1; Breyer, J., DOC; Souter, J., c/j; Stevens, J., dissent.) Because immediate objective of search

Case Name	Charge on Arrest	Authority for Arrest	Articles Seized	Warrant Clause	Exceptions to Warrant Clause	Decision
Ferguson v. City of Charleston, 532 U.S. 67 (2001)	Defendants were women whose blood was tested for presence of drugs by state hospital personnel pursuant to policy established by hospital personnel in conjunction with law enforcement and who, upon positive results, were arrested for violations of state narcotics laws; action filed under 42 U.S.C. § 1983 alleging seizure of blood violated Amd. IV	NA	Blood	No warrant	Special needs not applicable	Because immediate objective of search policy was to obtain evidence for law enforcement purposes, special needs exception did not apply and searches of patients' blood pursuant to policy violated Amd. IV. CCA reversed; remanded for determination of whether valid consent given. (6-3; Stevens, J., DOC; Kennedy, J., c/j; Scalia & Thomas, JJ., Rehnquist, C.J., dissent.)
Atwater v. City of Lago Vista, 532 U.S. 318, *reh. denied*, 533 U.S. 924 (2001)	Misdemeanor charges of driving without seatbelt, failure to secure children in seatbelts, driving without license, and failure to provide proof of insurance	Local police officer observed defendant driving vehicle in which, contrary to law, neither she nor her young children on front seat were wearing seatbelts	NA	No warrant	Probable cause to believe defendant has committed criminal offense in presence of law enforcement officer	Custodial warrantless arrest for misdemeanor charge, which might ultimately only result in fine, does not violate Amd. IV provided arrest is supported by PC. CCA affirmed. (5-4; Souter, J., DOC; O'Connor, Stevens, Ginsburg & Breyer, JJ., dissent.)
Arkansas v. Sullivan, 532 U.S. 769 (2001)	PWID methamphetamine, attempt to manufacture methamphetamine, possession of drug paraphernalia, unlawful possession of weapon, driving without registration and insurance documentation, and speeding	Defendant stopped for speeding and improperly tinted windshield; upon seeing defendant's license, officer realized that he had narcotics intelligence information on defendant; defendant arrested for driving and weapon offenses; inventory of defendant's car revealed methamphetamine and drug paraphernalia under armrest	Methamphetamine, roofing hatchet, and drug paraphernalia	No warrant	Inventory of automobile after arrest	Reiterating holding in *Whren v. United States,* 517 U.S. 806 (1996), subjective motivation of police officers in making arrest is not to be considered in determination of whether PC existed; arrest, for which PC exists, is not invalid because it was pretext for narcotics search; state courts may not interpret federal constitution to impose greater restrictions on police activities than those imposed by U.S. Supreme Court. Arkansas Supreme Court reversed; remanded. (9-0; per curiam; Ginsburg, Stevens, O'Connor, & Breyer, JJ., c/j.)

Case Name	Charge on Arrest	Authority for Arrest	Articles Seized	Warrant Clause	Exceptions to Warrant Clause	Decision
Kyllo v. United States, 533 U.S. 27 (2001)	Manufacturing marijuana	Police, suspecting defendant growing marijuana in home, used thermal imager to scan home; scan revealed areas that were hotter than other parts of home and other residences in triplex; based on tip from informant, defendant's utility bills, and scan, police obtained and executed search warrant leading to discovery of indoor growing operation involving more than 100 plants	Marijuana plants	Search warrant	None	Police use of technology that is not in public use, such as thermal imaging device used here, to explore details of home that would have otherwise have been unexplorable without physical intrusion constitutes search that is presumptively unreasonable in absence of search warrant. CCA reversed; case remanded for determination whether, without evidence provided by thermal scan, there was sufficient PC to support search warrant and, if not, whether any other basis existed for supporting admission of evidence produced as result of search warrant. (5-4; Scalia, J., DOC; Stevens, O'Connor & Kennedy, JJ., Rehnquist, C.J., dissent.)
United States v. Knights, 534 U.S. 112 (2001)	Conspiracy to commit arson, possession of unregistered destructive device, and felon in possession of ammunition	Defendant on probation for drug offense; condition of probation provided that he and his home and vehicle were subject to search without warrant at any time and by any police or probation officer; suspecting that defendant was involved in series of crimes, police, relying on terms of defendant's probation, searched his home without warrant	Incriminating evidence including detonation cord, ammunition, liquid chemicals, instruction manuals on chemistry and electrical circuitry, and brass padlock	No warrant	RAS	Touchstone of Amd. IV is reasonableness, and reasonableness of search is determined by balancing degree of intrusion upon individual's privacy against governmental interests involved; defendant's condition of probation authorizing searches significantly diminished his reasonable expectation of privacy; government has strong interest in seeing that probationers successfully complete probation and are reintegrated into society as well as justified concern that probationers are more likely to engage in criminal conduct than ordinary members of society; balance of interests requires no more than RAS to conduct search of home of probationer who is suspected of being engaged in criminal activity. CCA reversed; remanded. (9-0; Rehnquist, C.J., DOC; Souter, J., c/j.)

Case Name	Charge on Arrest	Authority for Arrest	Articles Seized	Warrant Clause	Exceptions to Warrant Clause	Decision
United States v. Arvizu, 534 U.S. 266 (2002)	PWID marijuana	Automobile, of type commonly used by drug smugglers, detected on unpaved road used only by ranchers, forest service personnel and smugglers trying to avoid border checkpoint at time when patrol agents were known to be heading back to checkpoint and not patrolling; patrol agent observed automobile substantially decrease speed upon sighting of agent's vehicle, driver appeared unnaturally stiff and failed to acknowledge presence of agent, knees of two of children in back seat appeared to be unusually high as if their feet were propped up on something on floor, children waved unnaturally to agent, and automobile appeared to avoid next checkpoint; agent, suspecting occupants of automobile of smuggling drugs across border, stopped defendant and searched automobile; search revealed more than 100 pounds of marijuana	More than 100 pounds of marijuana	No warrant	Sufficient RAS	To determine existence of RAS for investigatory stop of automobile, courts must look at TOC to decide if detaining officer had particularized and objective basis for suspecting illegal activity; this evaluative process allows officers to make use of own experience and training to draw inferences that might elude untrained person; under TOC standard, factors or acts considered by detaining officer should not be viewed in isolation inasmuch as acts of behavior might, when viewed separately, appear seemingly innocent but collectively might warrant investigation; while review of RAS determinations on appeal is de novo, appellate court should consider trial court's superior access to evidence. CCA reversed; remanded. (8-1; Rehnquist, C.J., DOC; Scalia, J., dissent.)

Case Name	Charge on Arrest	Authority for Arrest	Articles Seized	Warrant Clause	Exceptions to Warrant Clause	Decision
United States v. Drayton, 122 S. Ct. 2105 (2002)	Conspiracy to distribute cocaine and PWID cocaine	Defendants on Greyhound bus that made scheduled stop; passengers required to get off bus so that it could be refueled and cleaned; as passengers reboarded, driver checked their tickets and then left bus to complete paperwork; three plainclothes members of local police department, carrying concealed weapons and visible badges, allowed to board bus for routine drug and weapons interdiction effort; as one officer knelt in driver's seat, the other two went to back of bus and made their way forward; as they walked to front of bus, one officer asked individual passengers about travel plans and to identify baggage while second officer stood nearby; defendants asked to consent to search of bags and their persons and they did so; drug packages found on both defendants contained total of 778 grams of cocaine	Cocaine	No warrant	Consent	Even without basis for suspecting criminal wrongdoing, law enforcement officers do not violate Amd. IV merely by approaching individuals in public places and questioning them, asking for identification, or requesting consent to search if the individuals are willing to listen and officers do not use coercive means to induce cooperation; if reasonable person would feel free to terminate encounter, then there has been no seizure under Amd. IV; for most part, per se rules are inappropriate in Amd. IV context; proper inquiry in cases involving drug interdiction efforts on buses is whether reasonable person would feel free to decline officers' requests or otherwise end encounter; reasonable person test is objective and presupposes innocent person; no constitutional requirement that police must inform individuals of right to refuse when requesting permission to conduct warrantless consent search; TOC control, without placing extra weight on absence of warning of right to refuse; here, although officer did not advise defendants of right to refuse, TOC indicates that consent was voluntary and searches reasonable. CCA reversed. (6-3; Kennedy, J., DOC; Souter, Stevens, & Ginsburg, JJ., dissent.)

Case Name	Charge on Arrest	Authority for Arrest	Articles Seized	Warrant Clause	Exceptions to Warrant Clause	Decision
Board of Education v. Earls, 536 U.S. 822 (2002)	NA	Board of Education implemented drug testing policy requiring students involved in extracurricular activities to submit to drug testing; policy required pre-participation testing, random testing, and testing upon reasonable suspicion; testing done under circumstances to insure some privacy of student; testing designed to detect only use of illegal drugs and not medical conditions or presence of authorized prescription medications; results of testing not reported to law enforcement; action filed under 42 U.S.C. § 1983 by parents of students alleging policy, both on its face and as applied, violated Amd. IV.	Urine sample	No warrant	Special needs	Searches by public school officials, including collection of urine samples, implicate Amd. IV; public school drug testing policy must be reviewed for reasonableness, which is standard of constitutionality of government searches; while reasonableness usually requires showing of PC, this PC standard is unsuited to determination of reasonableness of administrative searches where government seeks to prevent development of hazardous conditions; in context of safety and administrative regulations, searches unsupported by PC may be reasonable when special needs beyond need for law enforcement make warrant and PC requirements impractical; warrant and finding of PC unnecessary in public school context; Amd. IV rights are different in public schools and reasonableness inquiry cannot disregard schools' custodial and tutelary responsibility for students; in public school environment, student's privacy interest is limited due to state's responsibility for maintaining discipline, health and safety; character of intrusion under policy is insignificant due to minimally intrusive means of collecting samples and limited use to which test results are put; no constitutional need to show specific or pervasive drug problem before suspiciousness drug testing may be conducted; reasonable for school board to enact policy in light of nationwide epidemic of drug use and evidence of drug use in district school; testing students who participate in extracurricular activities

Case Name	Charge on Arrest	Authority for Arrest	Articles Seized	Warrant Clause	Exceptions to Warrant Clause	Decision
Board of Education v. Earls (continued)						(continued) is reasonably effective means of addressing school board's legitimate concerns in preventing, deterring and detecting drug use; policy not violate Amd. IV. CCA reversed. (5-4; Thomas, J., DOC; Breyer, J., concurs; O'Connor, Souter, JJ., dissent; Ginsburg, Stevens, O'Connor, Souter, JJ., dissent.)
Kaupp v. Texas, 538 U.S. 626 (2003)	Murder	Suspect, who failed three lie detector tests, implicated 17-year-old Kaupp in a murder. Although lacking PC, police went to Kaupp's home at 3 a.m., woke him saying "we need to go and talk." Kaupp said "Okay." Police then handcuffed him, and took him, shoeless and in only his underwear, to police station where, after being given Miranda warnings, he admitted to participating in the crime. Texas Court of Appeals found Kaupp voluntarily consented to go with police.	Person	No warrant	Consent	Kaupp' s admissions were the fruit of an unlawful seizure. Kaupp's "okay" in response to the detective's statement "we need to go and talk" was not consent, but rather "'mere submission to a claim of lawful authority.'" Furthermore, placing him in handcuffs and removing him from his home shoeless and in his underwear, would have transformed any initial consensual encounter into a seizure. A confession obtained after an arrest that is not supported by PC must be suppressed unless it was "an act of free will" sufficiently independent of the illegal arrest. *Wong Sun v. United States*, 371 U.S. 471 (1963). Texas Court of Appeals vacated; remanded on *Wong Sun* issue. (9-0; per curiam.)

Case Name	Charge on Arrest	Authority for Arrest	Articles Seized	Warrant Clause	Exceptions to Warrant Clause	Decision
United States v. Banks, 540 U.S. 31 (2003)	Drug and firearms charges	Police executing search warrant for cocaine rapped on door, identified themselves and their purpose, and, after waiting 15 or 20 seconds, broke open door with a battering ram; search revealed weapons, crack cocaine, and other evidence of drug dealing.	Weapons, crack cocaine, and other evidence of drug dealing	Search warrant	None	Common law knock-and-announce requirement is designed to prevent damage to property by permitting homeowner to allow peaceful entry. However, where police have reasonable suspicion that giving notice may endanger officers or frustrate the purpose of the search, they may damage property to the extent reasonably necessary to gain immediate entry. The time period that police executing search warrant must wait before entering premises without permission after knocking and announcing their intent to search will vary depending on facts known to police in each case. Here the danger of the destruction of contraband created an exigency justifying forced entry and a wait of only 15 to 20 seconds was reasonable. The test is not how long it would take to get to the door, but how long it would take to destroy the cocaine. CCA reversed. (9-0; Souter, J., DOC.)
Maryland v. Pringle, 540 U.S. 366 (2003)	Possession of cocaine and PWID cocaine	Pringle was a front-seat passenger in a vehicle stopped for traffic law violations; driver consented to search of car; five bags of crack cocaine found behind back-seat armrest; $763 found in case in glove compartment; driver and both passengers arrested.	Cocaine and currency	No warrant	Consent	Although PC "must be particularized with respect to the person to be searched or seized," arrest here was constitutional because the totality of the circumstances (including large quantities of cash and drugs) created reasonable belief that defendant was engaged with the other occupants of the car in a common enterprise involving drug dealing. Maryland Court of Appeals reversed; remanded. (9-0; Rehnquist, C.J., DOC.)

Case Name	Charge on Arrest	Authority for Arrest	Articles Seized	Warrant Clause	Exceptions to Warrant Clause	Decision
Illinois v. Lidster, 540 U.S. 419 (2004)	DUI	Police operated checkpoint seeking information to help solve recent fatal hit-and-run accident; as Lidster approached checkpoint, he swerved, almost hitting officer; police pulled him over, smelled alcohol, and administered field sobriety tests.	Defendant	None	Information-seeking checkpoint	Distinguishing *Indianapolis v. Edmond*, 531 U.S. 32 (2000) (narcotics checkpoint), where the primary purpose of the roadblock was to discover *evidence* of criminal activity, here the primary purpose of the seizure was to seek information about a specific previously committed crime, not evidence. Balancing "the gravity of the public concerns served by the seizure" (solving homicide) against the "few seconds" of contact with police, the momentary seizure to ask for assistance in solving a crime was reasonable. Illinois Supreme Court reversed. (6-3; Breyer, J., DOC; Stevens, Souter & Ginsburg, JJ., concur in part & dissent in part.)
Groh v. Ramirez, 540 U.S. 551 (2004)	NA: Civil Rights Action	Although application for search warrant for weapons described items to be seized with specificity, the search warrant itself, prepared by ATF agent, did not describe the items to be seized or incorporate the application and thus was facially defective. Due to agent's error not caught by authorizing judge, the warrant described items to be seized as a "two story blue house." Agent was sued under § 1983 for violation of Amd. IV.	NA	Search warrant	NA	Amd. IV requires that search warrants describe with particularity the items to be seized; this requirement cannot be satisfied by a description contained in supporting documentation that is not incorporated by reference in the warrant and available at time search conducted. Search pursuant to a warrant that does not particularly describe the items to be seized is unconstitutional. Agent not entitled to qualified immunity because error was a "glaring defect." CCA affirmed. (5-4; Stevens, J., DOC; Kennedy, J., & Rehnquist, C.J., dissent; Thomas & Scalia, JJ., & Rehnquist, C.J., dissent.)

Case Name	Charge on Arrest	Authority for Arrest	Articles Seized	Warrant Clause	Exceptions to Warrant Clause	Decision
Hiibel v. Sixth Judicial District Court of Nevada, 542 U.S. 177 (2004)	Violation of stop and identify law	Officer was investigating report of fight; Hiibel repeatedly refused to identify himself and was arrested.	Person of defendant	No warrant	NA	State statute authorizing arrest of person who refuses to disclose his name during a valid investigating stop based upon reasonable suspicion does not violate Amd. IV. *Brown v. Texas*, 443 U.S. 47 (1979), distinguished. Nevada Supreme Court affirmed. (5-4; Kennedy, J., DOC; Stevens, J., dissents; Breyer, Souter & Ginsburg, JJ., dissent).
United States v. Flores-Montano, 541 U.S. 149 (2004)	Unlawful transportation of marijuana and PWID marijuana	Flores-Montano drove a vehicle to the Mexico-United States border; he was asked to leave his car at the U.S. border while it was inspected before entry; because the gas tank sounded solid, it was removed and disassembled; 81 pounds of marijuana were found and removed from the gas tank.	Marijuana	No warrant	Border search	*United States v. Ramsey*, 431 U.S. 606 (1977), held that routine searches of persons and their property at national borders, without probable cause or reasonable suspicion, are constitutionally reasonable. The removal, disassembly, and reassembly of a vehicle's fuel tank were therefore permissible intrusions during a search at the border. The distinction between "routine" and more intrusive searches made in *United States v. Montoya de Hernandez*, 473 U.S. 31 (1985), is not applicable to vehicles. CCA reversed; remanded. (9-0; Rehnquist, C.J., DOC; Breyer, J., concurs.)
Thornton v. United States, 541 U.S. 615 (2004)	PWID cocaine and firearms offenses	Prompted by driver's suspicious behavior, police ran a license tag check and learned that the tags did not match the vehicle; before police could pull the vehicle over, driver parked it and got out; police approached and discovered marijuana and crack cocaine during patdown search to which driver consented; driver arrested; search of vehicle incident to arrest revealed a handgun.	Marijuana, crack cocaine, and handgun	No warrant	Search incident to arrest	Even if arrestee was not in the vehicle at the time he was placed under arrest, police can conduct a search of the vehicle incident to that arrest, as long as the arrestee was a "recent occupant" of the vehicle. *New York v. Belton*, 453 U.S. 454 (1981), extended, but see *Arizona v. Gant* 129 S. Ct. 1710 (2009), significantly limiting application of *Belton*. CCA affirmed. (7-2; Rehnquist, C.J., DOC; O'Connor, J. concurs in part; Scalia and Ginsburg, JJ., concur; Stevens & Souter, JJ., dissent.)

Case Name	Charge on Arrest	Authority for Arrest	Articles Seized	Warrant Clause	Exceptions to Warrant Clause	Decision
Devenpeck v. Alford, 543 US. 146 (2004)	Violation of state privacy act and flashing headlights	Police suspected Alford, who had fitted his car with lights that flash at pre-set intervals, of being a police impersonator and stopped him; Alford had handcuffs, a police scanner, and a police radio in his car; officers noticed he had been tape recording their conversation during the stop and arrested him for violating the state privacy act. The charges were dismissed because taping police conversations did not violate that act. Alford filed § 1983 suit alleging police arrested him without PC.	NA	NA	NA	An officer's subjective reason for making an arrest (mistaken belief privacy act violation had occurred) was irrelevant where the facts known to the officer were sufficient to constitute PC to arrest for a different offense (impersonating an officer). Constitution does not require that a person be informed of the reason for his arrest at the time he is taken into custody. Because there was PC to arrest for impersonating an officer, arrest was lawful, although officer intended to arrest him for a different offense. CCA reversed, remanded. (8-0; Scalia, J., DOC; Rehnquist, C.J., took no part.)
Brosseau v. Haugen, 543 U.S. 194 (2004)	NA; Civil Rights Action	Police responded to call that Haugen, for whom a no-bond felony warrant had been issued, and another man were fighting outside a residence; Haugen fled the scene on foot and police pursued; Haugen returned to his vehicle and, as he was driving away, police fired a shot, wounding him; Haugen brought § 1983 action against police.	NA	NA	NA	Reiterating rule in *Tennessee v. Garner*, 471 U.S. 1 (1985), the seizure of an unarmed, non-dangerous suspect by the use of deadly force violates Amd. IV, but the use of deadly force to prevent the escape of a suspect who poses a threat of serious physical harm to police or others is not constitutionally unreasonable. Here the shooting by police was not "clearly" in violation of Amd. IV; police officer entitled to qualified immunity. CCA reversed, remanded. (8-1; per curiam DOC; Breyer, Scalia, & Ginsburg, JJ., concur; Stevens, J., dissents.)

Case Name	Charge on Arrest	Authority for Arrest	Articles Seized	Warrant Clause	Exceptions to Warrant Clause	Decision
Illinois v. Caballes, 543 U.S. 405 (2005)	Narcotics offense	Caballes stopped for speeding; while an officer wrote a warning ticket, a narcotics-detection dog was walked around the car by another officer; the dog alerted on the vehicle's trunk; search of trunk revealed marijuana.	Marijuana	No warrant	NA	Amd. IV not implicated where narcotics detector dog sniffs the exterior of a car for contraband during a valid traffic stop without prolonging the time "reasonably required" to make the "ordinary inquiries incident to such a stop" and write the traffic citation. Because there is no legitimate expectation of privacy with respect to contraband, the dog sniff is not a search. Thus, no justification for using dog is required. Illinois Supreme Court vacated; remanded. (6-2; Stevens, J., DOC; Souter, J., dissents; Ginsburg & Souter, JJ., dissent; Rehnquist, C.J. took no part.)
Muehler v. Mena, 544 U.S. 93 (2006)	NA: Civil Rights Action	During investigation of gang-related shooting, police obtained search warrant for home of suspect believed to be armed and dangerous; warrant authorized search for weapons and evidence of gang membership; Mena, a lawful permanent resident, was detained in handcuffs for three hours and interrogated by an INS agent about her immigration status; she filed § 1983 suit alleging length and manner of her detention was unreasonable.	Handgun, ammunition, marijuana, and gang paraphernalia	Search warrant	NA	Police have categorical authority to detain occupants of premises incident to execution of a search warrant for contraband so no justification for detention is needed even though Mena was not a suspect. Included in authority to detain is authority to use reasonable force to effectuate the detention. Here, the use of handcuffs for the duration of the search was reasonable because police were searching for weapons and evidence of gang membership and there were multiple occupants present. The questioning about Mena's immigration status did not constitute an additional seizure or turn a lawful seizure into an unlawful seizure because it did not prolong the seizure beyond the time needed to execute the search warrant. CCA vacated; remanded. (9-0; Rehnquist, C.J., DOC; Kennedy, J., concurs; Stevens, Souter, Ginsburg & Breyer, JJ., concur.)

Case Name	Charge on Arrest	Authority for Arrest	Articles Seized	Warrant Clause	Exceptions to Warrant Clause	Decision
United States v. Grubbs, 547 U.S. 90 (2006).	Receiving child pornography	Grubbs purchased videotape containing child pornography from Internet site operated by undercover law enforcement officer; police obtained anticipatory search warrant and arranged for controlled delivery of tape; Grubbs was detained after tape was delivered and admitted ordering it.	Videotape containing child pornography	Anticipatory search warrant	NA	Amd. IV does not prohibit an anticipatory search warrant based on "probable cause that at some future time (but not presently) certain evidence of crime will be located at a specified place." In most cases, a specified triggering condition must occur before warrant may be executed, because only then will there be PC to justify the search. The magistrate must find PC that the triggering condition will occur; however, the triggering condition need not be stated on face of warrant. In this case, the triggering condition (delivery of package) had occurred before warrant was executed. CCA reversed. (8-0; Scalia, J., DOC; Souter, Stevens, & Ginsburg, JJ. concur; Alito, J. took no part.)
Georgia v. Randolph, 547 U.S. 103 (2006)	Possession of cocaine	Randolph's estranged wife called police over child custody dispute. When police arrived, wife alleged Randolph used cocaine, which he denied; wife said there was evidence of drugs in the house; Randolph refused to consent to search; wife then gave permission for police to search the home; police found and seized straw with suspected cocaine residue; wife then withdrew consent and police obtained search warrant; execution of warrant revealed additional evidence of drug use.	Evidence of drug use, including straw with suspected cocaine residue	Search warrant	3d party consent	Police reliance upon invitation of one occupant to enter premises to search for evidence is not reasonable where co-tenant is present and objecting. *Illinois v. Rodriguez*, 497 U.S. 177 (1990) (defendant asleep at time of entry) distinguished. Second search pursuant to warrant invalid because based on evidence obtained pursuant to initial illegal entry and search. Georgia Supreme Court affirmed. (5-3; Souter, J., DOC; Stevens, J., concurs; Breyer, J., concurs; Roberts, C.J. & Scalia, J. dissent; Alito, J. took no part.)

Case Name	Charge on Arrest	Authority for Arrest	Articles Seized	Warrant Clause	Exceptions to Warrant Clause	Decision
Brigham City, Utah v. Stuart, 547 U.S. 398 (2006)	Contributing to delinquency of minor, disorderly conduct and intoxication.	Police responded to 3 a.m. call about a loud party; upon arrival, heard shouting from house and proceeded to investigate; police saw juveniles drinking beer in yard and an altercation taking place inside the house despite observed efforts of other people to stop it; police entered house to render assistance and made arrest.	Unspecified	No warrant	Exigent circumstances	Police may enter home without a warrant to render aid and restore order if there is an objectively reasonable basis for believing someone inside is seriously injured or imminently threatened with such injury. Even if police entered to make arrests, subjective motivations are irrelevant if objective facts create reasonable belief that assistance is needed to aid the injured and prevent further violence. Entry here was objectively reasonable. Utah Supreme Court reversed, remanded. (9-0; Roberts, C.J., DOC; Stevens, J., concurs).
Hudson v. Michigan, 547 U.S. 586 (2006)	Unlawful drug and firearm possession	Police executing search warrant announced their presence; after waiting only three to five seconds, they entered through unlocked door; search revealed drugs and a firearm.	Loaded gun and large quantities of drugs	Search warrant	NA	Because of the exclusionary rule's "substantial social costs," three conditions must be met before the suppression of evidence is justified. First, the constitutional violation must be the but-for cause of obtaining the evidence. Second, "the interest protected by the constitutional guarantee that has been violated [must be] served by suppression of the evidence." Third, the deterrent benefits of exclusion must outweigh its "substantial social costs." While proper knock-and-announce notice is required, none of the above conditions justify suppression. The evidence was not discovered as a result of the failure to give proper notice. No interest protected by the rule is served by suppression. Finally the substantial social cost of suppression outweighs any deterrent benefit in light of the fact that incentives for violating the Constitution are "minimal" because of "the increasing professionalism of police forces," the "new emphasis on internal

Case Name	Charge on Arrest	Authority for Arrest	Articles Seized	Warrant Clause	Exceptions to Warrant Clause	Decision
Hudson v. Michigan, 547 U.S. 586 (2006)						(continued) police discipline," and the "increasing use of various forms of citizen review." Michigan Court of Appeals affirmed. (5-4; Scalia, J., DOC; Kennedy, J., concurs; Breyer, Stevens, Souter, & Ginsburg, JJ., dissent.)
Samson v. California, 547 U.S. 843 (2006)	Possession of methamphetamine	As a statutory condition of Samson's parole, he agreed in writing to be subject to supicionless searches and seizures; search made solely because he was a parolee revealed methamphetamine.	Methamphetamine	No warrant	NA	The need to search parolees to prevent recidivism is great while parolees, because of their status, have diminished expectations of privacy. Thus, employing a simple balancing test, Court holds Amd. IV does not prohibit police from conducting warrantless and suspicionless search of parolees. California Court of Appeals affirmed. (6-3; Thomas, J., DOC; Stevens, Souter, & Breyer, JJ., concur.)
Scott v. Harris, 550 U.S. 372 (2007)	NA: Civil Rights Action	Police attempted to stop teenage driver going 73 mph in 55 mph zone. Teenager fled, driving recklessly, and police engaged in high speed pursuit reaching 90 mph. Patrol car ultimately rammed rear of fleeing vehicle at an angle causing it to crash, rendering teenager a quadriplegic; driver filed § 1983 suit against police alleging excessive force was used to make the arrest.	NA	No warrant	NA	*Tennessee v. Garner*, 471 U.S. 1 (1985), did not create rigid preconditions before police may lawfully use deadly force. Instead, the test is whether police acted reasonably under the particular circumstances. Police effort to terminate dangerous high-speed vehicle pursuit that poses danger to bystanders does not violate Amd. IV, even if it places the driver of the fleeing vehicle at risk of injury or death. CCA reversed. (8-1; Scalia, J., DOC; Ginsburg & Breyer, JJ., concur; Stevens, J., dissents.)

Case Name	Charge on Arrest	Authority for Arrest	Articles Seized	Warrant Clause	Exceptions to Warrant Clause	Decision
Los Angeles County v. Rettele, 550 U.S. 609 (2007)	NA: Civil Rights Action	Deputy sheriffs investigating identity theft ring obtained a valid search warrant to search several homes for documents and computer files. Targets of the investigation were African-American, one of whom owned a gun. Three months earlier, the home searched here had been sold to Max Rettele, who moved in with his girlfriend, Judy, and her 17-year-old son. All three are Caucasian. Deputies executing the search warrant were let in by the son, entered the bedroom with guns drawn and ordered Max and Judy out of bed, forcing them to stand naked and refusing to let Judy cover herself with a sheet while they searched. Rettele brought a civil rights action under § 1983.	NA	Search warrant	NA	Observing that "[v]alid warrants will issue to search the innocent," Court finds that, because probable cause does not require absolute certainty, police acted reasonably in executing the warrant. People of different races live together and the "possibility that an armed suspect might sleep with a weapon" that could be hidden in bedding justified the naked detention. CCA reversed, remanded. (Per curiam; Stevens, J., & Ginsburg, J. concurs; Souter, J. would deny petition for cert.)
Brendlin v. California, 551 U.S. 249 (2007)	Possessing and manufacturing methamphetamine	Brendlin was passenger in vehicle stopped without reasonable suspicion; dispatcher confirmed he was parole violator and he was arrested; search incident to arrest revealed drug paraphernalia	Drug paraphernalia	No warrant	Search incident to arrest	Because police have "unquestioned command of the situation" during a traffic stop, no reasonable passenger would believe she is free to leave, even if the stop is only for a traffic offense. Therefore passengers are seized the moment the car comes to a halt and have standing to challenge constitutionality of the stop. California Supreme Court vacated; remanded. (9-0; Souter, J., DOC).

Case Name	Charge on Arrest	Authority for Arrest	Articles Seized	Warrant Clause	Exceptions to Warrant Clause	Decision
Virginia v. Moore, 128 S. Ct. 1598 (2008)	PWID cocaine	Police had probable cause to arrest Moore, who was driving on a suspended license; although state law authorized only issuance of a summons, police made a custodial arrest; search of Moore's person incident to that arrest revealed $516 and 16 grams of crack cocaine.	Crack cocaine	No warrant	Search incident to arrest	The search incident to arrest exception applies only when police make a custodial arrest, *Knowles v. Iowa*, 525 U.S. 113 (1998). Under Virginia law, police are not authorized to make a custodial arrest for driving on a suspended license but are only authorized to issue a summons. Nevertheless, the Court holds that where there is probable cause to believe a crime has been committed in the officer's presence, a warrantless custodial arrest is reasonable under the Fourth Amendment. "It is not the province of the Fourth Amendment to enforce state law," which would lead to a lack of uniformity. Virginia Supreme Court reversed; remanded. (9-0; Scalia, J., DOC; Ginsburg, J. concurs because Virginia does not exclude evidence obtained in violation of its statutes).
Arizona v. Gant, 129 S. Ct. 1710 (2009)	Driving without license; possession of cocaine	Driving without license	Cocaine	No warrant	Search incident to arrest	*New York v. Belton*, 453 U.S. 454 (1981) established a bright line rule permitting police to make an automatic search of the passenger compartment of the car as an incident of the custodial arrest of the driver. Limiting *Belton*, the Court held that the search of a car incident to arrest is valid only if arrestee is unsecured and within reaching distance of the vehicle at the time of the search, or, there is reason to believe the car might contain evidence relevant to the crime for which the arrest is made. Evidence properly suppressed because at the time of search in this case, (1) arrestee had been hand-cuffed and locked in a patrol car; and

Case Name	Charge on Arrest	Authority for Arrest	Articles Seized	Warrant Clause	Exceptions to Warrant Clause	Decision
Arizona v. Gant (continued)						(continued) (2) no evidence of the offense of arrest (driving without license) could have been found in the car. Arizona Supreme Court affirmed. (5-4; Stevens, J. DOC; Scalia, J., concurs separately; Alito, J., dissents, joined by Roberts, C.J., Kennedy, and Breyer, J. in part; Breyer, J., dissents)
Herring v. United States, 129 S. Ct. 695 (2009)	Possession of weapon and drugs	Search incident to an arrest pursuant to warrant that had been withdrawn.	Narcotics and weapon	Warrant had been withdrawn	NA	Arresting officer reasonably relied upon neighboring county's police computer database, which erroneously showed outstanding warrant for defendant. Search incident to arrest on withdrawn warrant concededly illegal, but evidence admitted under good faith exception. Here police clerk's failure to update computer records was attenuated from the arrest and was an isolated, nonrecurring error due to negligence rather than deliberate or reckless misconduct. "To trigger the exclusionary rule, police conduct must be sufficiently deliberate that exclusion can meaningfully deter it and sufficiently culpable that such deterrence is worth the price." CCA affirmed. (5-4, Roberts, C.J. DOC; Ginsburg, Stevens, Souter, Breyer, JJ., dissent.)

Case Name	Charge on Arrest	Authority for Arrest	Articles Seized	Warrant Clause	Exceptions to Warrant Clause	Decision
Pearson v. Callahan, 129 S. Ct. 808 (2009)	Possession and distribution of drugs	Officers sent undercover civilian informant into residential trailer to make controlled buy of drugs; officers made warrantless entry into premises after informant signaled officers that sale had been concluded; officers seized drugs, paraphernalia, and marked currency. After state court held search illegal and reversed conviction, Callahan brought § 1983 action against officers.	Drugs, paraphernalia, marked money	No warrant	Consent	In a 42 USC § 1983 civil rights action, police officers have qualified immunity unless it can be shown that they violated a "clearly established" constitutional rule. Although officers entered plaintiff's home without a warrant, several state and federal courts have recognized an exception known as the "consent once removed doctrine," which provides that, where a homeowner permits either an undercover police officer or a confidential informant to enter his home, this consent to entry also applies to police officers who subsequently enter to make an arrest. Officers here were therefore entitled to qualified immunity because it was not clearly established that their entry was unconstitutional. *Saucier v. Katz*, 533 U.S. 194 (2001), which required courts to decide the merits of the constitutional claim before deciding the issue of qualified immunity, is overruled. Whether the consent once removed doctrine is valid thus still remains undecided. CCA reversed. (9-0; Alito, J., DOC).
Arizona v. Johnson, 129 S. Ct. 781 (2009)	Possession of firearm	During vehicle stop for minor traffic violation, officer learned back-seat passenger, who was wearing gang-associated clothing and had a scanner in his pocket, had been in prison and lived in a town known to have gang activity. Officer asked passenger to exit the car and patted him down, revealing a gun.	Firearm	No warrant	*Terry* weapons patdown	Following *Brendlin v. California*, 551 U.S. 249 (2007), Court holds that because a passenger is lawfully seized for the duration of a traffic stop, an officer who has reasonable suspicion that a passenger is armed and dangerous may conduct a frisk for weapons, without additional suspicion that the passenger is engaged in criminal activity. On remand, the state court is free to consider whether the officer had such a reasonable suspicion. Arizona Court of Appeals reversed, remanded. (9-0; Ginsburg, J. DOC).

Case Name	Charge on Arrest	Authority for Arrest	Articles Seized	Warrant Clause	Exceptions to Warrant Clause	Decision
Safford Unified School District v. Redding, 129 S. Ct. 2633 (2009)	NA; Civil Rights Action	Middle school student told school personnel that she had received contraband pills (ibuprofen) from fellow student Redding; search of Redding's backpack produced no contraband; administrative aide and nurse searched her outer garments, finding nothing, and then conducted what was deemed a strip search; no contraband was found. Redding's mother filed § 1983 action against school district and staff members.	NA	No warrant	Search by school officials	Strip search of 13-year-old girl for suspected contraband held unreasonable on the facts; school officials entitled to qualified immunity; remanded re reliability of school district. CCA reversed and remanded. (8-1 on legality of search; Souter, J., DOC; Stevens and Ginsburg JJ, dissent on immunity issue; Thomas, J. dissents on legality of search, concurs on immunity)
Michigan v. Fisher, 130 S. Ct. 546 (2009)	Assault with dangerous weapon, possession of firearm during commission of felony	Officers responding to complaint of a disturbance by a man "going crazy," observed damaged fence posts, broken house windows, and a truck parked in the driveway with its front smashed. There was blood on the hood, on clothes in the car, and on an outside door of the house. Officers saw defendant inside the house with a cut hand, screaming and throwing things. Asked if he needed medical attention, defendant told officers to get a warrant. When an officer entered house to investigate, defendant pointed a gun at him.	NA	No Warrant	Emergency aid	Following *Brigham City, Utah v. Stuart*, 547 U.S. 398 (2006), the Court concluded that the officer's warrantless entry was reasonable. The emergency aid exception requires only an "objectively reasonable basis" for believing that immediate medical assistance is needed (even if not for a life-threatening injury) or that persons are in danger. Here the officers could reasonably believe that Fisher needed medical assistance or that others in the house were in danger from his rage. Thus the Court reversed the state court decision affirming suppression of the officer's statement that Fisher had pointed a gun at him when he pushed open the door. Michigan Court of Appeals reversed, remanded. (7-2; PC, DOC; Stevens, J., & Sotomayor, 1. dissent)

Case Name	Charge on Arrest	Authority for Arrest	Articles Seized	Warrant Clause	Exceptions to Warrant Clause	Decision
City of Ontario v. Quon, 560 U.S. 746 (2010)	NA. 42 U.S.C. § 1983 action against police chief for reading transcripts of text messages on plaintiff's department-issued pager	NA	Text messages	No warrant	Administrative Search/Special Needs Doctrine	Police Chief's warrantless search of employee's text messages stored on government-issued device was reasonable. Assuming without deciding that employees have REP in their private electronic communications in a government workplace, such expectations are diminished. Search was for a legitimate, non-criminal, work-related purpose and was not excessive in scope. 9-0; Kennedy, J., DOC; Scalia, J., c/p, c/j. *See Riley v. California*, 134 S. Ct. 2473 (2014), *infra*, regarding cell phone searches.
Kentucky v. King, 563 U.S. 452 (2011)	Trafficking in marijuana	PC. Officer banged on door of suspected drug dealer's apartment, shouting "police, police" and upon hearing people moving inside, feared imminent destruction of evidence and kicked in the door, discovering drugs.	Marijuana and cocaine	No warrant	Exigent Circumstances	Police may manufacture exigent circumstances so long as the conduct that creates the "emergency" does not violate or threaten to violate the Fourth Amendment. Banging on door and yelling "police" was lawful conduct. PC was conceded.8-1; Alito, J., DOC; Ginsberg, J., dissent.
Camreta v. Greene, 563 U.S. 692 (2011)	NA. Civil rights action under 42 U.S.C. § 1983.	NA	NA	NA	NA	Supreme Court has jurisdiction to hear appeal of adverse Fourth Amendment ruling by officials granted qualified immunity in court below. Fourth Amendment issue, however, was now moot.5-4; Kagan, J., DOC; Scalia, J., concur; Sotomayor & Breyer, JJ., c/j only as to mootness; Kennedy & Thomas, JJ., dissent.

Case Name	Charge on Arrest	Authority for Arrest	Articles Seized	Warrant Clause	Exceptions to Warrant Clause	Decision
Ashcroft v. al-Kidd, 563 U.S. 731 (2011)	NA. *Bivens* action	Federal material witness statute, 18 U.S.C. § 3144, authorizes arrest of a person whose testimony is material in a criminal proceeding, upon showing that "it may become impracticable to secure the presence of the person by subpoena." *Bivens* action alleged Attorney General sought al-Kidd's detention on mere suspicion, without PC of criminal wrongdoing and without intending to call him as a witness.	NA	Arrest warrant	NA	Attorney General had qualified immunity from civil liability for alleged improper motive in seeking arrest warrant, because no precedent "clearly established" that pretextual use of the material witness statute to detain person suspected of links to terrorism, without actually intending to call him as a witness, was unconstitutional. Note: Constitutionality of statute not at issue.8-0; Scalia, J., DOC; Kennedy, J., concur; Ginsberg, Breyer & Sotomayor, JJ., c/p, c/j; Kagan, J., recused.
Davis v. United States, 564 U.S. 229 (2011)	Possession of a firearm by a convicted felon	Police arrested passenger for giving a false name during routine traffic stop. While sitting handcuffed in police car, auto search incident to arrest revealed gun in D's jacket pocket. Search occurred two years before this type of search was declared illegal in *Arizona v. Gant*, 556 U.S. 332 (2009).	Revolver	No warrant	Search incident to a valid custodial arrest (SIVA)	Evidence obtained during a search conducted in good faith and reasonable reliance on binding appellate precedent at the time of the search, but later ruled unconstitutional, is not subject to the exclusionary rule. Drawing a distinction between retroactivity and remedy, Court refuses to apply exclusionary rule to case on direct appeal at time new rule issued. 7-2; Alito, J., DOC; Sotomayor, J., c/j; Breyer & Ginsberg, JJ., dissent.
United States v. Jones, 565 U.S. 400 (2012)	Conspiracy to distribute cocaine	FBI installed GPS tracking device to the undercarriage of defendant's vehicle and monitored its movements for four months. Tracking data was used at trial to link defendant to drug stash house.	NA	Warrant obtained, but installation of GPS occurred after warrant had expired and while vehicle was outside issuing court's jurisdiction	NA	The installation of GPS tracking device on the defendant's car constituted a trespass upon a protected area (effects) and therefore was a "search." *Katz* REP test is not an exclusive test for search, but instead supplements common law trespass test. Standard of Fourth Amendment protection not decided.9-0; Scalia, J., DOC; Sotomayor, J., concurs joining Scalia, but also indicates agreement with Alito, Ginsberg, Breyer & Kagan, JJ., c/j, finding long-term monitoring violated D's REP under *Katz*.

Case Name	Charge on Arrest	Authority for Arrest	Articles Seized	Warrant Clause	Exceptions to Warrant Clause	Decision
Ryburn v. Huff, 565 U.S. 469 (2012)	NA. Civil rights action under 42 U.S.C. § 1983 NA. Civil rights action under 42 U.S.C. § 1983 alleging police executed a search warrant on suspect's mother's house without PC	NA	NA	No warrant	None	Officers had qualified immunity for warrantless entry because there was reasonable basis for fearing imminent violence after mother of suspect ran back into house after being asked about guns.9-0; per curiam.
Messerschmidt v. Millender, 565 U.S. 535 (2012)	NA. Civil rights action under 42 U.S.C. § 1983 for suspicionless strip search at jail after arrest for failure to appear at hearing to enforce a fine	NA	Shot gun and ammunition	Search warrant issued but alleged to be overbroad and not supported by PC	NA	It was not "entirely unreasonable" for officers to believe the warrant was valid and supported by PC.6-3; Roberts, C.J., DOC; Breyer, J., concur; Kagan, J., c/p, d/p; Sotomayor & Ginsburg, JJ., dissent.
Florence v. Burlington, 566 U.S. 318 (2012)		Bench warrant	NA. Strip search	No warrant	NA	Even defendants charged with minor offenses may be stripped searched without suspicion, if they enter the "general jail population." Court uses deferential standard under *Turner v. Safley*, 482 U.S. 78 (1987), finding intrusive strip search was "reasonably related to legitimate penological interest" in jail security, which outweighed inmate's privacy interest.5-4; Kennedy, J., DOC; Alito, J., Roberts, C.J., concur, noting Court leaves open exception for traffic offenders. Breyer, Kagan, Sotomayor & Ginsberg, JJ., dissent.
Reichle v. Howards, 566 U.S. 658 (2012)	NA. Civil rights *Bivins* action against Secret Service members claiming retaliatory arrest based on PC violated First Amendment	NA	NA	No warrant	NA	Qualified immunity granted because right to be free from a retaliatory arrest based on PC was not clearly established. Court declined to decide issue on the merits. 8-0; Thomas, J., DOC; Ginsburg & Breyer, JJ., c/j; Kagan J., took no part. *See also Lozman v. Riviera Beach*, 138 S.Ct. 1935 (2018).

Case Name	Charge on Arrest	Authority for Arrest	Articles Seized	Warrant Clause	Exceptions to Warrant Clause	Decision
Bailey v. United States, 568 U.S.186 (2013)	Possession of cocaine with intent to distribute; possession of a firearm by a felon	Defendant was seen leaving target premises just prior to execution of a search warrant and was stopped 0.7 miles away and brought back to premises where search revealed incriminating evidence.	Cocaine and a firearm	Search warrant	Seizure incident to execution of search warrant under *Michigan v. Summers*, 452 U.S. 692 (1981)	Suspicionless seizure and detention of persons not in the "immediate vicinity" of the premises targeted by search warrant are unreasonable. 6-3; Kennedy, J., DOC; Scalia, Ginsberg & Kagan, JJ., concur. Breyer, Alito, & Thomas, JJ., dissent.
Florida v. Harris, 568 U.S. 237 (2013)	Possessing pseudoephedrine for use in manufacturing methamphetamine	Positive alert by drug detector dog leading to search of vehicle, which revealed incriminating evidence	Pseudoephedrine pills	No warrant	Automobile exception	Drug detector dog, with expired certification, but recent successful training by local police department, was sufficiently reliable to provide probable cause despite failure to keep comprehensive records of dog's field performance, and two false alerts for which there was a plausible explanation.9-0; Kagan, J., DOC.
Clapper v. Amnesty Int'l USA, 568 U.S.398 (2013)	NA. Fourth Amendment challenge, brought under Declaratory Judgment Act, 28 U.S.C. § 2201, by non-citizen attorneys and journalists to § 1881a of the Foreign Intelligence Surveillance Act of 1978, which authorized surveillance of their electronic communications while not reasonably believed to be located in the U.S.	NA	NA	NA	NA	Plaintiffs lack Article III standing to challenge electronic surveillance because they cannot demonstrate injury in fact. The future economic and professional injury they claim (because of inability to locate witnesses, cultivate sources and communicate confidential information to clients) is not "certainly impending" and they cannot manufacture standing by incurring costs in anticipation of non-imminent harm.5-4; Alito, J., DOC; Breyer, Ginsberg, Sotomayor & Kagan, JJ., dissent.

Case Name	Charge on Arrest	Authority for Arrest	Articles Seized	Warrant Clause	Exceptions to Warrant Clause	Decision
Florida v. Jardines, 569 U.S. 1 (2013)	Drug trafficking	Based on anonymous tip that marijuana was being grown in defendant's home, a police drug detector dog physically intruded upon D's front porch and gave a positive alert for the presence of narcotics. A search warrant was obtained, which revealed several marijuana plants.	Marijuana plants	No warrant for dog's intrusion	NA	Police dog's entry upon front porch and area immediately surrounding home, for the purpose of investigating crime is a trespass upon defendant's curtilage and constitutes a search of the home.5-4; Scalia, J., DOC; Kagan, Ginsburg & Sotomayor, JJ., concur; Alito, Breyer, Kennedy, JJ., & Roberts, C.J., dissent.
Missouri v. McNeely, 569 U.S. 141 (2013)	Driving while intoxicated	After a lawful traffic stop, the officer noticed several signs of intoxication, including bloodshot eyes, slurred speech, and the smell of alcohol.	Blood of the defendant	No warrant	Exigent circumstances	The dissipation over time of alcohol in the bloodstream does not automatically constitute an exigent circumstance justifying warrantless and nonconsensual blood test. 5-4; Sotomayor, J., DOC; Roberts, C.J., Breyer & Alito, JJ., c/p, d/p; Thomas, J., dissent.
Maryland v. King, 569 U.S. 435 (2013)	NA. Challenge to suspicionless DNA test at county jail that matched arrestee to an unsolved rape	NA	DNA from defendant via cheek swab	No warrant	Search incident to arrest as part of routine booking procedure	Suspicionless and non-invasive DNA testing via cheek swab, that is uniformly administered to all detainees arrested for "serious" offenses, does not violate Fourth Amendment because it serves legitimate state interest in identifying arrestee, which outweighs detainees' privacy interests, which are diminished by custodial arrest. 5-4; Kennedy, J., DOC; Scalia, Ginsburg, Sotomayor & Kagan, JJ., dissent.
Stanton v. Sims, 571 U.S. 3 (2013)	NA. 42 U.S.C. § 1983 action by innocent resident injured by police during warrantless entry into her curtilage to pursue a misdemeanor suspect	NA	NA	No warrant	Hot pursuit	Declining to decide whether hot pursuit exception applies to misdemeanor suspects, Court held officer had qualified immunity because no "clearly established" rule established the exception did not apply.9-0; per curiam.

Case Name	Charge on Arrest	Authority for Arrest	Articles Seized	Warrant Clause	Exceptions to Warrant Clause	Decision
Fernandez v. California, 571 U.S. 292 (2014)	Infliction of corporal injury on a spouse	Police knocked on door after hearing screams from apartment. D's girlfriend answered, battered and bleeding, but D came to the door and objected after police asked for consent to search the apartment. D was arrested for assault and removed. An hour later police returned and obtained consent to search from girlfriend.	Butterfly knife and sawed-off shot gun	No warrant	Third-party consent	Objection to search by resident who is present, validly arrested and removed from premises, does not invalidate subsequent consent by cohabitant to search in resident's absence. 6-3; Alito, J., DOC; Scalia, J., concur; Thomas, J., c/j; Ginsberg, Sotomayor, & Kagan, JJ., dissent.
Navarette v. California, 572 U.S. 393 (2014)	Drug trafficking	Anonymous but detailed 911 tip gave license number, make, and model of pickup truck, which tipster claimed had just run her off the road. Seeing pickup truck on same highway 18 minutes later, officers followed and then stopped pickup, and smelled marijuana.	30 lbs. of marijuana discovered in pickup truck	No warrant	NA	Stop was valid. Under TOC, the detailed anonymous tip concerning ongoing criminal activity (DUI) by 911 caller, was sufficiently corroborated to provide reasonable suspicion that driver was intoxicated, despite observing no irregular driving after following pickup truck for five miles. 5-4; Thomas, J., DOC; Scalia, Ginsberg, Sotomayor & Kagan, JJ., dissent.
Tolan v. Cotton, 572 U.S. 650 (2014)	NA. Civil rights action under 42 U.S.C. § 1983 against officer who shot innocent unarmed man	NA	NA	NA	NA	In reviewing summary judgment, CCA erred in failing to view evidence in light most favorable to non-movant plaintiff.9-0; per curiam; Alito & Scalia, JJ., c/j.

Case Name	Charge on Arrest	Authority for Arrest	Articles Seized	Warrant Clause	Exceptions to Warrant Clause	Decision
Plumhoff v. Rickard, 572 U.S. 765 (2014)	NA. 42 U.S.C. § 1983 action for use of excessive force by surviving daughter of fleeing traffic offender. Following a high-speed chase, the driver and his passenger were killed after officers fired 15 shots into car at close range as driver attempted to again drive away after having spun out of control to a stop.	Reckless driving	NA	No warrant	Threat to public safety	1) Fourth Amendment not violated by use of deadly force to terminate "threat to public safety" created when minor traffic offender flees at high speed and engages in "outrageously reckless driving." 2) It is "reasonable" to shoot 15 times into the interior of the car to end the threat. Presence of passenger does not alter the calculus because driver cannot vicariously assert Fourth Amendment rights of passenger (if any exist). 3) Alternatively, police had qualified immunity. 8-1 first holding, 8-1 second holding, 9-0 third holding; Alito, J., DOC; Ginsberg, J., c/j; Breyer, J., j/p.
Riley v. California and *United States v. Wurie,* 573 U.S. 373 (2014)	*Riley:* possession of concealed weapon. *Wurie:* possessing crack cocaine with intent to distribute.	*Riley*: arrested for possession of concealed weapon. *Wurie:* arrested during commission of a crime.	*Riley:* cell phone and gang-related pictures stored on phone later used as evidence to convict of attempted murder. *Wurie:* number from call log in cell phone used to link D to drugs.	No warrant	*Riley:* SIVA; *Wurie:* SIVA	SIVA exception rejected.*Riley:* Absent a warrant or probable cause and exigent circumstances, police cannot access digital data in a cell phone found in the pants pocket of a person who has been arrested.*Wurie:* A warrant is required to obtain phone number from arrestee's cell phone's call log. 9-0; Roberts, C.J., DOC; Alito, J., c/j.
Carroll v. Carman, 135 S. Ct. 348 (2014)	NA. Civil rights action under 42 U.S.C. § 1983 claiming officers entered curtilage to attempt "knock and talk" instead of going to front door	NA	NA	No warrant	Implied consent	Officers granted qualified immunity because no "clearly established law" required them to first knock on front door before going to alternate sliding glass door facing side street, which appeared open to visitors.9-0; per curiam.

Case Name	Charge on Arrest	Authority for Arrest	Articles Seized	Warrant Clause	Exceptions to Warrant Clause	Decision
Heien v. North Carolina, 135 S. Ct. 530 (2015)	Possession of cocaine	Traffic stop was based on having only one functioning brake light, which was lawful under specific statute requiring only one brake light, but inconsistent with another statute requiring that rear lights (plural) be in good working order.	Two ounces of cocaine	No warrant	Consent to search car, which was fruit of stop based on mistake of law	An officer's objectively reasonable mistake of law due to ambiguity does not violate the Fourth Amendment. Consent therefore not tainted by unlawful stop, even though state court ruled driver committed no offense by driving with only one brake light. 8-1; Roberts C.J., DOC;Kagan & Ginsburg, JJ., concur; Sotomayor, J., dissent.
Grady v. North Carolina, 135 S. Ct. 1368 (2015)	NA. Appeal of order requiring recidivist sex offender, after completion of sentence, to wear GPS ankle bracelet "at all times" for rest of his life	NA	NA	No warrant	NA	Fourth Amendment applies to civil sex offender GPS monitoring program. Physically intruding upon a person's body with a device designed to acquire information is a search under *U.S. v. Jones* (2012). Remanded to determine reasonableness. 9-0; per curiam.
Rodriguez v. United States, 135 S. Ct. 1609 (2015)	PWID methamphetamine	Probable cause based on positive alert of drug detector dog approximately 7 or 8 minutes after valid traffic stop had been completed by return of documents and issuance of ticket.	Methamphetamine	No warrant	NA	NA Continued detention after the completion of a valid traffic stop, for purpose of using drug detector dog is an unlawful seizure absent RAS. State's claim that violation was *de minimis* is rejected. Remanded to determine if officer had RAS to detain for crime. 6-3; Ginsburg, J., DOC; Thomas, Alito & Kennedy, JJ., dissent.

Case Name	Charge on Arrest	Authority for Arrest	Articles Seized	Warrant Clause	Exceptions to Warrant Clause	Decision
San Francisco v. Sheehan, 135 S. Ct. 1765 (2015)	NA. Civil rights action under 42 U.S.C. §1983 by mentally disabled resident of group home for warrantless entry into her private room and use of excessive force	NA. At social worker's request, officers entered disturbed resident's room and were threatened with a kitchen knife. After retreating, and contrary to policy which required they wait for a trained negotiator, officers entered a second time by kicking down door and, after pepper spray failed, shot knife-wielding resident, who survived.	NA	No warrant	Emergency aid exception	First entry was lawful under emergency aid exception. Second entry was also lawful because it was "part of a single, continuous search or seizure" and did not require further justification. Use of deadly force was reasonable. Failure to follow policy did not negate immunity. 6-2; Alito, J., DOC; Scalia & Kagan, JJ. c/p, d/p. Breyer J., took no part.
City of Los Angeles v. Patel, 135 S. Ct. 2443 (2015)	NA. Ordinance requiring hotels and motels to allow police inspection of registry containing detailed information about guests, challenged as unconstitutional on its face under Fourth Amendment	NA	NA	No warrant	Administrative search/special needs doctrine	Fourth Amendment facial challenges are not barred or disfavored. City conceded inspection was a search. Ordinance unconstitutional on its face, because it provided no opportunity for pre-compliance review and no control on officer's discretion to demand inspection, which created intolerable risk of harassment of hotel operators and their guests. 5-4; Sotomayor, J., DOC;Scalia, Thomas, JJ., and Roberts, C.J., dissent; Alito & Thomas, JJ., dissent.
Mullenix v. Luna, 136 S. Ct. 305 (2015)	Civil rights action under 42 U.S.C. § 1983. Officer using rifle shot into car from overpass and killed fleeing misdemeanor offender whose probation had been revoked.	Arrest warrant	NA	Arrest warrant	NA	Officer entitled to qualified immunity because no precedent "clearly established" it was "beyond debate" that use of deadly force was unconstitutional in the circumstances.8-1; per curiam; Scalia, J., c/j; Sotomayor, J., dissent.

Case Name	Charge on Arrest	Authority for Arrest	Articles Seized	Warrant Clause	Exceptions to Warrant Clause	Decision
Utah v. Strieff, 136 S. Ct. 2056 (2016)	Possession of methamphetamine	Officer investigating suspicions about drug activity at a house stopped pedestrian seen leaving the house without RAS. Warrant check discovered outstanding arrest warrant.	Search incident to arrest on warrant revealed methamphetamine	Arrest warrant	Good faith and attenuation doctrine	Exclusionary rule does not apply. Where officer is investigating in good faith, the discovery of an outstanding arrest warrant attenuates the connection between an unlawful stop and fruits of a search incident to arrest on the arrest warrant. 5-3; Thomas, J., DOC; Sotomayor, J., dissent; Kagan & Ginsburg, JJ., dissent.
Birchfield v. North Dakota, 136 S. Ct. 2160 (2016)(Consolidated with *Bernard v Minn.* and *Beylund v. N. Dakota.)*	All arrested for DUI: *Birchfield* was prosecuted for crime of refusing to submit to warrantless blood draw. *Bernard* prosecuted for refusing breath test. *Beylund* consented to warrantless blood test after being advised refusal was a crime punishable by 90 days in jail and $1,000 fine.	Statutory. Crime to refuse to take breath/BAC test	Blood/breath	No warrant	SIVA	*Birchfield*: Blood tests must be authorized by a warrant unless there are exigent circumstances.*Bernard*: Breath tests are permitted without warrant under the search incident to valid custodial arrest exception (SIVA).*Beylund:* Remanded to determine whether consent was coerced by fear of prosecution for refusing to submit to unconstitutional blood test. 5-3; Alito, J., DOC; Sotomayor & Ginsburg, JJ., c/p, d/p; Thomas, J., d/p, c/j in part.
White v. Pauly, 137 S. Ct. 548 (2017)	NA. Civil rights action under 42 U.S.C. § 1983 for unreasonably using deadly force without proper warning	Officer, claiming he arrived late to an ongoing police action, fired into home from a position of safety without first giving warning.	NA	No warrant	NA	Fact-bound decision granted qualified immunity ruling that no precedent "clearly established" that officer could not presume other officers had given proper warnings. 8-0; per curiam.
Manuel v. City of Joliet, 137 S. Ct. 911 (2017)	NA. Civil rights action under 42 U.S.C. §1983, alleging unconstitutional pretrial detention based upon fabricated evidence	PC. Plaintiff claimed evidence technician falsified lab test showing substance was contraband.	A vitamin bottle containing pills	No warrant	NA	Fourth Amendment protects against unreasonable pretrial detention, which constitutes a continuing seizure until trial commences. Fourth Amendment protection is not extinguished by an indictment or judicial determination of probable cause.6-2; Kagan, J., DOC; Thomas and Alito, JJ., dissent.

Case Name	Charge on Arrest	Authority for Arrest	Articles Seized	Warrant Clause	Exceptions to Warrant Clause	Decision
County of Los Angeles v. Mendez, 137 S. Ct. 1539 (2017)	NA. Civil rights action under 42 U.S.C. § 1983 for warrantless entry and excessive use of force, resulting in $4 million award. 9th CCA affirmed finding that while use of force in self-defense was reasonable, the need to use such force was provoked by the warrantless entry.	Police, with only arrest warrant for third party, entered plaintiff's shack without a search warrant and without knocking or identifying themselves as police. Plaintiff, who was napping, picked up a gun and officers opened fire, severely injuring plaintiff and his wife.	NA	No search warrant	NA	9th Circuit's vague and subjective provocation rule could not be used to manufacture an excessive force claim that otherwise would not exist. Note: The use of deadly force in self-defense had been found reasonable below and was not at issue before the Court. Remanded to properly determine whether injuries were "proximately caused" by warrantless entry. 8-0; Alito, J., DOC.
Ziglar v. Abbasi, 137 S. Ct. 1843 (2017)	*Bivens* action by illegal aliens detained in New York by federal government after 9/11 terrorist attack, alleging harsh conditions of confinement, including frequent strip searches and abuse by guards	NA	NA	NA	NA	Special factors preclude extending judicially-created *Bivens* remedy to challenge conditions of confinement in "new context" involving national security.4-2; Kennedy, J., DOC;Thomas, J., c/p/c/j; Breyer & Ginsburg, JJ., dissent. Sotomayor & Kagan, JJ., recused; Gorsuch, J., took no part.
Hernandez v. Mesa, 137 S. Ct. 2003 (2017)	NA. *Bivens* action against Border Patrol Agent who shot across border, killing unarmed 15-year-old Mexican citizen	NA	NA	NA	NA	Case remanded to determine whether special factors preclude extending *Bivens* remedy to alleged unconstitutional cross-border shooting. 5-3; per curiam; Thomas, J., dissent; Breyer & Ginsburg, JJ., dissent.

Case Name	Charge on Arrest	Authority for Arrest	Articles Seized	Warrant Clause	Exceptions to Warrant Clause	Decision
District of Columbia v. Wesby, 138 S. Ct. 577 (2017)	NA. Civil suit under 42 U.S.C. §1983 for false arrest based on unlawful entry	Police responding to loud party complaint were admitted and observed drinking and debauchery in the unfurnished vacant house. Occupants scattered and hid. Police ultimately determined person who allegedly invited occupants to party had no permission from owner.	NA	No warrant	Consent	Police had PC under TOC to arrest 21 partygoers for unlawful entry into unfurnished vacant house, despite claimed invitation from prospective lessee, where occupants scattered and hid following consensual entry by police, who observed debauchery and lewd conduct and confirmed owner had not given permission. Police not required to rule out innocent explanation where, under TOC, there is a substantial chance of criminal activity. Police also had qualified immunity. 9-0; Thomas, J., DOC, Sotomayor, J., c/p, c/j; Ginsburg, J., c/j.
Collins v. Virginia, 138 S. Ct. 1663 (2018)	Possession of stolen property	Officer seeking speeding motorcyclist who escaped saw object covered with tarp parked in partially enclosed portion of driveway that abutted home. Officer walked up driveway, removed tarp, and discovered motor-cycle, which was stolen.	Motorcycle	No warrant	Automobile exception	Held: partially enclosed portion of driveway visible from street was curtilage and officer's warrantless trespass was not excused by the automobile exception. 8-1; Sotomayor, J., DOC; Thomas, J., concur; Alito, J., dissent.

Case Name	Charge on Arrest	Authority for Arrest	Articles Seized	Warrant Clause	Exceptions to Warrant Clause	Decision
Kinsela v. Hughes, 138 S. Ct. 1148 (2018)	NA. Civil suit under 42 U.S.C. §1983 for use of excessive force	NA. Three officers, responding to 911 call (erratic woman hacking tree with a knife) observed through chain link fence a calm woman in yard holding a kitchen knife down at her side, standing six feet from her roommate, who told officers to "take it easy." Although the mentally ill woman did not raise the knife or verbally threaten roommate, one officer, fearing roommate was in danger, fired four times without warning after the woman failed to acknowledge officer's presence and twice refused order to drop knife. Shooting occurred within one minute after arrival.	NA	No warrant	NA	Officer entitled to qualified immunity because no "clearly established" precedent informed a reasonable officer it was unconstitutional to use deadly force under the particular circumstances; 9-0; per curiam.
Dahda v. United States, 138 S. Ct. 1491 (2018)	Narcotics conspiracy	Federal agents intercepted mobile phone calls, one of which, although not used at trial, concerned a call made when both the target phone and listening post were outside the territorial jurisdiction of the issuing district court.	Mobile phone calls	Federal wiretap order	NA	Federal wiretap order purporting to authorize interception outside the territorial jurisdiction of issuing judge was not "insufficient on its face" in violation of 18 U.S.C. § 2518(10)(a)(ii). The defective language was surplusage because order was sufficient without it to authorize interception of the calls used at trial, which were within district court's jurisdiction. 8-0; Breyer, J., DOC; Gorsuch, J., took no part.
Byrd v. United States, 138 S. Ct. 1518 (2018)	PWID heroin	Driver of rental car, rented by friend, was stopped and trunk was searched, discovering heroin.	49 bricks of heroin	No warrant	NA. Police believed driver had no standing to object to search because he was not listed on rental agreement.	Driver in lawful possession and control of rental car has REP even if not listed as authorized driver on rental agreement.9-0; Kennedy, J., DOC;Thomas & Gorsuch, JJ., concur.

Case Name	Charge on Arrest	Authority for Arrest	Articles Seized	Warrant Clause	Exceptions to Warrant Clause	Decision
Lozman v. Riviera Beach, 138 S. Ct. 1935 (2018)	Civil rights action under 42 U.S.C. § 1983 for retaliatory arrest	Lozman, who had previously criticized city council members and filed a lawsuit against city, refused to leave podium during public comment period after being told to stop speaking; council ordered officer to arrest him for disrupting a public assembly.	NA	NA	NA	Presence of probable cause for arrest did not bar cause of action under 42 U.S.C. § 1983, which alleged retaliatory arrest was due to prior exercise of First Amendment rights and was made pursuant to an official policy to intimidate him from speaking. 8-1; Kennedy, J., DOC; Thomas, J., dissent.
Carpenter v. United States, 138 S. Ct. 2206 (2018)	Robbery	FBI obtained cell site location information ("CSLI") from cell phone records held by wireless carrier, revealing defendant's movements over 127-day period.	Business records of wireless carrier showing CSLI	No warrant	Third-party doctrine	Cell phone users have legitimate expectation of privacy in business records revealing past physical move-ments. Therefore, acquiring cell-site location information records from wireless carrier under Stored Comm-unications Act is a search and requires a warrant based upon probable cause. Third-party doctrine under *Smith v. Maryland*, 442 U. S. 735 (1979), and *United States v. Miller*, 425 U. S. 435 (1976), limited because of perva-sive nature of the cell phone user's privacy invasion and fact that user does not voluntarily assume the risk of disclosure. Narrow holding; does not address "real time" tracking, "tower dumps," security cameras, or national security surveillance techniques. 5-4; Roberts, C.J., DOC; Kennedy, Alito, Thomas, Gorsuch, JJ., dissent.

Case Name	Charge on Arrest	Authority for Arrest	Articles Seized	Warrant Clause	Exceptions to Warrant Clause	Decision
Sause v. Bauer, 138 S. Ct. 2561 (2018)	NA. Civil rights action under 42 U.S.C. §1983 brought on First Amendment grounds after petitioner's arrest for refusal to stop praying in her home	Disorderly conduct, interfering with law enforcement	NA	No warrant	Unclear whether consent granted	First Amendment claim for alleged violation of religious freedom demanded consideration under Fourth Amendment of the ground on which the officers were present in the apartment and the nature of any legitimate law enforcement interests that might have justified an order to stop praying at the specific time in question. 9-0; per curiam.
City of Escondido v. Emmons, 139 S. Ct. 500 (2019)	NA. Civil rights action under 42 U.S.C. § 1983 for excessive force in making misdemeanor arrest	NA	NA	No warrant	None	CCA defined "clearly established right" at too high a level of generality. Remanded. 9-0; per curiam.

INDEX

A

B

C

S

T

W

TABLE OF CASES

Case name	Page No.

Case name	Page No.

Case name	Page No.

Case name	Page No.

ABOUT THE AUTHORS, EDITORS, AND CONTRIBUTORS

From 1963 until his death in 1994, **William W. Greenhalgh** was both a professor of law at Georgetown University Law Center who taught Constitutional Criminal Procedure and director of the Prettyman-Stiller Legal Fellowship Program in the Law Center's graduate school.

In 1974, Professor Greenhalgh became director of the Criminal Justice Clinic at Georgetown, serving in that capacity until his death. He was widely regarded as a pioneer and champion of clinical legal education.

In 1977, Professor Greenhalgh was appointed the faculty advisor to the *American Criminal Law Review*. In addition, he was elected an officer of the American Bar Association Criminal Justice Section and chaired the section in 1982 and 1983. He also served as academic associate dean of the Law Center from 1972 to 1975 and as associate dean for clinical programs in 1975 and 1976. He earned his undergraduate and law degrees from the University of Virginia.

The author of many articles and books, Professor Greenhalgh was considered a leading authority on the Fourth and Sixth Amendments to the U.S. Constitution. In 1999, *American Criminal Law Review* published posthumously "In Defense of the 'Per Se' Rule: Justice Stewart's Struggle to Preserve the Fourth Amendment's Warrant Clause" (volume 31, page 1013), an article that Professor Greenhalgh and Mark J. Yost completed shortly before Professor Greenhalgh's death.

Charles E. Moylan, Jr., was a judge of the Maryland Court of Special Appeals from 1970 until his retirement in December 2000. A graduate of Johns Hopkins University and the University of Maryland School of Law, he served from 1964 to 1970 as state's attorney for Baltimore City. He taught at the University of Maryland and the University of Baltimore schools of law and continues to lecture on topics in criminal and constitutional law. Judge Moylan is the author of *Criminal Homicide Law*, *Maryland's Consolidated Theft Law and Unauthorized Use*, and *The Right of the People to Be Secure: An Examination of the Fourth Amendment*, and he also is the co-author of *Maryland Criminal Law Practice and Procedure*. He has contributed articles to such journals as the *Mercer Law Review*, *Southern Illinois University Law Journal*, *University of Baltimore Law Review*, and the *ABA Journal*.

Professor Emeritus **Laurence A. Benner** has been an active participant, educator, and consultant in the criminal justice arena for over four decades. *The Other Face of Justice*, which he co-authored, documented the systemic deficiencies of our system for providing counsel for the indigent accused. He has also written on a wide range of criminal justice issues, including the Fourth Amendment, interrogation law, habeas corpus, and racial disparity in the use of search warrants. A graduate of the University of Chicago Law School, Professor Benner practiced in Illinois and Michigan; was a Chief Public Defender; taught as a Clinician at the University of Chicago's Mandel Legal Aid Clinic; and was Managing Director of Criminal Justice Programs at California Western School of Law in San Diego, where he taught Criminal Procedure and Constitutional Law.

He is a Fellow of the American Bar Association, past chair of the ABA Criminal Justice Section's Defense Function Committee, and currently serves on the Section's Publication Board. He has been a consultant to numerous entities and governmental agencies, including the U.S. Justice Department, and the California Commission on the Fair Administration of Justice.

Amie L. Clifford serves as education coordinator for the South Carolina Commission on Prosecution Coordination. Prior to joining the Commission in November 2007, she was employed by the National District Attorneys Association as the Director of the National Center for Prosecution Ethics and as an assistant director of programs for the National College of District Attorneys. She has previously served as a Supreme Court Fellow at the U.S. Sentencing Commission, assistant solicitor in the Charleston County Solicitor's Office, assistant attorney general in the Criminal Appeals Section of the South Carolina Attorney General's Office, and staff attorney with Piedmont Legal Services, Inc. A 1982 graduate of the University of South Carolina School of Law, Ms. Clifford is a contributing author for *South Carolina Criminal Trial Techniques Handbook* (South Carolina Bar); she is also editor and contributing author for *Doing Justice: A Prosecutor's Guide to Ethics and Civil Liability* (2nd ed., 2007 National District Attorneys Association), and contributing author and editor for *The Fourth Amendment Handbook: A Chronological Survey of Supreme Court Decisions* (2nd ed.) (published in 2002 by the American Bar Association).

Carol Garfiel Freeman, a graduate of Wellesley College and Columbia Law School, clerked for U.S. District Judge Charles M. Metzner (S.D.N.Y.) and during her career has been an attorney in the U.S. Department of Justice, an assistant U.S. attorney for the District of Columbia, Deputy District Public Defender of Montgomery County, Maryland, a staff attorney for the U.S. District Court for the District of Columbia, and an attorney in private practice concentrating on state and federal criminal trials and appeals. Since 2005, Ms. Freeman has written the Cert Alert column for *Criminal Justice*, the quarterly magazine of the ABA's Criminal Justice Section. She is a former vice-chair for publications of the Criminal Justice Section and has also chaired the section's Book Publishing Board and Magazine Board. She has been active in various local and state bar associations and is the current president of the William B. Bryant American Inn of Court. Ms. Freeman was an editor of the Third Edition of the *Fourth Amendment Handbook.*

Sharon Rubinstein, a graduate of Cornell University and the University of Michigan Law School, has taught criminal law to undergraduates and was a consultant to the American Bar Association's Juvenile Justice Center. She has also worked as a reporter, with articles appearing in *Criminal Justice* magazine, *The Baltimore Sun*, *Business Week*, *Newsweek International*, and other publications. For nearly a decade, she was communications director for Advocates for Children and Youth in Baltimore and for the Maryland Juvenile Justice Coalition. She edited the first edition of the *Fourth Amendment Handbook* and co-edited the second and third editions.

Ria Moore Benedict, who contributed to some of the case briefs for the second edition, was formerly a legal writing instructor at Rutgers Law School, a clerk for the Honorable Arthur L. Burnett, Sr., in the Superior Court of the District of Columbia, an associate at Doepken, Keevican & Weiss in Pennsylvania, and a lawyer with the U.S. Department of Labor.

Andrew E. Taslitz is the immediate past Welsh S. White Distinguished Visiting Professor of Law at the University of Pittsburgh School of Law and is professor of law at the Howard University School of Law. He has also taught at the Duke University and Villanova University Schools of Law. He teaches criminal law, criminal procedure, evidence, free speech, terrorism and the law, professional responsibility, and advanced courses in those areas. He has published more than 100 scholarly works, including six books. His articles have been published in such journals as the *Georgetown Law Journal*, *Harvard Civil Rights–Civil Liberties Law Review*, *Fordham Law Review*, and *Northwestern University's Journal of Criminal Law and Criminology*. A major part of his research focuses on the Fourth Amendment to the U.S. Constitution. Indeed, his three most recent books are *Constitutional Criminal Procedure* (4th ed. 2010), published by Foundation Press; 1 *Mastering Criminal Procedure: Investigations* (2010), published by Carolina Academic Press; and *Reconstructing the Fourth Amendment: A History of Search and Seizure, 1789-1868* (paperback ed. 2009), published by New York University Press. Professor Taslitz is also the Reporter for the Committee on a Model Statute for the Electronic Recording of Custodial Interrogations of the Uniform Law Commission; a member of the ABA Committee on Transactional Surveillance Standards; a member of the ABA Criminal Justice Section's Governing Council; a member of its *Criminal Justice* periodical Editorial Board (and the board's former chair); chair of that section's Book Board, as well as having served as its Director of the Communications Division; formerly chair of its Committee on Race and Racism; and chair of the Eyewitness Identification Subcommittee of its Committee on Innocence and the Integrity of the Criminal Justice System.